The Message of the Wesleys

Francis Asbury Publishing Company was founded in 1980 by several members of the Asbury community in Wilmore. Kentucky. Its aim was to meet the spiritual needs of that segment of the evangelical Christian public that is Wesleyan in outlook and to communicate the Wesleyan message to the larger Christian community.

In 1983 Francis Asbury Publishing Company became a part of Zondervan Publishing House. Its aim remains the spread of the Wesleyan message through the publication of popular. practical. and scholarly books for all Wesleyan denominations.

FRANCIS ASBURY PRESS
Box 7
Wilmore. Kentucky 40390

The Message of
the Wesleys

A Reader of Instruction and Devotion

*Compiled and with
an introduction by
Philip S. Watson*

FRANCIS ASBURY PRESS
of Zondervan Publishing House

Grand Rapids. Michigan

THE MESSAGE OF THE WESLEYS

Copyright © 1984 by The Zondervan Corporation
Grand Rapids, Michigan

FRANCIS ASBURY PRESS is an imprint of Zondervan Publishing House
1415 Lake Drive, SE, Grand Rapids, Michigan 49506

Library of Congress Cataloging in Publication Data
Main entry under title:

The Message of the Wesleys.

Bibliography: p.
 1. Methodist Church—Addresses, essays, lectures. 2. Theology, Doctrinal—Addresses, essays, lectures. 3. Christian life—Methodist authors—Addresses, essays, lectures. I. Wesley, John, 1703-1791. II. Wesley, Charles, 1707-1788. III. Watson, Philip S. (Philip Saville), 1909-
BX8215.M47   1984   287   83-23290
ISBN 0-310-75031-8

Printed in the United States of America
84 85 86 87 88 89 90   9 8 7 6 5 4 3 2 1

Contents

Foreword   ix
Preface   xiii
List of Works Cited   xix
Abbreviations   xx

INTRODUCTION: ANATOMY OF A CONVERSION

I. *Discovery of a Message*   1
    Pentecost at Aldersgate   1
    Pilgrims' Progress   9
        Charles Wesley's Experience   11
        John Wesley's Experience   16

II. *Fulfilment of a Mission*   23
    "Methodism So Called"   23
    "Our Doctrines"   28
    "The Spirit and Discipline"   40

Notes to Introduction   53

PART ONE: INSTRUCTION IN THE FAITH

I. *The Mystery and Majesty of God*   59
    The Blessed Trinity   59
    His Inescapable Presence   64
    His All-Embracing Providence   66
    Our Knowledge of His Nature   70
    Our Ignorance of His Ways   71

II. *The Greatness and Littleness of Man*   75
    Existential Anxiety   75
    Cosmic Insecurity   77
    The Privilege of Humanity   78
    Our Fallen State   80

The Diseases of Human Nature 82
The Deceitfulness of Man's Heart 84
The Inhuman Folly of War 85
The Misery of Mankind 87
Original Sin 88

III. *The Mystery of Godliness* 91
For Sinners Only 91
The Gospel of the Kingdom 92
The Manifestation of the Son of God 95
The Centrality of the Atonement 99
The Liberating Work of Christ 100
The Renewing Power of the Spirit 102
Why God Let Adam Fall 104
What about the Heathen? 108

IV. *The Experience of Grace* 109
The Meaning of Grace 109
The Plan of Salvation 111
The Faith That Saves 112
Only Believe! 115
God's Part and Ours 117
Two Levels of Faith 119
The Assurance of Salvation 120
Varying Degrees of Faith 122
Variety in God's Working 124

Notes to Part One 127

PART TWO: GUIDANCE TO GLORY

I. *Waiting on God* 131
The Means of Grace 131
The Initiatory Sacrament 132
Works of Piety 134
(1) Prayer 134
(2) The Scriptures 135
(3) The Lord's Supper 136
(4) Fasting 138
(5) "Christian Confidence" 139
Works of Mercy 141
(1) Faith and Good Works 141
(2) The Reward of the Righteous 142
The Right Use of Such Means 145

II. *Christian Behaviour*   147
  Stewardship   147
  Self-Denial   148
  Temperance   149
  The Conduct of Business   151
  The Choice of a Career   152
  True Courtesy   153
  The Cultivation of the Mind   154
  The Use of Riches   155
  Leisure and Pleasure   157
  Cheerfulness   160
  Two Orders of Christians   161
  The Servant of the Lord   162

III. *Growth in Grace*   163
  The Pursuit of Holiness   163
  Stages in the Spiritual Life   165
  Christian Perfection   168
  The Imperfections of the Perfect   171
  "Treasure in Earthen Vessels"   174
  Varieties of Experience   177
  The Patience of Hope   181

IV. *Looking Towards Eternity*   187
  The Shadow of Death   187
  The Intermediate State   189
  A Prospect of Paradise   191
  The Communion of Saints   193
  Judgment   196
  The Fateful Choice   198
  A Foretaste of Hell   199
  A Vision of Heaven   201
  The New Creation   203

Notes to Part Two   207

EPILOGUE: *A Meditation on the Lord's Prayer*   211

Select Bibliography   223

Foreword

There is no more frustrating and futile exercise than to wonder how different things would be if circumstances or events had been other than they were; frustrating because we sense from our later perspective what might have been, and futile because we know it can never be. Yet when one reflects on the already tremendous impact John and Charles Wesley have had on the history of the Christian Church, it is difficult to refrain from musing about what might have been John written "Institutes" rather than sermons, tracts and letters. He did not do so, and the lack of such a systematic presentation has resulted in people knowing his thought only in a general and fragmented fashion.

Philip Watson has rendered an invaluable service to the spiritual descendants of the Wesleys in *The Message of the Wesleys*. Intending to reintroduce readers to the lives and teachings of John and Charles Wesley and, at the same time, to provide a volume that would serve as a devotional guide, Watson has made available to preachers and laity an extremely useful and useable anthology. The organization of material into two major divisions—instruction and practical guidelines for life—reflects not only the spirit of the Wesleyan revival but also the pattern of Pauline literature, thus reminding the reader again that the Wesleys sought and found in Scripture the foundations for faith and practice. The documentation of the edited passages from John Wesley's writings provides ample opportunity for the interested student to pursue the extended statement or related context. The inclusion of many of Charles' hymns does more than add a devotional dimension to this book: it indicates the profound role his poetry had in the theological education of the early Methodist societies.

The rationale for reprinting this excellent work is established clearly by Watson in his introduction: "Wesley's Methodist descendants . . . all too often talk about Wesley's warmed heart without any reference to the fire that warmed it" (page 6). The fire that warmed his heart was his rediscovery of the biblical truth that had earlier ignited Luther—justification by grace through faith. The kindling for Wesley's burning heart came from his theological discoveries—faith, instantaneous conversion, and the witness of the Spirit giving assurance to the believer.

However, one must not confuse the kindling with the backlog. Years before Aldergate, John Wesley had already perceived that holiness is the essence of biblical Christianity. As he later wrote to a young disciple, "None are or can be saved but those who are by faith made inwardly and outwardly holy" (page 163). He had seen it; he had committed himself to seek it; he had disciplined his life rigorously to achieve it; he had proclaimed it at Oxford in 1733 in his sermon "The Circumcision of the Heart"; and Aldersgate brought it into sharp focus in a moment of personal realization.

Wesley's theology is a theology of holiness. God had created man *imago dei,* which means, in part, that originally man bore the image of God's holiness—he was like God, But the tragedy of sin had destroyed that holiness. Consequently, "there is, in the heart of every child of man, an inexhaustible fund of ungodliness and unrighteousness, so deeply and strongly rooted in the soul, that nothing less than almighty grace can cure it" (page 84). For Wesley, it is this accurate appraisal of man's sinful condition that constitutes the fundamental distinction between Christianity and every other religion (see his sermon "Original Sin"). This sinfulness Wesley characterized as spiritual sickness, for the healing of which the Great Physician gave himself. This healing of the soul, the prime objective of redemption, is the restoration of holiness, the putting off of the old nature and the putting on of the new nature, "which—after God is created in righteousness and true holiness" (Eph. 2:24).

Sanctification, the process of making people holy, is therefore the heart of th Gospel. It is the *real change* that God effects in a believer through the Holy Spirit, who "breaks the power of canceled sin" and restores the image of God. This sanctifying work of the Spirit produces that holiness without which "no man shall see the Lord" (Heb. 12:14). Holiness is "the true wedding garment' [Matt. 22:12], the only qualification for glory" (page 163).

In Wesley's understanding of Scripture, sanctification begins in the new birth and involves both process and event in human experience. It is evidenced in the one born of God by a genuine love for God, love expressed in voluntary obedience to the known laws of God. But holiness begun is not holiness completed. Entire sanctification is that gracious work of God in which the believer's heart is cleansed "by the inspiration of the Holy Spirit" so that he might perfectly love God and worthily magnify His holy name; it is the circumcision of the heart "from all evil dispositions" (page 166); it is "having 'the mind that was in Christ' " (page 163); it is loving God with all the heart and all the soul. In conjunction with this love, Wesley used the term "Christian perfection," a term that drew and has drawn strong criticism and continuous misunderstanding. But he refused to negotiate the use of "perfection" because it is scriptural. He would not "send the Holy Ghost to school, and teach Him to speak who made the tongue" (page 169). "Perfection" means "completeness," and to love God with all the heart is to be perfect as our Father in heaven is perfect (Mt. 5:48). However, such perfection "still admits of a thousand degrees" (page 184).

(It would seem that the real conflict generated by the word "perfection" has to do with whether one conceives of it from the perspective of Greek philosophical language or of Hebrew thought. In the former there is the connotation of an "absolute" in which there can be no degrees. In Hebrew thought such abolutism is not the focus of the word. Rather, the idea of "wholeness" or "integrity" strikes more at the heart of its meaning. Thus, "Asa's heart was perfect with the Lord all his days" [I Kg. 15:14] and Job was called "a perfect and an upright man, one that feareth God, and escheweth evil [Job 1:8]. In this latter sense Wesley found it possible to speak of a biblical perfection in which there are degrees of perfectness.)

Holiness is the perfection of love, and love is the fulfilling of the law (Rom. 14:10). Holiness is "having the mind of Christ," and Christ was sacrificial in his love for all the world. Early in their ministerial loves, both John and Charles understood their pursuit of God to be intimately related with caring for the downtrodden. Consequently, social action was integral to the disciplines of the Holy Club. It led both of the brothers to Georgia, and it continued its significant place in their lives after their transformations in 1738. John's statements on "the inhuman folly of war" (pages 85-86) are indicative of the social passion that prohibited his isolating grace to personal religious experience. To love God is to love God's. How could holiness be anything less?

The message of the Wesleys is the message of holiness, a very simple message. Yet it is exceedingly complex, related to every facet of human existence. Some will not accept it; many in the church of the Wesleys' day would not. For the early Methodists it was the grand *depositum* that God had entrusted to them and for which they had the responsibility of promulgation. For every Christian it is the mandate of Scripture: "For God has not called us for uncleanness, but in holiness. Therefore whoever disregards this, disregards not man but God, who gives his Holy Spirit to you" (I Th. 4:7-8).

Dr. Watson died in 1983. It is fitting that he assigned the rights to *The Message of the Wesleys* to Asbury College. Since 1890 when it was founded as Kentucky Holiness College, Asbury has sought to proclaim through its graduates the Wesleyan message of scriptural holiness. In 1923 the college gave birth to Asbury Theological Seminary, which has been responsible for training more Wesleyan preachers and missionaries over the past fifty-eight years than any other graduate institution in America.

The Message of the Wesleys is being reprinted in the confidence that this message is still vital to the Church. Our hope is that in reading the message many will sense a hungering and thirsting for holiness in themselves. Such will bring the spiritual renewal our world so desperately needs.

WILLIAM B. COKER

Professor of Bible
Asbury College

Preface

John and Charles Wesley are well known by name as leading figures in the Evangelical Revival of the eighteenth century and as founders of the movement that has since developed into the world-wide Methodist Church. Yet one need not read very far in their writings to discover how dim and distorted their image has become for the greater part even of their Methodist successors, not to mention those of other denominations who know of them only as the originators of Methodism. In particular, their quality of mind, the range and depth of their thought, the true nature of the ideas and ideals that inspired their work—these are all too often either wholly unknown or represented by garbled fragments that only misrepresent them. This is true despite a renewal of interest in them in recent years, which has resulted in a number of scholarly studies of different aspects of their theology, as well as several slighter and more popular collections of material extracted from their works.

Consequently, in an age that is notoriously bewitched by the "contemporary" and the superficially "relevant," it is hardly surprising if the Wesleys are not commonly regarded as having anything particularly significant to say to us today. Yet to one who has the patience to listen to them they have a great deal to say, including much that could not well be brought within the limits of this volume, which is deliberately focused on their most central concerns.

The purpose of this book is therefore twofold. First of all, as a "*Wesley* Reader" it is intended to be a kind of re-introduction of the Wesleys, presenting them as it were in person and (to use current theological jargon) "without myth." For example, it seeks to dispose of the romanticism and sentimentality that are commonly associated with John Wesley's "strangely warmed" heart; it corrects the impression which modern Methodists sometimes give that he equated temperance with teetotalism and teetotalism with the essence of Christianity; and it furnishes plenty of evidence that when he said of

xiii

himself and his Methodists, "We think and let think," he was far from advocating the kind of muddle-headedness and indifference to sound doctrine that is too often symbolised by this overworked quotation. Admittedly,he would never allow even the soundest doctrine to become a substitute for "inward religion" and the realities of Christian experience; but neither would he be satisfied with any "religious experience," no matter how inward and warm-hearted, that was not consonant with sound Christian doctrine.

In this connexion I trust that the whole tenor of the book exposes the fallacy of the idea that John Wesley was "no theologian." Oddly enough, no one ever seems to have thought of saying this about Charles—perhaps because it is taken for granted that theology and the poetic gift simply do not go together. But it has too often been said about John, who is held (greatly to his credit) to have been instead a man of "practical religion," much too busy to waste his time in theologising. This has furnished a splendid excuse for theological indolence among his followers, and it no doubt largely explains why we still have so few reputable studies of his thought, while there are whole shelves of historical and biographical writing about him.

It is, of course, true that neither of the Wesleys was a systematic theologian in the sense of one who seeks to elaborate a detailed, comprehensive, and logically ordered system of doctrine. But John's thinking was thoroughly systematic in the sense of being logical and coherent; and while he dealt in detail with only a limited number of doctrines, which he found from time to time needed special attention, it should be observed that he had a perfect genius for putting his finger on what was—and is—vital and essential, so that all his preaching and teaching revolved around one unmistakable centre: the love of God revealed in Christ and imparted to men by the Holy Spirit. And the doctrine that John expounded in his sermons, tracts, and treatises, Charles set forth also in his hymns, which were one of the chief means by which the minds of their followers were enlightened as well as their hearts warmed. Although there were certain differences of accent between the two brothers and, on one or two occasions, sharp differences of opinion between them, on the central issues they were entirely at one, and it is their united witness that is represented in this book.

In the Introduction I have ventured to give my own interpretation of the emergence of the Wesleys as leaders of the Revival and of their theory and practice of what to them was essential Christianity, although the jibe of an early critic led to its being called Methodism. This furnishes a context and background for the remainder of the book, where the Wesleys are allowed to speak for themselves with only an occasional editorial comment. Broadly speaking, Part I exhibits the basic doctrinal convictions that underlay their whole evangelistic enterprise, while Part II illustrates the practical application and outworkings of the doctrine. It will easily be seen, however, that doctrine and practice belong inseparably together for the Wesleys, so that their expositions of the Christian faith are always in touch with the realities of life, and their directions for Christian living with the firmly grasped substance of the faith. In that sense, the Wesleys were indeed men of "practical religion."

This brings us to the second, though by no means secondary, purpose of this book—its practical purpose as a "Reader of *Instruction and Devotion.*" It has more than once been alleged that Protestantism has produced "no devotional literature"—a charge which on any showing is at least highly exaggerated. But naturally everything depends on what "devotional literature" is supposed to be. If it is literature designed to foster "the life of God in the soul of man"—to borrow with Wesley the title of a famous work of Puritan edification—then Protestantism has produced such literature in abundance and in large variety. Protestantism not only gave the Bible to the common man in his own tongue, but its scholars and theologians gave him commentaries on it, to assist him in applying its teaching to his life, and its preachers and teachers supplied him with printed sermons, tracts, and treatises on the spiritual life. They wrote and published journals describing their own spiritual pilgrimage for the help and encouragement of others; they gave personal spiritual counsel in letters; and they produced collections of hymns setting forth the doctrines of the faith and describing the varieties of spiritual experience. Such literature was available and was widely used, both by individuals privately and by family and other groups, through generation after generation of Protestants till the widespread decline of piety in recent times. To such literature the Wesleys made a notable contribution, from which most of the material for the present volume has been directly drawn.

That the Wesleys were men of the eighteenth century may suggest to some that they are unlikely to have much of relevance to say to us in the twentieth. But their times were not as different from our own nor were they themselves as unacquainted with the problems of "modern man" as we are apt to imagine. Our generation is not the first to have discovered the insignificance of man in the vastness of the universe, nor even the first to feel its very existence threatened by a universal holocaust (see pp. 75-78). And if, as we are often told, it is because "modern man is not worrying about his sins" that he is unresponsive to the gospel with its message of forgiveness and grace, this, too, is a problem of which the Wesleys were not unaware (see pp. 80-81, 91-92). Besides this, they lived in a time of wars and rumours of war, of rebellions and revolutions; a time of "rapid social change," of swiftly expanding population and the shifting of its centres from rural areas to new industrial towns; and a time of new and exciting developments (which they welcomed) in the sciences, including the establishment of a new cosmology.

There is not much that is new—fundamentally new—under the sun, but perhaps in one major respect the situation of modern man is novel. We live today, for the first time in history, in an "affluent society"—actually so in the West, potentially everywhere else. In consequence, it is becoming more urgently necessary to teach people how to use their increasing leisure than to inculcate the ancient virtues of hard work and thrift, and on this subject there is little direct guidance to be found either in the Wesleys or in any of the spiritual mentors of the past. Even so, it has not been difficult to discover in them more material that is relevant to the present-day conduct of life than could well be included in this volume.

But be that as it may, the most important thing about the Wesleys is that they were men of God, men who knew God and knew how to lead others to the knowledge of God; and such knowledge is neither the product nor the property of any one century. This book is therefore designed to enable us to listen to their instruction and to emulate their devotion. Not that we should seek to reproduce in ourselves their experiences, for both of them (as we shall see) give warnings against the attempt to pattern our own experience on someone else's. Nor should we suppose that the "plan of salvation" which John describes in some detail represents a series of stages through which we must necessarily pass in an orderly and uninterrupted progression. For although his doctrine is quite clear and definite, he is anything but doctrinaire in his application of it, as his letters above all make plain but as may also be discerned in the very sermons where he sets it out with such logical precision.

I have not attempted to produce a critical text of the many passages quoted, since that was unnecessary for the purposes of this book. In cases of divergence between the Jackson edition of John Wesley's *Works* and the Standard editions of his *Sermons, Journal,* and *Letters,* I have simply taken the version that seemed clearest and most pertinent. (On pp. 199f, for example, one of the "Letters to a Young Disciple" in the Jackson edition has been preferred to the two letters to Philothea Briggs by which it is represented in the Standard edition.) I have dealt similarly with the variant versions of the hymns that appear in the different collections I have used. It should perhaps also be mentioned that few of the hymns have been quoted in full, and that some of the verses selected in any given instance may well be missing from one or other of the sources cited. Wherever a reference to the source of a hymn is given, it may be taken to be by Charles Wesley unless another author is named.

In a number of cases I have abridged or condensed the Wesleys with almost as much freedom as John Wesley used when he published other people's work, but I believe without in any way altering their meaning. In order to avoid disfiguring the pages with ellipses, however, I have rarely indicated the omission of any of their material. My aim has been to produce a readable volume for those who may be interested in the subject but have neither the time nor inclination to work through the sources to which a scholar or research student must naturally turn. The occasional insertion of editorial matter has been marked by the use of square brackets, but obviously printer's errors have been corrected silently.

With regard to spelling, punctuation, and capitalisation, Wesley's (or his printer's) practice varied at different periods, and I have therefore freely modernised them as far as seemed desirable. If even so the punctuation seems by modern standards at times excessive, I suggest that the experiment of reading aloud may show the reason for it. The original punctuation appears to have been designed largely for rhetorical purposes, and there is no doubt that Wesley *heard* is often more effective then Wesley silently read. In a day when the ability to read was rarer than it is now and books were scarcer, Mr. Wesley's publications must often have been read aloud. Even his brother's hymns were so read, for they were "lined out"—read out line by line by the preacher or precentor for the congregation to sing after him.

I have not felt it necessary to track down all the biblical and literary quotations and allusions in which the work of both the Wesleys abounds. The biblical references are as a rule not too difficult to trace with the aid of a Concordance to the Authorised or King James Version, but the literary sources, for which we have no such aid, are often very elusive. Whether from the Bible or elsewhere, John Wesley usually quotes from memory, and therefore not always accurately; and with Charles we have the added complication of a poet's licence. It should also be noted that quotations from the Psalms are almost always from the older, Prayer Book Version, which differs considerably from the King James Version.

The following chapters are arranged so as to present a developing theme when the book is read straight through. They are also divided up into short sections, which can be turned to as interest may dictate in any few moments of leisure. If this is done, however, it will be well to bear in mind that the import of any one section may be more fully understood in the light that can be shed on it by others. There is material here, not only for perusal, but for study; and what John Wesley said of his *Explanatory Notes on the Old Testament* might very well be said of the present volume also: "It is no part of my design to save either learned or unlearned men from the trouble of thinking. On the contrary, my intention is to make them think, and assist them in thinking."

My special thanks are due to Professor Edmund Perry of Northwestern University and to my colleagues at Garrett, Professors William E. Hordern and Ernest W. Saunders, for patiently bearing with my Wesleyan enthusiasm and for much helpful advice; to professor Merrill R. Abbey for generously reading the manuscript at short notice; and to President Dwight E. Loder for unfailing encouragement and a lightened teaching load that enabled me to meet my deadline.

PHILIP S. WATSON

Garrett Theological Seminary
Aldersgate Day, 1963

List of Works Cited

Hildebrandt, F., ed. *The Wesley Hymn Book*, London, 1960; Kansas City, Mo., 1963.

The Methodist Hymnal. Official Hymnal of the Methodist Church. Nashville, 1932.

The Methodist Hymn Book. London, 1933.

Wesley, Charles. *The Journal of the Rev. Charles Wesley, M.A.*, ed. Thomas Jackson. London, 1849. 2 vols.

———. *The Journal of the Rev. Charles Wesley, M.A.*, 1736-39, ed. John Telford. London, 1909.

Wesley, John. *The Journal of the Rev. John Wesley, A.M.*, Std. edn., ed. Nehemiah Curnock. London, 1938. 8 vols.

———. *The Letters of the Rev. John Wesley, A.M.*, Std. edn., ed. John Telford. London, 1931. 8 vols.

———. *Wesley's Standard Sermons,* ed. and annot. Edward H. Sugden. London, 1921-56. 2 vols.

———. *The Works of the Rev. John Wesley, A.M.,* with the Last Corrections of the Author, ed. Thomas Jackson. London, 1829-31. 14 vols.

———. *A Collection of Hymns for the Use of the People Called Methodists.* London, 1780. Revised with a new suppl., London, Wesleyan Conference Office, 1876.

——— and Charles Wesley. *Hymns on the Lord's Supper.* Bristol, 1745. Reprinted in *The Eucharistic Hymns of John and Charles Wesley* by J. E. Rattenbury, London, 1948.

Abbreviations

AMH	*The* (American) *Methodist Hymnal*
CW	Charles Wesley
CWJ(J)	*The Journal of the Rev. Charles Wesley, M.A.* (Jackson ed.)
CWJ(T)	*The Journal of the Rev. Charles Wesley, M.A.* (Telford ed.)
HLS	*Hymns on the Lord's Supper*
HPCM	*A Collection of Hymns for the Use of the People Called Methodists*
HPCM(S)	Supplement to *HPCM*
JW	John Wesley
JWJ	*The Journal of the Rev. John Wesley, A.M.*
L	*The Letters of the Rev. John Wesley, A.M.*
Large Minutes	"Minutes of Several Conversations between the Rev. Mr. Wesley and Others"
MHB	*The* (British) *Methodist Hymn Book*
Minutes	"Minutes of Some Late Conversations between the Rev. Mr. Wesley and Others"
S	Sermon
SS	*Wesley's Standard Sermons*
W	*The Works of the Rev. John Wesley, A.M.*
WHB	*The Wesley Hymn Book*

Anatomy of a Conversion

* * *

I

Discovery of a Message

PENTECOST AT ALDERSGATE

On a day late in February, 1738, in a lodging in Oxford, two young men were engaged in serious conversation. One of them, an Anglican clergyman, lay in bed suffering from a severe attack of pleurisy. His name was Charles Wesley. The other, who had come to visit his sick friend, was a minister of the Moravian Church, who was intending to go shortly as a missionary to America. His name was Peter Böhler.

The conversation turned very soon to the deep things of the Christian faith and life, and Peter Böhler led it to the point where he asked Charles Wesley what reason he had for hoping to be saved. The answer Charles gave was simple and direct. He said: "Because I have used my best endeavours to serve God." At this Peter Böhler shook his head, and although he made no spoken comment, his silence was more eloquent than words. After he had gone, Charles Wesley wrote in his *Journal:* "I thought him very uncharitable, saying in my heart, 'What, are not my endeavours a sufficient ground of hope? Would he rob me of my endeavours? I have nothing else to trust to.'"[1]

Charles Wesley's attitude was very human—all too human. "I've done my best," people say, "I've done my best, and what more can God require of me?" Yet few people have such a best, such endeavours to rely on, as Charles Wesley had.

Ten years or so earlier, he had resolved to devote all his time and talents to the service of God. He had gathered around him a few like-minded friends, including his own brother, John, and together they had formed a little religious society, which soon became mockingly known as the Holy Club. They had pledged themselves to daily Bible-study and prayer and to weekly attendance at Holy Communion. They had given themselves unsparingly to works of charity—visiting the sick and those in prison, feeding the hungry, clothing the naked, and teaching the children of the poor. They had also earned themselves a certain amount of unpopularity by their devotion to such a rigorous role of life and had been called by a variety of derisive names, such as Bible-moths, Sacramentarians, and *Methodists*.[2] And in all this Charles Wesley had played his part; indeed he had done more. Of his own free will he had refused an offer of flourishing estates in Ireland, owned by a childless cousin who wished to make him his heir. Instead he had gone, with his brother and two other friends from the Holy Club, to Georgia in order to serve God under the rude and rigorous conditions of the newly opened British colony there. They went, as John explains, "not to avoid want, God having given us plenty of temporal blessings, nor to gain riches or honour, which we trust he will ever enable us to look on as no other than dung and dross; but singly this—to save our souls, to live wholly to the glory of God."[3]

Surely, then, Charles Wesley had reason to say that he had "used his best endeavours to serve God"; and what endeavours they were! So was not Peter Böhler "very uncharitable" to suggest, even by silence, that he had no ground of hope for salvation in them? What had Peter in mind?

If he had spoken, his argument might have run something like this: "Charles, that is sheer pride. Indeed, it's worse, it's unbelief; for it's entirely contrary to the gospel. You know what St. Paul says: 'By grace you have been saved through faith; and this is not your own doing, it is the gift of God—not because of works, lest any man should boast. For we are his workmanship, created in Christ Jesus for good works'—*for* them, Charles, not *by* them!—'which God prepared beforehand that we should walk in them.' Do you really think that man can purchase his salvation by his good works and endeavours? Is God's kingdom put up for sale, like wares on a market-stall? If it were, do you really think you would have enough to be able to pay for it?" (Charles Wesley did not think so, of course; he only hoped, and rather uncertainly at that. He was far from sure, as many people are today.)

However, Peter Böhler's argument would go on: "If you have used your time and talents in the service of God, does this deserve praise or reward from him? Doesn't our Lord tell us something about this?

'When you have done all that is commanded you, say, "We are unworthy servants; we have only done our duty."' After all, who gave you your time and talents? To whom do you owe them? Don't you owe your very existence, your life, with all your powers of body and soul, everything you have and are—don't you owe it to God alone, who created you? 'It is he that hath made us, and not we ourselves.' Shall *we*, then, who did not and could not give ourselves even our earthly, temporal life, imagine that we can rely on ourselves for eternal life and blessedness? How can we, especially when we remember how imperfect our service of God has been? How much we have left undone that we ought to have done! How often we have done what we ought not to have done! No, Charles, there is no health in us that we should look to ourselves for salvation. We must look to Christ, and to God in Christ, to his mercy, his forgiving and renewing grace, and to that alone."

Not until the beginning of May did Peter Böhler convince Charles Wesley of all this—though some weeks earlier he had persuaded John, with whom he had also been in touch since February. By this time Charles was lodging in London. He had still not fully recovered from his illness, and although he was at last persuaded of the truth of Peter Böhler's teaching, he had still not made it truly his own. He was "convinced of unbelief." For it is possible to believe, even fervently, in the doctrine of salvation by faith without having that faith in Christ of which the doctrine speaks, the faith that saves. This was John Wesley's situation, too, for he also was convinced that the doctrine was true and was preaching it regularly at the time, while knowing that he himself was without saving faith. Like Charles, he was convinced of unbelief.

John appears to have been more prepared than his brother for Peter Böhler's message as a result in particular of experiences he had had with other Moravians both on shipboard and in Georgia. During a violent storm at sea, for example, he observed that a group of Moravian emigrants alone among both passengers and crew seemed unafraid; and he tells us: "I asked one of them afterwards, 'Were you not afraid?' He answered, 'I thank God, no.' I asked, 'But were not your women and children afraid?' He replied mildly, 'No; our women and children are not afraid to die.'"[4]

This reply shook John Wesley even more than the storm had done. Then, a few days after his landing in Georgia, some searching questions were put to him during a conversation he had with another Moravian, August Gottlieb Spangenberg, that still further disturbed him. "[He asked me]! 'Does the Spirit of God bear witness with your spirit that you are a child of God?' I was surprised, and knew not what to answer. He observed it and asked, 'Do you know Jesus Christ?' I paused, and said, 'I know he is the Saviour of the world.' 'True,' replied he, 'but do you know he has saved you?' I answered, 'I hope he has died to save me.' He only added, 'Do you know yourself?' I said, 'I do.' But I fear they were vain words."[5]

John Wesley had thus long been questioning his own spiritual state before he met Peter Böhler, and yet he was far from easily persuaded by Peter, as his *Journal* shows. He says:

In my return to England, January 1738, being in imminent danger of death, and very uneasy on that account, I was strongly convinced that the cause of that uneasiness was unbelief; and that the gaining a true, living faith was the "one thing needful" for me. But still I fixed not this faith on its right object. I meant only faith in God, not faith in or through Christ. Again, I knew not that I was wholly void of this faith; but only thought I had not enough of it. So that when Peter Böhler, whom God prepared for me as soon as I came to London, affirmed of true faith in Christ (which is but one) that it had those two fruits inseparably attending it, "dominion over sin and constant peace from a sense of forgiveness," I was quite amazed, and looked upon it as a new gospel. If this was so, it was clear I had not faith. But I was not willing to be convinced of this. Therefore I disputed with all my might, and laboured to prove that faith might be where these were not; for all the scriptures relating to this I had been long since taught to construe away. Besides, I well saw no one could, in the nature of things, have such a sense of forgiveness and not *feel* it. But I felt it not. If, then, there was no faith without this, all my pretensions to faith dropped at once.[6]

It was, he tells us, on March 5 that he was first "clearly convinced of unbelief, of the want of that faith whereby we are saved";[7] and yet he was still slow to accept what Peter Böhler maintained concerning faith as a gift and work of God. In particular, he "could not understand how this faith should be given in a moment; how a man could *at once* be thus turned from darkness to light, from sin and misery to righteousness and joy in the Holy Ghost."[8] He seems not to have been fully convinced of this until near the end of April, when (in company with Charles) he met Peter Böhler once more.

When I met Peter Böhler again [he writes], he consented to put the dispute upon the issue which I desired, namely, Scripture and experience. I first consulted the Scripture. But when I set aside the glosses of men and simply considered the words of God, comparing them together, endeavouring to illustrate the obscure by the plainer passages, I found they all made against me, and was forced to retreat to my last hold, "that experience would never agree with the *literal interpretation* of those scriptures. Nor could I therefore allow it to be true, till I found some living witnesses of it." He replied, he could show me such at any time; if I desired it, the next day. And accordingly the next day he came again with three others, all of whom testified, of their own personal experience, that a true, living faith in Christ is inseparable from a sense of pardon for all past and freedom from all present sins. They added with one mouth that this faith was the gift, the free gift of God; and that he would surely bestow it upon every soul who earnestly and perseveringly sought it. I was now thoroughly convinced; and, by the grace of God, I resolved to seek it unto the end, (1) by absolutely renouncing all dependence, in whole or in part, upon *my own* works or righteousness; on which I had really grounded my hope of salvation, though I knew it not, from my youth up; (2) by adding to the constant use of all the other means of grace continual prayer for this very thing, justifying, saving faith, a full reliance on the blood of Christ shed for *me;* a trust in him as *my* Christ, as *my* sole justification, sanctification and redemption.[9]

Let us, however, now return to Charles Wesley, still a sick man in his lodging in London. On May 17, he received a visit from a new Moravian friend, William Holland, who brought with him a copy of Martin Luther's *Commentary on St. Paul's Epistle to the Galatians.* They read it together, then afterwards Charles read it alone. He found it, he says, "nobly full of faith,"[10] and he read it eagerly, himself longing and labouring to believe. He recognised in Luther's teaching a doctrine identical with that of the Articles and Homilies of his own Church and was astonished that he should ever have thought this a new doctrine.[11] Then at length he came to Luther's exposition of Galatians 2:20, where St. Paul speaks of "the Son of God who loved me, and gave himself for me." Here is part of what he read:

Who is this "me"? Even I, wretched and damnable sinner, so dearly beloved of the Son of God that he gave himself for me. If I, then, through works or merits could have loved the Son of God, and so come unto him, what needed he to deliver himself for me?... If I, being a wretch and a damned sinner, could be redeemed by any other price, what needed the Son of God to be given for me? But because there was no other price, either in heaven or in earth, but Christ the Son of God, therefore it was most necessary that he should be delivered for me. Moreover, this he did of inestimable love; for Paul says, "who loved me." For he delivered neither sheep, ox, gold, nor silver, but even God himself entirely and wholly, "for me," even for "me," I say, a miserable and wretched sinner.

Read therefore with great vehemency these words, "ME" and "FOR ME," and so inwardly practise with thyself, that thou with a sure faith mayest conceive and print this "ME" in thy heart, and apply it unto thyself, not doubting but that thou art of the number of those to whom this "ME" belongeth; also that Christ hath not only loved Peter and Paul, and given himself for them, but that the same grace also which is comprehended in this "ME" as well pertaineth and cometh unto us as unto them. For as we cannot deny but that we are all sinners, and are constrained to say that through the sin of Adam we are all lost [and] subject to the wrath and judgment of God, so can we not deny but that Christ died for our sins, that he might make us righteous. For he died, not to justify the righteous, but the unrighteous, and to make them the friends and children of God, and inheritors of all heavenly gifts. Therefore, when I feel and confess myself to be a sinner through Adam's transgression, why should I not say that I am made righteous through the righteousness of Christ, especially when I hear that he loved me and gave himself for me?[12]

That was what Charles read, and the message of it struck home. By prayer and meditation and by conversing with Christian friends, he sought to follow Luther's counsel and apply St. Paul's word to himself. Three days later he was enabled to do so, and on Sunday, May 21, the day of Pentecost, he rose from his convalescent couch, freed from the pain and weakness of his pleurisy and thoroughly happy in God. That, however, was not the end of the story but only a new beginning, as we shall see.

Late the following Wednesday evening, an excited little group of people made their way to Charles's lodging. John was at their head, and he burst in on his surprised and overjoyed brother, exclaiming: "I believe!"[13]—as if he said, "I too believe, Charles; I now believe as you do"—for he had heard, two days before, what he calls "the surprising news that my brother had found rest to his soul."[14]

John had come from the meeting of that religious society in Aldersgate Street, to which, as he tells us, he had gone "very unwillingly." He had been in the same distress of soul as Charles. He was convinced of the truth of the doctrine of salvation by faith and, at the same time, of his own lack of faith—"convinced of unbelief." He was preaching faith to others but not possessing it himself. In Aldersgate Street, however, he heard someone read Luther's *Preface to the Epistle to the Romans,* and Luther clinched matters for him as he had already done for Charles. "About a quarter before nine, while he was describing the change which God works in the heart through faith in Christ, I felt my heart strangely warmed. I felt I did trust in Christ, Christ alone for salvation; and an assurance was given me that he had taken away *my* sins, even *mine,* and saved *me* from the law of sin and death."[15]

Wesley's Methodist descendants, I fear, all too often talk about Wesley's warmed heart without any reference to the fire that warmed it. They even exhort People to warmth, as if a man could generate his own heat, instead of speaking words aflame with the love of God in Christ, which might kindle an answering fire. Let us then listen to some of the words that John Wesley heard that night:

Doing the works of the law [Luther says] and fulfilling the law are two very different things. The work of the law is everything that one does or can do, towards keeping the law of his own free will or by his own powers. But since under all these works and along with them there remains in the heart dislike for the law, and the compulsion to keep it, these works are all wasted and of no value. That is what St. Paul means when he says: "By the works of the law no man becomes righteous before God." To fulfil the law, however, is to do its works with pleasure and love, and to live a godly and good life of one's own accord, without the compulsion of the law. This pleasure and love for the law is put into the heart by the Holy Ghost. But the Holy Ghost is not given except in, with and by faith in Jesus Christ. And faith does not come save only through God's word or gospel, which preaches Christ, that he is God's Son and a man, and has died and risen again for our sakes.

Hence it comes that faith alone makes righteous and fulfils the law; for out of Christ's merit it brings the Spirit, and the Spirit makes the heart glad and free as the law requires that it shall be. Faith, however, is a divine work in us. It changes us and makes us to be born anew of God (John 1.); it kills the old Adam and makes altogether new and different men, in heart and spirit and mind and powers, and it brings with it the Holy Ghost. O, it is a living, busy, active, mighty thing, this faith, and so it is impossible for it not to do good works incessantly. It does not ask whether there are good works to do, but before the question rises it has already done them, and is always at the doing of them.

Faith is a living, daring confidence in God's grace, so sure and certain that a man would stake his life on it a thousand times. This confidence in God's grace and knowledge of it, makes a man glad and bold and happy in dealing with God and with all his creatures; and this is the work of the Holy Ghost in faith. Hence a man is ready and glad, without compulsion, to do good to everyone, to serve everyone, to suffer everything, in love and praise of God, who has shown him this grace; and thus it is impossible to separate works from faith, as impossible as to separate heat and light from fire.[16]

"As impossible as to separate heat and light from fire." That is why the Wesleys' evangelical conversion, or pentecostal experience, or call it what you will, was not the end but only a new beginning. "I began," writes John in his *Journal*, "to pray with all my might for those who had in a more especial manner despitefully used me and persecuted me. I then testified openly to all there what I now first felt in my heart."[17] That was the immediate and spontaneous fruit of the warning of his heart.

John and Charles Wesley now no longer merely hoped for salvation; they had received it and were sure of it. And they were sure, not on the basis of their own good works and "best endeavours," not on the basis of their own righteousness, but on the basis of God's righteousness, God's work through Christ for them and in them. Not that their assurance always remained equally clear and strong, and they sometimes held the gift of God with weak and trembling hands, as we shall see; but they never afterwards let it go. Nor did they cease from their good works and their devoted service of God and man. On the contrary, they only now truly began. They began their lifelong, tireless pursuit of those "good works which God had prepared beforehand" for them to walk in.

Not for a moment did they leave off any of the tasks they had assumed before—their Bible-study and constant prayer and frequent attendance at Holy Communion, their visiting of the sick and those in prison, feeding the hungry, clothing the naked, teaching, preaching, exhorting, rebuking, comforting. But all was now done with a new heart and mind. They were not now seeking anxiously to save their own souls but rather yielding themselves in grateful obedience to God, to be instruments in his hand for the salvation of others; and this, not by their own "best endeavours," but by the limitless resources and mighty power of the Holy Ghost given unto them. It was no longer their own work, but God's work in and through them.

Sometimes modern Christians look back wistfully to the days of the Wesleys and the Evangelical Revival and lament that "times have changed" and "things don't happen now as they did then." That is just what John Wesley said when Peter Böhler was trying to convince him of the reality of salvation by faith. Even when he was persuaded that this was the teaching of the New Testament and the experience of the first Christians, he argued: "Thus, I grant, God wrought in the first ages of Christianity; but times are changed. What reason have I to believe he works in the same manner now?" But he was "beat out of this retreat," he says, "by the concurring evidence of several living witnesses, who testified God had thus wrought in themselves."[18] Then, on May 24, he found confirmation in his own experience of what the New Testament and the "living witnesses" had taught him. He found that although the times might have changed, God had not nor had God's plan of salvation, and the same resources that were available to the first Christians were available also to him. And the same resources are available still today for us, by the same grace of God and the same "living, busy, active, mighty faith," the all-victorious faith of Paul, of Luther, of Peter Böhler and the Wesleys.

This faith, of which the seeds were first planted by our Lord in the days of his flesh, came to full flower first at Pentecost, when the Holy Spirit was poured out on the Apostles. It has withered and revived countless times since then, and it blossomed again at Whitsuntide, the anniversary of Pentecost, in May, 1738, in the experience of John and Charles Wesley. To celebrate it, Charles wrote a hymn, which the two brothers sang together after John's confession of faith on the evening of May 24. In these verses they expressed both their gratitude to God

and their dedication to the mission that was to occupy them for the rest
of their lives.

Where shall my wondering soul begin?
    How shall I all to heaven aspire?
A slave redeemed from death and sin,
    A brand plucked from eternal fire,
How shall I equal triumphs raise,
    Or sing my great Deliverer's praise?

O how shall I the goodness tell,
    Father, which thou to me hast showed?
That I, a child of wrath and hell,
    I should be called a child of God,
Should know, should feel, my sins forgiven,
    Blest with this antepast of heaven!

And shall I slight my Father's love?
    Or basely fear his gifts to own?
Unmindful of his favours prove?
    Shall I, the hallowed cross to shun,
Refuse his righteousness to impart,
    By hiding it within my heart?

Outcasts of men, to you I call,
    Harlots and publicans and thieves!
He spreads his arms to embrace you all;
    Sinners alone his grace receives;
No need of him the righteous have;
    He came the lost to seek and save.

Come, O my guilty brethren, come,
    Groaning beneath your load of sin!
His bleeding heart shall make you room,
    His open side shall take you in;
He calls you now, invites you home;
    Come, O my guilty brethren, come![19]

PILGRIMS' PROGRESS

That the experience of John and Charles Wesley in May, 1738, was a
decisive turning-point in their lives is indisputable. The traditional
understanding of it as the authentic starting-point of the Methodist
Revival is also entirely proper. Yet its essential significance has often
been obscured, especially when undue attention has been paid to the

temperature of John Wesley's "strangely warmed" heart. Methodists have in consequence often been accused (and not always unjustly) of teaching "salvation by feeling." They have even at times appeared to substitute a rather vague, general notion of "religious experience" for faith in Jesus Christ. But such charges cannot lie against the Wesleys.

In a letter written in 1771, John says: "Many years since, I saw that 'without holiness no man shall see the Lord.' I began following after it, and inciting all with whom I had any intercourse to do the same. Ten years after, God gave me a clearer view than I had before of the way how to attain this—namely, by faith in the Son of God. And immediately I declared to all, 'We are saved from sin, we are made holy, by faith.'"[20] The same point is made elsewhere, thus:

Q. What was the rise of Methodism, so called?

A. In 1729, two young men, reading the Bible, saw they could not be saved without holiness, followed after it, and incited others to do so. In 1737, they saw holiness comes by faith. They saw likewise that men are justified before they are sanctified; but still holiness was their point. God then thrust them out, utterly against their will, to raise a holy people.[21]

What this means can be expressed as follows: (1) From the inception of the Holy Club (and in John's case even earlier[22]) both the Wesleys were engaged in the pursuit of holiness. By holiness they meant nothing else but the love of God and man, or "the mind that was in Christ." They were seeking to fulfil the great twofold commandment: "Thou shalt love the Lord thy God with all thy heart and mind and soul and strength; and thou shalt love thy neighbour as thyself." (2) But they were seeking to cultivate this love in themselves by their own devotion and "best endeavours." Just as Luther had sought to fulfil the commandment by becoming a monk and observing the rule of his order, so they had sought it by the discipline of the Holy Club and the renunciation involved in going to Georgia. (3) Then from the Moravians, especially Peter Böhler, and from Luther himself, they learned that the holiness and love which they sought was not to be found by the way of their own "good works" but by faith in Christ alone; and in May, 1738, they took their first trembling but excited steps along that way. (4) "But still holiness was their point." The goal they had set themselves long before remained still their goal. The way of faith must lead to love filling the heart and governing the life, or it was no true faith. "Faith working by love" was for them the sum and substance of Christianity and, indeed, of all true religion.[23]

It is true that the Wesleys were interested in "feeling" and "experience"; but the experience with which they were concerned was that of living faith in Christ, and what they wanted to "feel" was the fruit of that faith—love, peace, and joy, but above all, love. At Pentecost, 1738, they began to enter into this experience, taking, as we have said, "their first trembling but excited steps" along the way of faith. But this was only the beginning for them, and for days, weeks, and even months afterwards, they were beset by recurrent doubts and uncertainties, and had to wrestle with very contrary feelings. The following extracts from their writings reveal a continual struggle for faith and the gradual triumph of faith over feeling.

Charles Wesley's Experience.[24]

[*Evening of May 21*] . . . I now found myself at peace with God, and rejoiced in hope of loving Christ. My temper for the rest of the day was mistrust of my own great, but before unknown, weakness. I saw that by faith I stood; by the continual support of faith, which kept me from falling, though of myself I was ever sinking into sin.

Mon., May 22. Under [Christ's] protection I waked next morning, and rejoiced in reading the 107th Psalm, so nobly describing what God had done for my soul. Today I saw him chiefly as my King, and found him in his power: but saw little of the love of Christ crucified, or of my sins past; though more, I humbly hope, of my own weakness and his strength. I had many evil thoughts darted into my mind, but I rejected them immediately (yet not I).

Tue., May 23. I waked under the protection of Christ, and gave myself up, soul and body to him. At nine I began an hymn upon my conversion, but was persuaded to break off, for fear of pride. Mr. Bray coming, encouraged me to proceed in spite of Satan. I prayed Christ to stand by me, and finished the hymn.

Wed., May 24. Being to receive the sacrament today, I was assaulted by the fear of my old accustomed deadness; but soon recovered my confidence in Christ, that he would give me so much sense of his love now, as he saw good for me. I received [the sacrament] without any sensible devotion.

At eight [in the evening] I prayed by myself for love; with some feeling, and assurance of feeling more. Towards ten, my brother was brought in triumph by a troop of our friends, and declared "I believe." We sang the hymn with great joy, and parted with prayer. At midnight I gave myself up to Christ; assured I was safe, sleeping or waking.

Thur., May 25. I commended myself to Christ, my Prophet, Priest, and King. Before communicating, I left it to Christ, whether or in what measure he would please to manifest himself to me in this breaking of bread. I had no particular attention to the prayers. . . . At the same time, I felt great peace and joy; and assurance of feeling more, when it is best.

Soon after I was a little cast down, by feeling some temptation, and foreseeing more; but God lifted me up by his word: "Fear not: for I have redeemed thee, I have called thee by thy name; thou art mine. When thou passest through the waters, I will be with thee. . . . "; (Isa. 43:1f.). This promise was fulfilled in me when under frequent motions of sin I looked up to Christ, and found them beaten down continually.

Fri., May 26. . . . I dined with great liberty of spirit, being amazed to find my old enemy, intemperance, so suddenly subdued, that I have almost forgot I was ever in bondage to him. In the evening I broke through my own great unwillingness, and at last preached faith in Christ to an accidental visitant.

Sat., May 27. I felt a motion of anger, from a trifling disappointment; but it was no sooner felt than conquered. I received the sacrament: still no sensible love; but comfort.

Trinity Sunday, May 28. I rose in great heaviness, which neither private nor joint prayer could remove. At last I betook myself to intercession for my relations, and was greatly helped and enlarged herein; particularly in prayer for a most profligate sinner. I spent the morning with James Hutton, in prayer, and singing and rejoicing.

Thur., June 1. I was troubled today that I could not pray, being utterly dead at the sacrament.

Fri., June 2. I was still unable to pray; still dead in communicating; full of a cowardly desire of death.

Sat., June 3. My deadness continued, and the next day increased. I rose exceeding heavy and averse to prayer; so that I almost resolved not to go to church. When I did go, the prayers and sacrament were exceeding grievous to me; and I could not help asking myself, "Where is the difference between what I am now, and what I was before believing?" I immediately answered, "That the darkness was not like the former darkness, because I was satisfied there was no guilt in it; because I was assured it would be dispersed; and because, though I could not find I loved God, or feel that he loved me, yet I did and would believe he loved me notwithstanding."

In the evening Mr. Brown, Holland, and others called. I was very averse to coming among them, but forced myself to it, and spent two or three hours in singing, reading, and prayer. This exercise a little revived me; and I found myself much assisted to pray.

We asked particularly that, if it was the will of God, some one might now receive the atonement. While I was yet speaking the words, Mr. Brown found power to believe. He rose and told me my prayer was heard, and answered in him. We were all full of joy and thanksgiving. Before we parted,

I prayed with Mr. Brown, and praised God, to the great confirmation of my faith. The weight was quite taken off. I found power to pray with great earnestness, and rejoiced in my trials having continued so long, to show me that it is then the best time to labour for our neighbour, when we are cast down, and most unable to help ourselves.

Tue., June 6. In the evening I read Luther, as usual, to a large company of our friends. Mr. Burton was greatly affected. My inward temptations are, in a manner, uninterrupted. I never knew the energy of sin, till now that I experience the superior strength of Christ.

Wed., June 7. I found myself this morning under my [heavenly] Father's protection; and reading Matt. 7, "Ask and ye shall receive," I asked some sense of his love in the sacrament. It was there given me to believe assuredly that God loved me, even when I could have no sense of it. Some imperfect perception of his love I had, and was strengthened to hope against hope, after communicating.

Thur., June 8. . . . . At three I took coach for Blendon, with Mr. Bray; and had much talk with a lady about the fall, and faith in Christ. She openly maintained the merit of good works. I would all who oppose the righteousness of faith were so ingenuous: then would they no longer seek it as it were by the works of the law.

Sun., June 11. . . . . After prayers we joined in intercession for Mr. and Mrs. Delamotte; then for poor Hetty. I received much comfort in reading Luther.

[After church, we] joined in prayer for a poor woman in despair, one Mrs. Searl, whom Satan had bound these many years. I saw her pass by in the morning, and was touched with a sense of her misery. After pleading his promise of being with us to the end of the world, we went down to her in the name of Jesus. I asked her whether she thought God was love; and not anger, as Satan would persuade her. Then I preached the gospel, which she received with all imaginable eagerness. When we had for some time continued together in prayer, she rose up another creature, strongly and explicitly declaring her faith in the blood of Christ, and full persuasion that she was accepted in the Beloved. Hetty then declared that she could not but believe that Christ died for her, even for her. We gave thanks for both, with much exultation and triumph.

Wed., June 14. . . . . Poor Hetty was tempted to imagine she did not believe, because she had not been affected exactly in the same manner with others. We used a prayer for her, and parted.

Thur., June 22. I comforted Hetty, under a strong temptation because she was not in all points affected like other believers, especially the poor; who have generally a much larger degree of confidence than the rich and learned.

Mon., July 10. At Mr. Sparks's request, I went with him, Mr. Bray, and Mr. Burnham, to Newgate; and preached to the ten malefactors under sentence of death; but with a heavy heart. My old prejudices against the possibility of a death-bed repentance still hung upon me; and I could hardly hope there was mercy for those whose time was so short. But in the midst of my languid discourse, a sudden spirit of faith came upon me, and I promised them all pardon in the name of Jesus Christ, if they would then, as at the last hour, repent and believe the gospel. Nay, I did believe they would accept of the proffered mercy, and could not help telling them, "I had no doubt but God would give me every soul of them."

Wed., July 12. I preached at Newgate to the condemned felons, and visited one of them in his cell, sick of a fever; a poor Black that had robbed his master. I told him of One who came down from heaven to save lost sinners, and him in particular; described the sufferings of the Son of God, his sorrows, agony, and death. He listened with all the signs of eager astonishment; the tears trickled down his cheeks while he cried, "What! was it for me? Did God suffer all this for so poor a creature as me?" I left him waiting for the salvation of God.

Sat., July 15. I preached there again with an enlarged heart; and rejoiced with my poor happy Black; who now *believes* the Son of God loved him, and gave himself for him.

Tue., July 18. . . . At night I was locked with Bray in one of the cells. We wrestled in mighty prayer. All the criminals were present; and all delightfully cheerful. Joy was visible in all their faces. We sang:

> Behold the Saviour of mankind,
> Nailed to the shameful tree!
> How vast the love that him inclined
> To bleed and die for thee![25]

Wed., July 19. . . . At half-hour past nine their irons were knocked off, and their hands tied. I went in a coach with Sparks, Washington, and a friend of Newington's. By half-hour past ten we came to Tyburn, waited till eleven: then were brought the children appointed to die. I got upon the cart with Sparks and Broughton. I prayed first, then Sparks and Broughton. We had prayed before that our Lord would show there was a power superior to the fear of death. They were all cheerful; full of comfort, peace, and triumph; assuredly persuaded Christ had died for them, and waited to receive them into paradise.

The Black had spied me coming out of the coach, and saluted me with his looks. As often as his eyes met mine, he smiled with the most composed, delightful countenance I ever saw. Read caught hold of my hand in a transport of joy. Newington seemed perfectly pleased. Hudson declared he was never better, or more at ease, in mind and body. None showed any natural terror of death: no fear, or crying, or tears. All expressed their desire of our following them to paradise. I never saw such calm triumph, such incredible indifference to dying. We sang several hymns; particularly,

> Behold the Saviour of mankind,
> Nailed to the shameful tree;

and the hymn entitled "Faith in Christ," which concludes:

> A guilty, weak, and helpless worm,
> Into thy hands I fall:
> Be thou my life, my righteousness,
> My Jesus, and my all.[26]

We prayed him, in earnest faith, to receive their spirits. I could do nothing but rejoice: kissed Newington and Hudson; took leave of each in particular. Mr. Broughton bade them not be surprised when the cart should draw away. They cheerfully replied they should not; expressed some concern how we should get back to our coach. We left them going to meet their Lord, ready for the Bridegroom. When the cart drew off, not one stirred or struggled for life, but meekly gave up their spirits. Exactly at twelve they were turned off. I spoke a few suitable words to the crowd; and returned, full of peace and confidence in our friends' happiness. That hour under the gallows was the most blessed hour of my life.

> O the goodness of God,
> Employing a clod
> His tribute of glory to raise!
> His standard to bear,
> And with triumph declare
> His unspeakable riches of grace.

> All honour and praise
> To the Father of grace,
> To the Spirit and Son I return!
> The business pursue
> He hath made me to do,
> And rejoice that I ever was born.

> In a rapture of joy
> My life I employ,
> The God of my life to proclaim;
> 'Tis worth living for this,
> To administer bliss
> And salvation in Jesus' name.

> My remnant of days
> I spend in his praise.
> Who died the whole world to redeem:
> Be they many or few.
> My days are his due.
> And they all are devoted to him.[27]

John Wesley's Experience.[28]

[*Evening of May 24*]. . . . It was not long before the enemy suggested, "This cannot be faith; for where is thy joy?" Then was I taught that peace and victory over sin are essential to faith in the Captain of our salvation; but that, as to the transports of joy that usually attend the beginning of it, especially in those who have mourned deeply, God sometimes giveth, sometimes withholdeth them, according to the counsels of his own will.

Thur., May 25. The moment I awaked, "Jesus, Master," was in my heart and in my mouth; and I found all my strength lay in keeping my eye fixed upon him, and my soul waiting on him continually. . . . Yet the enemy injected a fear, "If thou dost believe, why is there not a more sensible [perceptible] change?" I answered (yet not I), "That I know not. But this I know, I have now 'peace with God.' And I sin not today, and Jesus my Master has forbid me to take thought for the morrow."

"But is not any sort of fear," continued the tempter, "a proof that thou dost not believe?" I desired my Master to answer for me, and opened his Book upon those words of St. Paul, "Without were fightings, within were fears." Then, inferred I, well may fears be within me; but I must go on, and tread them under my feet.

Mon., May 29. I set out for Dummer with Mr. Wolf, one of the first-fruits of Peter Böhler's ministry in England. I was much strengthened by the grace of God in him. Yet was his state so far above mine, that I was often tempted to doubt whether we had one faith. But without much reasoning about it, I held here: "Though his be strong and mine weak, yet that God hath given some degree of faith even to me, I know by its fruits. For I have constant peace; not one uneasy thought. And I have freedom from sin; not one unholy desire."

Sun., June 4. Was indeed a feast-day. For from the time of my rising till past one in the afternoon, I was praying, reading the Scriptures, singing praise, or calling sinners to repentance. All these days I scarce remember to have opened the New Testament, but upon some "great and precious promise." And I saw more than ever that the gospel is in truth but one great promise, from the beginning of it to the end.

Tue., June 6. I had still more comfort, and peace, and joy; on which I fear I began to presume. For in the evening I received a letter from Oxford, which threw me into much perplexity. It was asserted therein, "That no doubting could consist with the least degree of true faith; that whoever at any time felt any doubt or fear was not weak in faith, but had no faith at all. . . ."

Begging of God to direct me, I opened my Testament on I Cor. 3:1ff., where St. Paul speaks of those whom he terms "babes in Christ," who were "not able to bear strong meat," nay (in a sense) "carnal"; to whom nevertheless he says, "Ye are God's building, ye are the temple of God." Surely, then, these men had some degree of faith; though it is plain, their faith was but weak.

Wed., June 7. I determined, if God should permit, to retire for a time into Germany. I had fully proposed, before I left Georgia, so to do, if it should please God to bring me back to Europe. And now I clearly saw the time was come. My weak mind could not bear to be thus sawn asunder. And I hoped the conversing with these holy men the Moravians, at Herrnhut, who were themselves living witnesses of the full power of faith, and yet able to bear with those that are weak, would be a means under God of so establishing my soul, that I might go on from faith to faith, and "from strength to strength."[29]

[Before leaving for Germany Wesley preached the University Sermon at Oxford on the afternoon of Sunday, June 11. This was the sermon on Salvation by Faith, which afterwards became the first of the Standard Sermons. Not a mean achievement for one who at the time was so "weak in faith"!]

Sun., Sept. 17. I began again to declare in my own country the glad tidings of salvation, preaching three times, and afterwards expounding the Holy Scripture to a large company in the Minories. On *Monday* I rejoiced to meet with our little society, which now consisted of thirty-two persons. The next day I went to the condemned felons in Newgate, and offered them free salvation.

Mon., Oct. 9. I set out for Oxford. In walking I read the truly surprising narrative of the conversions lately wrought in and about the town of Northampton, in New England [under the ministry of Jonathan Edwards]. Surely "this is the Lord's doing, and it is marvellous in our eyes." An extract from this I wrote to a friend, concerning the state of those who are "weak in faith." His answer, which I received at Oxford on *Saturday* the 14th., threw me into great perplexity. . . .

Sun., Oct. 29. . . . In the evening, being troubled at what some said of "the kingdom of God within us," and doubtful of my own state, I called upon God, and received this answer from his word: "He himself also waited for the kingdom of God" [Luke 23:51]. "But should not I wait in silence and retirement?" was the thought that immediately struck into my mind. I opened my Testament again, on those words, "Seest thou not how faith wrought together with his works? And by works was faith made perfect" [James 2:22].[30]

[*Mon., Oct. 30. John wrote in a letter to his brother Samuel:*] By a Christian I mean one who so believes in Christ as that sin hath no more dominion over him; and in this obvious sense of the word I was not a Christian till May the '24th last past. For till then sin had the dominion over me, although I fought with it continually; but surely then, from that time to this it hath not, such is the free grace of God in Christ.

If you ask by what means I am made free (though not perfect, neither infallibly sure of my perseverance), I answer, by faith in Christ; by such a sort or degree of faith as I had not till that day. My desire of this faith I knew long before, though not so clearly till Sunday, January the 8th last.[31]. . . . Some measure of this faith, which bringeth salvation or victory over sin, and which implies peace and trust in God through Christ, I now enjoy by his free mercy; though in very deed it is in me but as a grain of mustard seed: for the πληοφπρία πίστεως—the seal of the Spirit, the love of God shed abroad in my heart, and producing joy in the Holy Ghost—this witness of the Spirit I have not; but I patiently wait for it. And having seen and spoken with a cloud of witnesses abroad as well as in my own country, I cannot doubt but that believers who wait and pray for it will find these scriptures fulfilled in themselves. My hope is that they will be fulfilled in me. I build on Christ, the Rock of Ages; on his sure mercies described in his Word; and on his promises, all which I know are yea and amen. Those who have not yet received joy in the Holy Ghost, the love of God, and the plerophory of faith (any or all of which I take to be the witness of the Spirit with our spirit that we are the sons of God), I believe to be Christians in that imperfect sense wherein I may call myself such; and I exhort them to pray that God would give them also "to rejoice in the hope of the glory of God," and to feel "his love shed abroad in their hearts by the Holy Ghost which is given unto them."[32]

Thur., Jan. 4, 1739—One who had had the form of godliness many years wrote the following reflections:

My friends affirm that I am mad, because I said I was not a Christian a year ago. I affirm I am not a Christian now. Indeed, what I might have been I know not, had I been faithful to the grace then given, when, expecting nothing less, I received such a sense of the forgiveness of my sins as till then I never knew. But that I am not a Christian at this day I as assuredly know as that Jesus is the Christ.

For a Christian is one who has the fruits of the Spirit of Christ, which (to mention no more) are love, peace, joy. But these I have not. I have not any love of God. I do not love either the Father or the Son. Do you ask, how do I know whether I love God? I answer by another question, "How do you know whether you love me?" Why, as you know whether you are hot or cold. You *feel* this moment that you do or do not love me. And I *feel* this moment I do not love God; which therefore I *know* because I *feel* it. There is no word more proper, more clear, or more strong.

Wed., Jan. 10. I preached at Basingshaw church *Saturday* the 13th. I expounded to a large company at Beech Lane. *Sunday* the 14th, after preaching at Islington, I expounded twice at Mr. Sims's in the Minories.

Sun., Feb. 4. I preached at St. Giles's on "Whosoever believeth on Me, out of his belly shall flow rivers of living water." How was the power of God present with us! I am content to preach here no more.[33]

Fri., Mar. 2. It was the advice of all our brethren that I should spend a few days at Oxford, whither I accordingly went on *Saturday* the 3rd. A few names I found here also who had not denied the faith, neither been ashamed of their Lord, even in the midst of a perverse generation. And every day we were together we had convincing proof, such as it had not before entered into our hearts to conceive, that "He is able to save unto the uttermost all that come to God through him."

Thursday the 15th. I set out early in the morning, and in the afternoon came to London. During my stay here. . . . I received, after several others, a letter from Mr. Whitefield, and another from Mr. Seward, entreating me in the most pressing manner to come to Bristol without delay. This I was not at all forward to do.

Sat., Mar. 31. In the evening I reached Bristol, and met Mr. Whitefield there. I could scarce reconcile myself at first to this strange way of preaching in the fields, of which he set me an example on Sunday; having been all my life (until very lately) so tenacious of every point relating to decency and order, that I should have thought the saving of souls almost a sin if it had not been done in a church.

Sun., Apr. 1. In the evening I began expounding our Lord's Sermon on the Mount (one pretty remarkable example of field-preaching, though I suppose there were churches at that time also) to a little society which was accustomed to meet once or twice a week in Nicholas Street.

Mon., Apr. 2. At four in the afternoon I submitted to be more vile, and proclaimed in the highways the glad tidings of salvation, speaking from a little eminence in a ground adjoining to the city, to about three thousand people. The scripture on which I spoke was this (is it possible any one should be ignorant that it is fulfilled in every true minister of Christ?), "The Spirit of the Lord is upon me, because he hath anointed me to preach the gospel to the poor. He hath sent me to heal the broken-hearted; to preach deliverance to the captives, and recovery of sight to the blind; to set at liberty them that are bruised, to proclaim the acceptable year of the Lord."[34]

Shall I, for fear of feeble man,
The Spirit's course in me restrain?
Or, undismayed, in deed and word
Be a true witness for my Lord?

Saviour of men, thy searching eye
Doth all my inmost thoughts descry;
Doth aught on earth my wishes raise,
Or the world's pleasures or its praise?

The love of Christ doth me constrain
To seek the wandering souls of men;
With cries, entreaties, tears, to save,
To snatch them from the gaping grave.

My life, my blood, I here present,
If for thy truth they may be spent:
Fulfil thy sovereign counsel, Lord;
Thy will be done, thy name adored.

Give me thy strength, O God of power;
Then, let winds blow or thunders roar,
Thy faithful witness will I be:
'Tis fixed; I can do all through thee![35]

More than a decade later, John Wesley wrote in a reply to a critic who
had commented adversely on several passages in his *Journal:*

[You quote me as saying:] ". . . . I cannot find in myself the love of God or
of Christ. Hence my deadness and wanderings in public prayer. Hence it is
that even in the Holy Communion I have rarely any more than a cold
attention. Hence, when I hear of the highest instance of God's love, my
heart is still senseless and unaffected. Yea, at this moment (October 14,
1738) I feel no more love to him than one I had never heard of."
      To any who knew something of inward religion I should have observed
that this is what serious divines mean by desertion. But all expressions of this
kind are jargon to you. So, allowing it to be whatever you please, I ask only,
Do you know how long I continued in this state? How many years, months,
weeks, or days? If not, how can you infer what my state of mind is now from
what it was above eleven years ago?
      Sir, I do not tell you or any man else that "I cannot now find the love of
God in myself"; or that now, in the year 1751, I rarely feel more than a cold
attention in the Holy Communion: so that your whole argument built upon
this supposition falls to the ground at once.[36]

Yet nearly a quarter of a century after this, he wrote to a certain
correspondent: "I feel more want of heat than light. I value light; but it

is nothing compared to love."[37] And after another decade he wrote yet again:

I do not remember to have heard or read anything like my own experience. Almost ever since I can remember, I have been led in a peculiar way. I go on in an even line, being very little raised at one time or depressed at another. Count Zinzendorf observes there are three different ways wherein it pleases God to lead his people: some are guided in almost every instance by apposite texts of Scripture; others see a clear and plain reason for everything they are to do; and yet others are led not so much by Scripture or reason as by particular impressions. I am very rarely led by impressions, but generally by reason and by Scripture. I see abundantly more than I feel. I want to feel more love and zeal for God.[38]

John Wesley's heart may have been "strangely warmed" at Aldersgate, but it was only warm, not hot, and it was strange for it even to be warm. John seems clearly never to have experienced the intensity of feeling that he knew thousands of others did; and there is a remarkable letter to his brother Charles, written in 1766, in which he declares he never had any love for God, nor any real faith. "And yet," he says:

I dare not preach otherwise than I do, either concerning faith or love, or justification, or perfection. And yet I find rather an increase than a decrease of zeal for the whole work of God and every part of it. I am Φερόμενος [borne along], I know not how, that I can't stand still. I want all the world to come to ὸὺ οὐκ οἶδα [Him whom I do not know]. Neither am I impelled to this by fear of any kind. I have no more fear than love. Or if I have [[any fear, it is not that of falling]] into hell but of falling into nothing.[39]

But the man who could write thus could also translate Johann Andreas Rothe's great hymn, *"Ich habe nun den Grund gefunden,"* and could put into his translation the depth of feeling that the following verses express:

> O Love, thou bottomless abyss,
> My sins are swallowed up in thee!
> Covered is my unrighteousness,
> Nor spot of guilt remains on me,
> While Jesus blood through earth and skies
> Mercy, free, boundless mercy! cries.
>
> With faith I plunge me in this sea,
> Here is my hope, my joy, my rest;
> Hither, when hell assails, I flee,
> I look into my Saviour's breast:

Away, sad doubt and anxious fear!
Mercy is all that's written there.

Though waves and storms go o'er my head,
　　Though strength, and health, and friends be gone,
Though joys be withered all and dead,
　　Though every comfort be withdrawn,
On this my steadfast soul relies—
Father, thy mercy never dies.

Fixed on this ground will I remain,
　　Though my heart fail and flesh decay;
This anchor shall my soul sustain,
　　When earth's foundations melt away:
Mercy's full power I then shall prove,
Loved with an everlasting love.[40]

II

Fulfilment of a Mission

"METHODISM SO CALLED"

When John Wesley traveled up and down the United Kingdom for fifty years, covering six thousand miles a year on horseback or by coach, holding conferences, forming societies, and preaching in all some forty thousand sermons, he had no intention of founding a new church, still less a sect. The very idea was repugnant to him, and it was even more repugnant to Charles. They were clergymen of the Church of England, and most of those working with them, as John tells us in his *Short History of Methodism* [ca. 1764], were "Church of England men." They loved the doctrine, the liturgy, and the discipline of the Church of England and did not willingly vary from it in any instance.[1] Nevertheless, they were called (though not by their own choice) "Methodists," and the movement they led possessed distinct characteristics of its own—largely shaped by John Wesley. It could be argued, indeed, that Wesley himself succeeded in making the People called Methodists into a distinct and eventually separate body.

The reasons for this were not of course doctrinal. For Methodism, as Wesley again and again insisted, was nothing else but "the religion of the Bible, the Primitive Church, and the Church of England,"[2] and with the doctrinal standards of the Church of England they had no quarrel. Their teaching was wholly in harmony with that of the Articles, the Homilies, and the Book of Common Prayer. It was in fact the common doctrine of Christendom, presented with certain particular emphases that were characteristically but by no means exclusively Methodist. What became chiefly important for the distinct and separate life of Methodism was Wesley's organization of his followers into societies, which were linked together in a strongly unified "Connexion." This was very necessary if the work of the Methodist Revival was not to be largely dissipated, but it was almost inevitable that it should result in the creation of the Methodist Church. No doubt, if the Church of England had possessed more imagination, not to mention Christian insight and charity, Methodism (at least in

Britain) might have developed into an Order within that Church; but in the circumstances that could not be.

How impossible it was can be illustrated from a letter written by Wesley in the last year of his life to the Bishop of Lincoln:

> The Methodists in general, my Lord, are members of the Church of England. They hold all her doctrines, attend her service, and partake of her sacraments. They do not willingly do harm to anyone, but do what good they can to all. To encourage each other herein they frequently spend an hour together in prayer and mutual exhortation. Permit me then to ask, *Cui bono,* "for what reasonable end," would your Lordship drive these people out of the Church? Are they not as quiet, as inoffensive, nay as pious, as any of their neighbours—except perhaps here and there an hairbrained man who knows not what he is about? Do you ask, "Who drives them out of the Church?" Your Lordship does; and that in the most cruel manner—yea, and the most disingenuous manner. They desire a licence to worship God after their own conscience. Your Lordship refuses it, and then punishes them for not having a licence! So your Lordship leaves them only this alternative, "Leave the Church or starve." And is it a Christian, yea a Protestant bishop, that so persecutes his own flock? I say, *persecutes;* for it is persecution to all intents and purposes. You do not burn them indeed, but you starve them. And how small is the difference! And your Lordship does this under colour of a vile, execrable law, not a whit better than that *de haeretico comburendo* [concerning the burning of heretics]. So persecution, which is banished out of France, is again countenanced in England! O my Lord, for God's sake, for Christ's sake, for pity's sake, suffer the poor people to enjoy their religious as well as civil liberty![3]

At the same time, it cannot be overlooked that Wesley instituted a discipline for both the preachers and the members of the Methodist Societies which was not that of the Church of England and over which the authorities of that Church had no control. He gave them Lovefeasts and Watchnight Services and Tickets of Membership, following precedents he found in the Early Church; and he gave them a Covenant Service that was all their own. He revised the Articles of Religion and the Book of Common Prayer for the Methodists in America *(The Sunday Service of the Methodists),* and what was still more fateful, he ordained preachers to minister to them—an action that had repercussions also in Britain. He also published a series of hymn books, notably one entitled *A Collection of Hymns for the Use of the People Called Methodists* (1780), which, with their successors, became the Prayer book and liturgy of Methodism, nourishing the souls both of the individual Christian and the Society. With all this, it was virtually impossible that the People called Methodists should not come to feel themselves a distinct if not separate body, especially when they met with all kinds of unfriendliness from many of the bishops and clergy. There were in consequence periodic agitations among them in favour of separation from the Church; and although Wesley successfully resisted these, so that British Methodism did not become explicitly a separate denomination till long after his death, he was forced towards the end of his life to bow to the logic of events and assist in the setting up of The Methodist Church in America.

Nevertheless, in all that he did, Wesley had, in his own words, only "one point in view—to promote, so far as I am able, vital, practical religion; and by the grace of God to beget, preserve, and increase the life of God in the souls of men."[4] "It is not our care, endeavour, or desire, to proselyte any from one man to another; or from one church (so called), from one congregation or society, to another—we would not move a finger to do this, to make ten thousand such proselytes—but from darkness to light, from Belial to Christ, from the power of Satan to God. Our one aim is to proselyte sinners to repentance, the servants of the devil to serve the living and true God."[5] "We look upon ourselves, not as the authors or ringleaders of a particular sect or party (it is the farthest thing from our thoughts), but as messengers of God to those who are Christians in name, but Heathens in heart and life, to call them back to that from which they are fallen, to real, genuine Christianity. We are therefore debtors to all these, of whatever opinion or denomination; and are consequently to do all that in us lies, to please all for their good to edification. We look upon the Methodists (so called) in general, not as any particular party (this would exceedingly obstruct the grand design for which we conceive God has raised them up), but as living witnesses, in and to every party, of that Christianity which we preach, which is hereby demonstrated to be a real thing, and visibly held out to all the world."[6]

The majority of the Methodists, it is true, were Anglicans; but it was a peculiar glory of Methodism, in Wesley's view, that while it was a religious society within the Church of England, it was one to which members of any church might belong, the only condition of membership being "a real desire to save their soul."[7] "By Methodists," he said, "I mean a people who profess to pursue (in whatsoever measure they have attained) holiness of heart and life, inward and outward conformity in all things to the revealed will of God; who place religion in a uniform resemblance of the great object of it; in a steady imitation of Him they worship, in all his imitable perfections; more particularly, in justice, mercy, and truth, or universal love filling the heart and governing the life."[8] In order to pursue such an end, it was not necessary that men should renounce their existing ecclesiastical allegiance. And just as Wesley always exhorted the Methodist Anglicans to be loyal to their own Church, so he encouraged the Methodist Presbyterians, Baptists, Congregationalists, and Quakers to do the same. Indeed, he regarded it as highly undesirable that they should do anything else, for Methodism could fulfil its true function only as an interdenominational society, not as a separate denomination. "The Methodists," he insisted, "are to spread life among all denominations; which they will do till they form a separate sect."[9]

"But," said some of his critics, "you form a Church within a Church, whose members in South Britain profess to belong to the Church of England, and those in North Britain to the Church of Scotland; while yet they are inspected and governed by Teachers who are sent, continued, or removed, by Mr. W." To which Wesley replied: "All this is in a certain sense very true. But let us see what it amounts to. 'You form a Church within a Church'; that is, you raise up and join together witnesses of real Christianity, not among Mahometans and Pagans, but within a Church by law established. Certainly so. And that Church, if she knew her own interest, would see she is much obliged to us for so doing."[10] Not, however, that Wesley ever maintained that the members of his Methodist Societies were the only "witnesses of real Christianity," nor, indeed, that they could alone be called Methodists. "There are many thousand Methodists in Great Britain and Ireland," he wrote to a correspondent in Sweden in 1769, "which are not formed into Societies. Indeed, none are but those (or rather a part of those) who are under the care of Mr. Wesley. These at present contain a little less than thirty thousand persons."[11] In other words, one could be a Methodist in John Wesley's understanding of the term, not only without leaving one's own denomination, but without becoming a member of the Methodist Society. All that was necessary was that one should be seriously pursuing "holiness in heart and life."

Wesley was, however, early accused of breaches of ecclesiastical order on account of the methods he employed: his open-air preaching, his permitting of laymen to preach, his use of extempore prayer, and his working in other men's parishes. But to all such charges he had a ready answer.

"You ask, 'How is it that I assemble Christians, who are none of my charge, to sing psalms and pray and hear the Scriptures expounded?' and think it hard to justify doing this in other men's parishes, upon catholic principles. Permit me to speak plainly. If by catholic principles you mean any other than scriptural, they weigh nothing with me. I allow no other rule, whether of faith or practice, than the Holy Scriptures; but on scriptural principles I do not think it hard to justify whatever I do. God in Scripture commands me, according to my power, to instruct the ignorant, reform the wicked, confirm the virtuous. Man forbids me to do this in another's parish: that is, in effect, to do it at all; seeing I have now no parish of my own, nor probably ever shall. Whom, then, shall I hear, God or man? 'If it be just to obey man rather than God, judge you. A dispensation of the gospel is committed to me; and woe is me if I preach not the gospel.' Suffer me now to tell you my principles in this matter. I look upon all the world as my parish; thus far, I mean, that in whatever part of it I am I judge it meet, right and my bounden duty, to declare unto all that are willing to hear, the glad tidings of salvation. This is the work which I know God has called me to; and sure I am that his blessing attends it."[12]

"It is true in some things we vary from the rules of our Church; but no further than we apprehend is our bounden duty. It is upon a full conviction of this that we. . . permit laymen whom God has called to preach. I say *permit,* because we ourselves have hitherto viewed it in no other light. It is not clear to us that presbyters so circumstanced as we are may *appoint* or *ordain* others, but it is that we may *direct* as well as *suffer* them to do what we conceive they are *moved* to *by the Holy Ghost.* It is true that in ordinary cases both an *inward* and an *outward* call are requisite. But we apprehend there is something far from *ordinary* in the present case. And upon the calmest view of things, we think they who are only called of God and not of man have *more* right to preach than they who are only called of man and not of God. Now, that many of the clergy, though called of man, are not called of God to preach his gospel is undeniable, (1) because they themselves utterly disclaim, nay, ridicule, the inward call; (2) because they do not know what the gospel is, of consequence they do not and cannot preach it. Dear sir, coolly and impartially consider this, and you will see on which side the difficulty lies. I see those running whom God hath not sent, destroying their own souls and those that hear them. I see the blind leading the blind and both falling into the ditch. Unless I warn in all ways I can these perishing souls of their danger, am I clear of the blood of these men? Soul-damning clergymen lay me under more difficulties than soul-saving laymen."[13]

As to attacks on his open-air preaching and use of extempore prayer, Wesley writes: "I have often replied: (1) It were better for me to die than not to preach the gospel of Christ; yea and in the fields, either where I may not preach in the church or where the church will not contain the congregation. (2) That I use the Service of the Church every Lord's Day, and it has never yet appeared to me that any rule of the Church forbids my using extemporary prayer on other occasions." He then proceeds:

But methinks I would go deeper. I would inquire, what is the end of all ecclesiastical order? Is it not to bring souls from the power of Satan to God, and to build them up in his fear and love? Order, then, is so far valuable as it answers these ends; and if it answers them not, it is nothing worth. Now I would fain know, where has order answered these ends? Not in any place where I have been—not among the tinners in Cornwall, the keelmen at Newcastle, the colliers in Kingswood or Staffordshire; not among the drunkards, swearers, Sabbath-breakers of Moorfields, or the harlots of Drury Lane. They could not be built up in the fear and love of God while they were open, barefaced servants of the devil; and such they continued, notwithstanding the most orderly preaching both in St. Luke's and St. Giles's Church. One reason whereof was, they never came near the church, nor had any desire or design to do so, till, by what you term 'breach of order' they were brought to fear God, to love him, and to keep his commandments. It was not, therefore, so much the want of order as of the knowledge and love of God which kept those poor souls for so many years in open bondage to an hard master. And indeed, wherever the knowledge and love of God are, true order will not be wanting. But the most apostolical order, where these are not, is less than nothing and vanity."[14]

It is true, Wesley admits, "I still believe 'the Episcopal form of Church government to be both scriptural and apostolical': I mean, well agreeing with the practice and writings of the Apostles. But that it is prescribed in Scripture I do not believe. This opinion (which I once heartily espoused) I have been heartily ashamed of ever since I read Dr. Stillingfleet's *Irenicon*. I think he has unanswerably proved that neither Christ nor his Apostles prescribed any particular form of Church government, and that the plea for the divine right of Episcopacy was never heard of in the primitive Church. But were it otherwise, I would still call these 'smaller points than the love of God and mankind.'"[15]

"OUR DOCTRINES"

Let us now turn to look at the characteristic teaching of the Wesleys and their Methodism. As we do so, it should of course be constantly borne in mind that this rests solidly upon the doctrinal heritage of the Christian centuries. The great and fundamental doctrines of the Trinity, the Incarnation, the Atonement, the Holy Spirit, and the Church are unquestioningly presupposed in all John Wesley's sermons, tracts, and treatises, and they are frequently celebrated in Charles Wesley's hymns. At the same time, there are other doctrines, corollaries of these, that are singled out for special emphasis and that must be regarded as of the very essence of Methodism. John Wesley often spoke of them as "our doctrines,"not as implying that they were in any way exclusively Methodist (for they were and are not), but that Methodists had a special responsibility for them.

Wesley produced no specific formulation of those doctrines, though he summarised them again and again in a variety of ways. The following, from a reply to misrepresentations of a critic in the public press, is an example:

The fundamental doctrine of the people called Methodists is, Whosoever will be saved, before all things it is necessary that he hold the true faith—the faith which works by love; which, by means of the love of God and our neighbour, produces both inward and outward holiness. This faith is an evidence of things not seen; and he that thus believes is regenerate, or born of God; and he has the witness in himself (call it assurance or what you please): the Spirit itself witnesses with his spirit that he is a child of God. "From what scripture" every one of these propositions "is collected" any common Concordance will show. "This is the true portraiture of Methodism," so called. "A religion superior to this" (the love of God and man) none can "enjoy," either in time or in eternity.[16]

In what follows, however, we shall review Wesley's teaching in terms of a simple fourfold formula, which, although not Wesley's own, admirably represents his mind and is rather more comprehensive than any single statement of his. It is this: (1) All men need to be saved; (2) all men can be saved; (3) all men can know they are saved; (4) all men can be saved to the uttermost.

We shall also draw on Charles Wesley's hymns to illustrate aspects of this teaching, and to show what was perhaps the most effective single means the Wesleys devised for instilling it into their people. These hymns expound the great catholic doctrines of the faith and interpret evangelical experience; and so long as they were sung—together with some of Isaac Watts and Philip Doddrige—the Methodists could not have a bad theology, whatever they heard preached from the pulpit. In the Preface to *A Collection of Hymns for the Use of the People Called Methodists,* John Wesley describes the book as "a little body of experimental and practical divinity," and claims that it contains "all the important truths of our most holy religion, whether speculative or practical, . . . carefully ranged under proper heads, according to the experience of real Christians."[17] By contrast with modern hymn books, whose table of contents usually resembles that of a treatise on systematic theology, Wesley's arrangement is far more 'existential.' The Methodists learned their theology by singing it, and they sang it not only into their heads but their hearts.

(1) All men need to be saved.

Why do they? Because all men are sinners. All men are either self-indulgent sinners like the Prodigal Son, or self-righteous sinners like his Elder Brother, or else, like most of us, they are something of both. As St. Paul says, "All have sinned and fall short of the glory of God."

This doctrine was not popular in the eighteenth century—the Age of Enlightenment. The prevailing temper of the time was one of optimistic humanism, cheerful faith in the possibilities of man. All that men needed, it was generally believed, was more knowledge, more education, more enlightenment, and then their problems would be solved. Against this Wesley set the ancient Christian doctrine of "original sin."[18] Certainly he agreed that men need more education and enlightenment, but they need more than that. They need salvation, a deep and radical deliverance from sin—from their estrangement from God—and this is something they cannot get for themselves. They need to be saved, they need a Saviour. Even good men need him, as John and Charles Wesley themselves had found.

It is strange how latter-day Methodism seems often to have forgotten that good men need to be saved. The typical example of conversion has come to be that of the drunkard made sober, and it hardly appears that the sober man has anything to be saved from. Yet the founders of Methodism had never been drunkards, nor had they indulged in any other kind of reprehensible behaviour. They were not Prodigals; they were good men. They were in fact Christian Pharisees, as both of them confess:

> A goodly, formal saint
> I long appeared in sight,
> By self and nature taught to paint
> My tomb, my nature, white.
> The Pharisee within
> Still undisturbed remained,
> The strong man, armed with guilt of sin,
> Safe in his palace reigned.
>
> But O, the jealous God
> In my behalf came down;
> Jesus himself the stronger showed,
> And claimed me for his own;

My spirit he alarmed,
And brought into distress;
He shook and bound the strong man armed
In his self-righteousness.[19]

It is not surprising, then, that Wesley's hymn book opens with a section "Exhorting Sinners to Return to God," which includes among others the following:

Sinners, turn, why will ye die?
God, your Maker, asks you why?
God, who did your being give,
Made you with himself to live;
He the fatal cause demands,
Asks the work of his own hands,
Why, ye thankless creatures, why
Will ye cross his love, and die?[20]

This hymn, incidentally, also inculcates the doctrine of the Trinity, the second line of the second verse being "God, your Saviour, asks you why?" and of the third, "God, the Spirit, asks you why?" It then concludes with a verse too strong to be included in modern hymn books:

Dead, already dead within,
Spiritually dead in sin,
Dead to God while here you breathe,
Pant ye after second death?
Will you still in sin remain,
Greedy of eternal pain?
O ye dying sinners, why,
Why will you forever die?[21]

Then follows another, longer section, in which the strong reasons are set forth why sinners should return to God. It begins with hymns describing "The Pleasantness of Religion" and "The Goodness of God," then moves on to the awful solemnity of "Death," "Judgment," "Heaven," and "Hell." Interestingly, there is only one hymn on hell, and even those on death and judgment more often strike a note of confident hope and joyful expectation than of fear and gloom. The Wesleys knew well how to warn men of the peril in which sin and ungodliness involved them, but they also knew that merely to frighten them would not save them; they must be won by the love and mercy of God. Hence, while the first part of the hymn on hell begins:

> Terrible thought! shall I alone,
> Who may be saved—shall I—
> Of all, alas! whom I have known,
> Through sin for ever die?

the second part is in another key:

> Ah, no! I still may turn and live,
> For still his wrath delays;
> He now vouchsafes a kind reprieve,
> And offers me his grace.[22]

(2) All men can be saved.

How can they? Only one answer is possible: through Jesus Christ and his atoning work.

> Jesus comes with all his grace,
> Comes to save a fallen race;
> Object of our glorious hope,
> Jesus comes to lift us up![23]

Consequently, the exhortation to return to God becomes an invitation to come to Jesus, to respond to his love and grace.

> To save what was lost, from heaven he came;
> Come, sinners, and trust in Jesus's name;
> He offers you pardon, he bids you be free:
> If sin be your burden, O come unto me![24]

> Ye thirsty for God, to Jesus give ear,
> And take, through his blood, a power to draw near;
> His kind invitation ye sinners embrace,
> Accepting salvation, salvation by grace.[25]

But here again was a doctrine that ran counter to eighteenth-century sentiment, and that in two directions.

First, men under the influence of rationalism and Deism could make no sense of the Atonement because they had no sense of sin. They could see no need of a Mediator between man and God because they had no awareness of the tragic depth of man's estrangement from God.[26] Secondly, men of Calvinistic sympathies, although they accepted the Atonement, could not approve of Wesley's way of preaching it. With their doctrine of predestination, they held that

Christ did not die for all men but only for the elect, so that for the rest of men there was no possibility of salvation. By contrast, Wesley insisted that "God wills all men to be saved" and that Christ died for all so that all may come to him and be saved, if only they will.

> Father, whose everlasting love
> Thy only Son for sinners gave,
> Whose grace to *all* did freely move,
> And sent him down *the world* to save;
>
> Help us thy mercy to extol,
> Immense, unfathomed, *unconfined;*
> To praise the Lamb who died for *all,*
> The *general* Saviour of mankind.
>
> The *world* he suffered to redeem;
> For *all* he hath the atonement made;
> For *those that will not come to him,*
> The ransom of his life was paid.[27]

Wherever we find phrases like those here italicised in a Wesley hymn, we may suspect it was written with a consciously anti-Calvinist intent.

But how do we, how can we, respond to Wesley's invitation to "come to Christ"? Nowadays it is often suggested that there are many different ways, almost as many as there are different people. But Wesley knows of only one way, the way of repentance and faith. For however different from one another we human beings may be, we are all alike in this, that we are sinners in need of salvation. And we can find salvation only as we acknowledge and confess that we are sinners (which is repentance) and believe that Jesus Christ came into the world to save sinners, and therefore to save *us* (which is faith).

> He dies to atone for sins not his own;
> Your debt he hath paid, and your work he hath done.
> Ye all may receive the peace he did leave,
> Who made intercession: My Father, forgive!
>
> For you and for me he prayed on the tree;
> The prayer is accepted, the sinner is free.
> That sinner am I, who on Jesus rely,
> And come for the Pardon God cannot deny.
> My pardon I claim; for a sinner I am,
> A sinner believing in Jesus's name. . . . [28]

That is repentance and faith; that is the way of salvation.

Not that it is easy to repent and believe, even when we see that we need to and even when we want to. We are so apt to be sorry for ourselves rather than for our sins, repenting because they have found us out rather than because we ever committed them; and when we are truly penitent, we find it easier to believe that Christ is the Saviour of the world than that he is *ours*. Wesley therefore teaches us to pray for the gift of repentance and faith.

> O that I could repent!
>   O that I could believe!
> Thou by thy voice the marble rent,
>   The rock in sunder cleave!
> Thou by thy two-edged sword,
>   My soul and spirit part,
> Strike with the hammer of thy word,
>   And break my stubborn heart!
>
> Saviour, and Prince of peace,
>   The double grace bestow;
> Unloose the bands of wickedness,
>   And let the captive go:
> Grant me my sins to feel,
>   And then the load remove;
> Wound, and pour in, my wounds to heal,
>   The balm of pardoning love.[29]

When this happens and we do repent and believe, then we are saved—and we can know we are saved.

(3) All men can know they are saved.

Notice here that Wesley says "can" know, not that they "must" know. He does not hold that a man cannot be saved unless he knows, as if knowing and being sure of it were a condition of salvation. What he contends is that everyone who is saved *can* have knowledge of it, and it is desirable that he should. We have no right to say that a person who is not sure is therefore not saved, but we do have a right to tell him he can be sure and to urge and help him to find assurance.[30]

But what is it precisely that a man knows when he knows he is saved, and how does he know? First of all, he knows that he is "justified"; that is to say, he is pardoned and accepted by God, so that there is no estrangement between him and God any more. He knows that he has "received the adoption"; he is accepted by God as a child of God, and he knows God as his heavenly Father. He knows that he has been "born again"; he has started life afresh as a child of God by the power of the Spirit of God. For salvation means not only forgiveness, it means also the gift of the Holy Spirit. That is what a man knows, who knows that he is saved.

As to how he knows, the answer lies in the gift of the Spirit. "The Spirit himself bears witness with our spirit that we are children of God." It is by the Holy Spirit, the Spirit of God and of Christ, that we are enabled to pray to God just as Jesus did, saying "Abba, Father." And it is by the same Spirit we are enabled to live as children of God should, so that "the fruit of the Spirit" is seen in our lives: "love, joy, peace, patience, kindness, goodness, faithfulness, gentleness, self-control." Here, in the witness of the Spirit and the fruit of the Spirit, is the heart of the Wesleyan doctrine of "assurance."

> How can a sinner know
> His sins on earth forgiven?
> How can my gracious Saviour show
> My name inscribed in heaven?
>
> What we have felt and seen
> With confidence we tell,
> And publish to the sons of men
> The signs infallible.
>
> His Spirit to us he gave,
> And dwells in us we know;
> The witness in ourselves we have,
> And all its fruits we show.[31]

Is this an arrogant claim? There are those who say it is. They hold we have no right to be so cocksure; the most we have any right to is a "sober trust" that we "may" be saved; and to claim "assurance" is to be guilty of overweening self-confidence. (The eighteenth century accused the Methodists of "enthusiasm," religious fanaticism, because of it.) But this is a complete misunderstanding. Wesleyan assurance is as far as possible removed from *self*-confidence. It is the very opposite of *self*-confidence, for it is confidence in *God,* and in God alone. It is an assurance concerning God, who in Christ has shown himself a good and gracious Father to us and has given us the Spirit of sonship, of which the fruit can be seen in our lives. Furthermore, it is an assurance regarding our *present* standing with God, not an infallible guarantee of our future destiny. It is no more that than falling in love and getting married is a guarantee of a permanently happy marriage—though they would be strange lovers who were not firmly convinced that they were going to be "happy ever after."

From this assurance springs the joyfulness of all true Methodist piety, and the lyrical quality of countless Wesley hymns.

> O what shall I do my Saviour to praise,
> So faithful and true, so plenteous in grace,
> So strong to deliver, so good to redeem
> The weakest believer that hangs upon him.
>
> How happy the man whose heart is set free,
> The people that can be joyful in thee!
> Their joy is to walk in the light of thy face,
> And still they are talking of Jesus's grace.[32]
>
> My God, I am thine;
>   What a comfort divine,
> What a blessing to know that my Jesus
>   is mine!
> In the heavenly Lamb
> Thrice happy I am,
> And my heart it doth dance at the sound
>   of his name.[33]

(4) All men can be saved to the uttermost.

The work of salvation is not completed with "conversion," that is, with justification, adoption, the new birth, or even with assurance. These things are only the beginning from which we must go on, Wesley insists, to "entire sanctification" or "Christian perfection."

Sanctification means being made holy, and holiness is in Wesley's view, as we have seen, nothing else but love. It is love for God with all our heart and mind and soul and strength, in response to the love he has shown to us in Christ; and it is love for our neighbour "as ourselves," so that we treat our neighbour in the way that God in Christ has treated us, showing to him the same Spirit of love. But this, of course, is something we cannot do of ourselves, in our own strength and by our own resources. It is God's work in us that we must seek to have him do. In the hymn book, therefore, Wesley includes a whole series of hymns under the heading "For Believers Seeking Full Redemption" (i.e., "Entire Sanctification"). Here are some examples:

> Purge me from every evil blot;
>   My idols all be cast aside;
> Cleanse me from every sinful thought,
> From all the filth of self and pride.

Give me a new, a Perfect heart,
  From doubt, and fear, and sorrow free;
The mind which was in Christ impart,
  And let my spirit cleave to thee.[34]

What! never speak one evil word,
  Or rash, or idle, or unkind!
O how shall I, most gracious Lord,
  This mark of true perfection find?

Thy sinless mind in me reveal,
  Thy Spirit's plenitude impart;
And all my spotless life shall tell
  The abundance of a loving heart.[35]

I want thy life, thy purity,
  Thy righteousness brought in;
I ask, desire, and trust in thee,
  To be redeemed from sin.

Anger and sloth, desire and pride,
  This moment be subdued!
Be cast into the crimson tide
  Of my Redeemer's blood![36]

Sanctification is begun in us, Wesley teaches, as soon as ever we receive God's gift of pardon and the Holy Spirit. But it is only begun, and most of us have a long way to go before it is completed. Most of us, indeed, are unlikely to attain perfect holiness till we are on our death-beds, though many might attain it earlier, if only they were earnest enough in seeking it. In the meantime, however, the process of being made holy involves us in conflict with all that is unholy, not only in the world around us, but more especially in ourselves. If we have peace with God, we must inevitably be at war with the world, the flesh, and the devil. Hence, Wesley appropriately includes in his hymn book a large selection of hymns "For Believers Fighting, Watching, Praying," and also "For Persons Convinced of Backsliding." For sometimes even soundly converted Christians fall away from true repentance and faith and need to begin again. But they can neither begin nor continue in their own strength. They must always look to Jesus and the power of his Spirit for salvation from beginning to end. And if they "backslide," it is to him they must turn in order to be restored.

O Jesus, full of truth and grace,
  More full of grace than I of sin,

> Yet once again I seek thy face;
>   Open thine arms and take me in,
> And freely my backslidings heal,
> And love the faithless sinner still.
>
> Thou know'st the way to bring me back,
>   My fallen spirit to restore;
> O for thy truth and mercy's sake,
>   Forgive, and bid me sin no more;
> The ruins of my soul repair.
> And make my heart a house of prayer.
>
> Ah! give me, Lord, the tender heart
>   That trembles at the approach of sin;
> A godly fear of sin impart,
>   Implant, and root it deep within,
> That I may dread thy gracious power,
> And never dare to offend thee more.[37]

There are many ups and downs on the Christian's pilgrimage through this mortal life, but there is never any need for despair. We may very well have no confidence in ourselves, but we can and should have every confidence in our Lord. If we have not, Wesley will help us to find it by singing and praying about it.

> I am never at one stay,
>   Changing every hour I am;
> But thou art, as yesterday,
>   Now and evermore the same;
> Constancy to me impart,
> Stablish with thy grace my heart.
>
> Give me faith to hold me up,
>   Walking over life's rough sea,
> Holy, purifying hope
>   Still my soul's sure anchor be;
> That I may be always thine,
> Perfect me in love divine.[38]

This does not mean that anyone can become an absolutely perfect *person* in this life. The perfection Wesley teaches is not the perfection of angels or of Adam "before the Fall;" it is *Christian perfection.* It means being as good Christians as God can make us before he takes us out of this sinful world into heaven. It does not mean freedom from all kinds of unintentional faults, defects, and failings; but it does mean such a surrender to the love of God in Christ that we never intentionally do or say, think or even feel, anything out of harmony with the mind and Spirit of Christ. Even a "babe in Christ," a beginner on the Christian way, is of course free from any conscious, wilful acts of disobedience to God; he does not commit outward sin. But the mature, the "perfect" Christian is freed also from inward sin, from evil thoughts and tempers, from all passions and desires that are contrary to love. If this seems impossible to us, Wesley insists that "all things are possible to him. That can in Jesu's name believe." Then he says:

> The most impossible of all
>   Is, that I e'er from sin should cease;
> Yet shall it be, I know it shall;
>   Jesus, look to thy faithfulness!
> If nothing is too hard for thee,
> All things are possible to me.[39]

Christian perfection is sometimes described by Wesley as "total resignation to the will of God"—what a modern evangelist might call "complete surrender." But unlike some modern evangelists (and some of his contemporaries also), Wesley does not ask for or expect any such completeness of surrender at the moment of conversion. On the contrary, he believes it rarely if ever happens so soon. In fact, as we have said, with most people it does not happen till they are on their death-beds; and even when it happens earlier, it often has to happen more than once before it becomes a quite settled state in this life. Those, therefore, who have, or think they have, attained to Christian perfection have no grounds for complacency. They have not attained it by any virtue of their own but only by the grace of God, and only as they depend, moment by moment, on the grace of God can they retain it. On the other hand, those who have not yet attained it, or have attained and lost it, need never despair so long as they are seeking it. God, who has begun a good work in them by forgiving their sins and giving them his Holy Spirit, will surely bring it in his own time and way to completion.

> Thou who didst so greatly stoop
>   To a poor virgin's womb,
> Here thy mean abode take up;
>   To me, my Saviour, come!
> Come, and Satan's works destroy,
>   And let me all thy Godhead prove,
> Filled with peace, and heavenly joy,
>   And pure eternal love.[40]

> Jesus, the First and Last
>   On thee my soul is cast:
> Thou didst thy work begin
>   By blotting out my sin;
> Thou wilt the root remove,
>   And perfect me in love.
>
> Yet when the work is done,
>   The work is but begun:
> Partaker of thy grace,
>   I long to see thy face;
> The first I prove below,
>   The last I die to know.[41]

"THE SPIRIT AND DISCIPLINE"

Salvation, as Wesley always insists, is God's work in us, not our own achievement. But how does God do this work? What does it mean for practical purposes?

The first thing to be said here is that, just as Wesley's Methodists shared the same catholic and evangelical faith as other Christians, so they shared the habit of Public and private worship, using the same means of grace as the rest of Christ's Church. The reading and hearing of the Word of God, participation in the gospel sacraments, the practice of private and corporate prayer, and fasting—these "ordinances of God" they found to be the chief means by which God's salvation is brought to us, his grace made available to us; and the use of these means was an essential part of the Methodist discipline.[42]

Here again, however, there were certain particular emphases that were characteristically though not exclusively Methodist. The importance of preaching, for example, was stressed as it has not everywhere been. I cannot find that Wesley anywhere speaks of preaching explicitly as a means of grace, but he holds that wherever the gospel of Christ is preached, "the kingdom of God is at hand" as certainly as when Christ himself first spoke those words; for our risen Lord is present, according to his promise, with those who preach in his name.[43] The Christian preacher speaks God's word, not his own; he is an ambassador of God, a co-worker with God.

> God, the offended God most high,
>   Ambassadors to rebels sends;
> His messengers his place supply,
>   And Jesus begs us to be friends.

Us, in the stead of Christ, they pray,
Us, in the stead of God, intreat,
To cast our arms, our sins, away,
And find forgiveness at his feet.[44]

There is great need of such preachers, and therefore we are taught to pray:

Convert, and send forth more
Into thy Church abroad;
And let them speak thy word of power,
As workers with their God.[45]

Thy only glory let them seek;
O let their hearts with love o'erflow!
Let them believe, and therefore speak,
And spread thy mercy's praise below.[46]

Another characteristic feature of the Wesleyan understanding of the means of grace concerns the sacrament of Holy Communion, the Lord's Supper. This sacrament, as Wesley sees it, is not intended only for those who are established in the faith, or even for those only who are converted. It is also a "converting ordinance," to which those may and should be encouraged to come who are not yet converted but are only seekers after true repentance and saving faith. Wesley himself led countless throngs of those who responded to his preaching in field or market-place to the Table of the Lord, in order that there they might meet the Saviour of whom he had been telling them.

Come, to the Supper come,
Sinners, there still is room;
Every soul may be his guest,
Jesus gives the general word;
Share the monumental feast,
Eat the supper of your Lord.

In this authentic sign
Behold the stamp divine:
Christ revives his sufferings here,
Still exposes them to view;
See the Crucified appear,
Now believe he died for you.[47]

How strange that among the successors of those first Methodists (and among other Christians, too) there are those who do not attend

Holy Communion because they are not "good enough"! As if anyone
ever were or could be "good enough"! As if it were not for sinners that
Christ died! It was indeed for sinners that he died, and both converted
and unconverted sinners have perpetual need of him. They should
therefore take every opportunity, as Wesley insists in his sermon on
The Duty of Constant Communion,[48] of meeting him in the sacrament
that he has ordained. There the crucified and risen Lord himself is
present and presides, imparting to all who truly seek him a share in his
own eternal and blessed life. As we approach his Table, we sinners
may well say:

> Saviour, and can it be
> That thou shouldst dwell with me?
> From thy high and lofty throne,
> Throne of everlasting bliss,
> Will thy majesty stoop down
> To so mean a house as this?
>
> I am not worthy, Lord,
> So foul, so self-abhorred,
> Thee, my God, to entertain
> In this poor, polluted heart:
> I, a frail and sinful man;
> All my nature cries: Depart![49]

Yet as we come away, we can joyfully and thankfully confess:

> O the depth of Love divine,
> Th' unfathomable grace!
> Who shall say how bread and wine
> God into man conveys!
> *How* the bread his flesh imparts,
> *How* the wine transmits his blood,
> Fills his faithful people's hearts
> With all the life of God![50]

The Wesleys and their Methodists have no theory as to "the manner
how" Christ is present in the sacrament; they only know from rich
experience "the fact that" he is present, and they rejoice to meet him
there.[51]

But besides the resources common to all Christians, the first
Methodists had certain spiritual helps peculiar to themselves. There
were short daily services on weekdays (at five in the morning and six or
seven in the evening) with preaching, prayer, and singing; a Sunday
morning service (beginning between nine and ten) that concluded with

Holy Communion and a Sunday evening meeting of the Society; the weekly "Class" Meeting; and a quarterly review of the members by the Wesleys or their Assistants, in the light of the conditions of membership. As we have said, anyone could become a member who sincerely desired to "save his soul"; but he must evince the sincerity of his desire by "avoiding all known sin, doing good after his power, and attending all the ordinances of God"; otherwise his membership would be terminated.[52] For, as Wesley held, "it was a true saying, which was common in the ancient Church, 'The soul and the body make a man; and the Spirit and discipline make a Christian.'"[53]

Out of this vital union of "the Spirit and discipline" there emerged five features which, though again not exclusively Methodist, became specially characteristic of the Methodist movement. They may be described as: Spiritual Fellowship, Lay Ministry, Active Evangelism, Social Concern, and what Wesley calls "Catholic Spirit."

(1) Spiritual Fellowship.

The Wesleys gathered their followers together, as we have said, into Societies. As they saw it, no man could find his way to heaven by himself, and Christians could not be isolated, solitary souls.

> Woe to him whose spirits droop,
>   To him who falls alone!
> He has none to lift him up,
>   To help his weakness on:
> Happier we each other keep,
>   We each other's burdens bear;
> Never need our footsteps slip,
>   Upheld by mutual prayer.[54]

Christianity, after all, is a religion of love; and not of self-love but love of one's brethren and neighbours in Christ. "Fellowship" has therefore always been a key word in Methodism, and in original Methodism it was much more than a word. In order to make and keep it a living reality, Wesley divided his Societies up into Classes. These were groups of not more than a dozen members, who met together once a week under the leadership of one of their own number for conversation on the spiritual life.

The Class Meetings were not study circles, not discussion groups, and least of all were they debating societies. They were Christ-centered fellowships. Their members were taught to take seriously our Lord's promise that he would be present in the midst wherever two or three were gathered together in his name. Hence, when they met in Class, they would sing:

> Jesus, we look to thee.
> Thy promised presence claim!
> Thou in the midst of us shalt be,
> Assembled in thy name:
> Thy name salvation is,
> Which here we come to prove;
> Thy name is life, and health, and peace,
> And everlasting love.[55]

Then they could go on to share their Christian experience with one another—their troubles and triumphs on the Christian way, or on their quest for that way. Sometimes they confessed their sins to one another, sometimes took one another to task, but always with the aim of helping one another to grow in grace, in faith and hope and love. Their varying degrees of spiritual maturity enabled them all the more to help one another by mutual conversation and prayer, and it was of course understood that no one ever gossiped about anything that was said in Class.

The purpose of the Class Meeting is perhaps nowhere better expressed than in these verses of Charles Wesley's:

> Help us to help each other, Lord,
> Each other's cross to bear,
> Let each his friendly aid afford,
> And feel his brother's care.
>
> Help us to build each other up,
> Our little stock improve;
> Increase our faith, confirm our hope,
> And perfect us in love.
>
> Then, when the mighty work is wrought,
> Receive thy ready bride:
> Give us in heaven a happy lot
> With all the sanctified.[56]

Always there is the perspective of heaven, both in John Wesley's preaching and in Charles's hymns. Always there is a goal ahead of us to be aimed at, a goal that has been reached by so many of God's people already, and by many known to us. Methodists used to be so accustomed to singing about heaven that they looked forward to going there and being reunited with their friends. "Our people die well,"

said Wesley, and for those who died he taught the ones who remained
to sing:

> Rejoice for a brother deceased,
>   Our loss is his infinite gain;
> A soul out of prison released,
>   And freed from its bodily chain.
>
> Our brother the haven hath gained,
>   Out-flying the tempest and wind,
> His rest he hath sooner obtained,
>   And left his companions behind.
>
> There all the ship's company meet
>   Who sailed with the Saviour beneath,
> With shouting each other they greet,
>   And triumph o'er trouble and death.[57]

Not that heaven is a far distant place, nor are those who have reached it
far separated from us who are still on the way. They are one with us in
the communion of saints.

> Let all the saints terrestrial sing,
>   With those to glory gone;
> For all the servants of our King,
>   In earth and heaven, are one.
> One family we dwell in him,
>   One Church, above, beneath,
> Though now divided by the stream,
>   The narrow stream of death.[58]

Wesley's Methodists have a range of vision that is not bounded by the
horizons of this world. But they are not otherworldly in the bad sense
of having no concern for this world and its affairs, as we shall see.

(2) Lay Ministry.

In the Class Meeting, Methodism gave a practical demonstration of
the Priesthood of All Believers. For the Leader of the Class, like its
other members, was a layman—or woman. The Class was a group of
Christian laity ministering to one another in holy things. Moreover,
the Leaders of the several Classes in a Society were responsible for the
spiritual oversight of the Society as a whole, and they exercised
discipline in it under the direction of the minister, who was one of
Wesley's "Travelling Preachers." These Preachers, whom Wesley

appointed to serve in wide circuits throughout the United Kingdom and in distant America, were themselves also for the most part laymen; and so, too, were the "Local Preachers" who served when the Itinerant was away on his travels.

Methodism had a very high regard for the ordained ministry, but it had no room for clericalism. Clericalism arises from a secularised view of the laity, when men forget that the laity are the *laos,* or *People* of God, among whom the clergy are simply the duly appointed leaders—leading laymen in fact. Then the laity are regarded as "lay" in the sense of "not professionally qualified," while the clergy with their professional qualifications are allowed to claim a virtual monopoly of spiritual competence and responsibility. But in true Methodism there can be no such monopoly. It was not for preachers or leaders only, but "For Believers Fighting," that Wesley gave words like these to sing:

> Shall I, for fear of feeble man,
> The Spirit's course in me restrain?
> Or, undismayed, in deed and word
> Be a true witness for my Lord?
>
> The love of Christ doth me constrain
> To seek the wandering souls of men;
> With cries, entreaties, tears, to save,
> And snatch them from the gaping grave.[59]

Nor do the hymns "For Believers Working" have reference to "church work" only.

> Forth in thy name, O Lord, I go,
> My daily labour to pursue,
> Thee, only thee, resolved to know
> In all I think, or speak, or do.
>
> The task thy wisdom hath assigned
> O let me cheerfully fulfil,
> In all my works thy presence find,
> And prove thine acceptable will.[60]

And the hymns "For the Head of a Household" assign a spiritual task to both parents and employers:

> Master supreme, I look to thee
> For grace and wisdom from above;
> Vested with thy authority,
> Endue me with thy patient love:

That, taught according to thy will
  To rule my family aright,
I may the appointed charge fulfil,
  With all my heart, and all my might.

O could I emulate the zeal
  Thou dost to thy poor servants bear!
The troubles, griefs, and burdens feel
  Of souls entrusted to my care:

In daily prayer to God commend
  The souls whom Jesus died to save;
And think how soon my sway may end,
  And all be equal in the grave![61]

(3) Active Evangelism.

Methodism could not be other than an evangelistic movement. The gospel, the good news of salvation, as John and Charles Wesley had found it, had to be told. They could not keep it to themselves. Nor could thousands of others who found it through their ministry. Very fittingly, therefore, the first hymn in their hymn book was:

O for a thousand tongues to sing
  My great Redeemer's praise,
The glories of my God and King,
  The triumphs of his grace!

Look unto him, ye nations, own
  Your God, ye fallen race;
Look, and be saved through faith alone,
  Be justified by grace.[62]

It was the Aldersgate experience and the knowledge of Christ he received there that led John Wesley to say, "I look upon all the world as my parish,"[63] and Charles to write:

O for a trumpet voice,
  On all the world to call!
To bid their hearts rejoice
  In him who died for all;
For all my Lord was crucified,
  For all, for all my Saviour died![64]

Methodism began as a mission to the lost sheep of the Church of England,[65] for whom the Wesleys prayed:

> Jesu, thy wandering sheep behold!
> See, Lord, with tenderest pity see
> The sheep that cannot find the fold,
> Till sought and gathered in by thee.
>
> Thou, only thou, the kind and good
> And sheep-redeeming shepherd art:
> Collect thy flock, and give them food,
> And pastors after thine own heart.[66]

They also prayed for the clergy, the ordained priests and pastors of the flock:

> Jesu, the word of mercy give,
> And let it swiftly run;
> And let the priests themselves believe,
> And put salvation on.[67]

But Methodism could not limit its concern to the Church of England, or even to the English nation. The Wesleys had been brought up in a missionary-minded home; they had been—briefly and unsuccessfully, it is true—missionaries themselves; and above all, they knew that the gospel of God was the message for the whole world. So Methodists were given hymns to sing "For the Heathen" and "For the Jews" and for the entire race of men.[68]

(4) Social Concern.

Together with evangelism and missionary outreach, there went hand in hand social concern. It is true that when the early Methodists met in Class or Society they would sometimes sing:

> In Jesu's name, behold, we meet,
> Far from an evil world retreat,
> And all its frantic ways;
> One only thing resolved to know,
> And square our useful lives below
> By reason and by grace.

But the next verse of the hymn reminded them, if they needed it, that Christians are not called to turn their backs on the world in its need but to minister to it:

> Not in the tombs we pine to dwell,
> Not in the dark monastic cell,

> By vows and grates confined;
> Freely to all ourselves we give,
> Constrained by Jesu's love to live
> The servants of mankind.[69]

Wesley told his people that God had raised them up, "Not to form any new sect; but to reform the nation, particularly the Church; and to spread scriptural holiness over the land."[70] He also told them that "Christianity is essentially a social religion"[71] and that there is "no holiness but social holiness."[72] For holiness means love, the love of God and one's neighbour, which cannot but move us to seek to do all possible good to all mankind. Moreover, while ministering to men's souls is of primary importance, there are also temporal and material needs of men that must be met in the Spirit of Christ.

> Thy mind throughout my life be shown,
> While listening to the sufferer's cry,
> The widow's and the orphan's groan.
> On mercy's wings I swiftly fly,
> The poor and helpless to relieve,
> My life, my all, for them to give.[73]

Wesley's own social concern was actively manifested in innumerable ways. We recall, for example, his tracts and sermons on the use of money and possessions; his pamphlets against smuggling, bribery at elections, intemperance; his plea for government action to deal with unemployment and the high cost of food;[74] his support of the anti-slavery campaign; his opening of medical dispensaries for the poor; his educational enterprises; his orphanage; and his home for aged widows—to mention no more.[75] And he sought to teach his people,

> By word and by deed,
> The bodies in need,
> And souls to relieve,
> And freely as Jesus hath given to give.[76]

In these ways, no less than in his preaching of sermons and building up of his Societies, he saw the fulfilment of his vocation:

> To serve the present age,
> My calling to fulfil:
> O may it all my powers engage
> To do my Master's will![77]

(5) "Catholic Spirit."

This is the final mark of all true Methodism and one that is stamped on every aspect of it. In his sermon under this title,[78] Wesley defines it as "catholic or universal love." It is love for God and all mankind, especially our fellow-Christians. It is the antidote to the sectarian spirit that he attacks in a companion sermon entitled "A Caution against Bigotry."[79] Wesley's Methodism is the sworn foe of all sectarianism.

This does not mean that Wesley objected fundamentally to the existence of different Christian denominations. He believed them to be inevitable—in a fallen world. We cannot all think alike, and therefore we cannot all worship alike. There are bound to be diverse expressions of the Christian faith and life. What is more, each of us is bound to think his own denomination the best there is; otherwise, we would presumably not belong to it. But there is a difference between believing our own to be the best and believing it to be the only right one. That is sectarianism; that is bigotry. It means in effect that we equate our way of seeing things and doing things with God's way, as if the work of God could not be rightly done, if done at all, in any other way. Against this attitude Wesley warns us, reminding us of our Lord's rebuke to his disciples when they told him they had forbidden a man to cast out demons "because he followeth not with us."

Charles Wesley also castigates this attitude in brief but telling terms:

> Ye different sects, who all declare,
> "Lo, here is Christ!" or, "Christ is there!" .
>
> Your stronger proofs divinely give,
> And show me where the Christians live.
>
> Your claim, alas! ye cannot prove,
> Ye want the genuine mark of love.[80]

Here is the essential point, the one thing needful: "the genuine mark of love." Without this you may well have a sect but not the true Church of Jesus Christ.

This is the whole substance of Wesley's sermon on "Catholic Spirit," for which he takes as his text Jehu's words to Jehonadab in II Kings 10:15: "Is thine heart right, as my heart is with thy heart? . . . If it be, give me thine hand." Wesley is here preaching no mere heartiness nor even that "religion of the warm heart" which is sometimes supposed to be Methodism. He certainly holds that the state of a man's heart is more important than his theological opinions or mode of worship, but it is with the rightness rather than the warmth of the heart that he is concerned. A catholic spirit is more than mere cordiality. Jehu's words in Wesley's sermon mean (in brief): Do you believe in Jesus Christ and in God through him, and does your faith lead you to love God and your neighbour—every man—as Christ has commanded? If so, or if you are sincerely seeking to have it so, then give me your hand. That is to say, accept me as your brother in Christ; pray for me, provoke me to love and good works, join with me in the work of God as far as ever you can.

In a letter to a brother clergyman in 1763, Wesley wrote:

I am not satisfied with "Be very civil to the Methodists, but have nothing to do with them." No; I desire to have a league offensive and defensive with every soldier of Christ. We have not only one faith, one hope, one Lord, but are engaged directly in one warfare. We are carrying the war into the devil's own quarters, who therefore summons all his hosts to war. Come, then, ye that love him, to the help of the Lord, to the help of the Lord against the mighty![81]

In this same warfare Christians of all denominations (if they know their business) are perpetually engaged, and there was never more need for unity among them than today. Let each, then, be as attached as he will to his own opinions (whether liberal, conservative, or neo-orthodox) and as devoted to his own mode of worship (Anglican or Free Church, Catholic or Protestant); but let him be still more clear that the most essential thing about Christians (unless they are merely nominal Christians) is not their denominational allegiance or theological position but simply the fact that they are Christians—members of Christ, children of God, and therefore friends and brothers of his own.

> Christ, our Head, gone up on high,
> Be thou in thy Spirit nigh:
> Advocate with God, give ear
> To thine own effectual prayer!
>
> One the Father is with thee;
> Knit us in like unity;
> Make us, O uniting Son,
> One, as thou and he are one![82]
>
>
> Sweetly may we all agree,
> Touched with loving sympathy;
> Kindly for each other care;
> Every member feel its share.

Wounded by the grief of one,
Now let all the members groan;
Honoured if one member is,
All partake the common bliss.

Love, like death, hath all destroyed,
Rendered all distinctions void;
Names, and sects, and parties fall:
Thou, O Christ, art all in all![83]

Notes to Introduction

I. DISCOVERY OF A MESSAGE

1 *CWJ*(J)I.82 = *CWJ*(T) 134f. [24 Feb. 1738].
2 CW explains "the harmless nickname of Methodist" as due to his and his friends' resolve "to observe the method of study prescribed by the Statutes of the University." (See Frank Baker, *Charles Wesley as Revealed by His Letters* [London, 1948], p. 14.) JW gives a fuller account in S.132 (W.VII.421): "The regularity of their behaviour gave occasion to a young gentleman of the College to say, 'I think we have got a new set of Methodists'—alluding to a set of Physicians, who began to flourish at Rome about the time of Nero, and continued for several ages. The name was new and quaint; it clave to them immediately; and from that time, both these four young gentlemen, and all that had any religious connexion with them, were distinguished by the name of *Methodists*."
3 *JWJ*.I.109 = W.I.17 [14 Oct. 1735].
4 *JWJ*.I.143 = W.I.2 [25 Jan. 1736].
5 *JWJ*.I.151 = W.I.23 [8 Feb. 1736].
6 *JWJ*.I.471 = W.I.101f. The "imminent danger of death" to which JW refers was occasioned by a storm at sea, the latest of a series on both the outward and the homeward voyages, which made a deep and lasting impression on him.
7 *JWJ*.I.442 = W.I.86.
8 *JWJ*.I.454 = W.I.91 [22 Apr. 1738].
9 *JWJ*.I.471f. = W.I.102 [24 May 1738].
10 *CWJ*(J)I.88 = *CWJ*(T) 142 [17 May 1738].
11 *Ibid.*
12 Martin Luther, A *Commentary on St. Paul's Epistle to the Galatians*, ed. P. S. Watson (Winchester, N.J., London, 1953), pp. 177f. and 179f.
13 *CWJ*(J)I.95 = *CWJ*(T) 153 [24 May 1738].
14 *JWJ*.I.464 = W.I.96 [21 May 1738]. JW adds: "His bodily strength returned also from that hour."
15 *JWJ*.I.475f. = W.I.103 [24 May 1738].
16 *Works of Martin Luther, Translated with Introductions and Notes* (Philadelphia, Pa., 1932), VI.449f. and 451f.
17 *JWJ*.I.476 = W.I.103.
18 W.VIII.367. Cf. *JWJ*.I.454f. = W.I.91.
19 *HPCM* 30; *MHB* 361; *WHB* 35.
20 *L*.V.258: to the Countess of Huntingdon [19 June 1771].

[21] *W.*VIII.300 (large Minutes). The date 1737 stands in the original text, though one might have expected 1738.

[22] From 1725, when he first read Thomas à Kempis' *Christian Pattern* (*The Imitation of Christ*) and Jeremy Taylor's *Rules of Holy Living and Holy Dying.* See *L.*IV.298f.(= JWJ.V.117; *W.* III.212f.): to John Newton [14 May 1765]; cf. also *W.* VII.421 (S.132).

[23] In this they are not so different from Luther as is often supposed. For Luther himself can say: "If there is not love, neither is there faith, but mere hypocrisy" (*Luthers Werke,* [Kritische Gesamtausgabe, Weimar, 1883ff.], XXXVI.474, 10f.). And see my article on "Luther and Sanctification" in the *Concordia Theological Monthly,* Apr., 1959, and "Wesley and Luther on Christian Perfection" in the *Ecumenical Review,* Apr., 1963.

[24] The material in this section consists of extracts from *CWJ*(J)I.92-123 = *CWJ*(T) 149-94.

[25] *HPCM* 22; *MHB* 193; *AMH* 136. Samuel Wesley senr.

[26] *HPCM*(S) 786. Isaac Watts.

[27] *HPCM* 231; *MHB* 874; *WHB* 2 ("A Birthday Hymn").

[28] The material in this section consists of extracts from JW's *Journal* and *Letters.*

[29] *JWJ.*I.476-84*W.*I.103-6.

[30] *JWJ.*II.70-97*W.*I.158-63.

[31] Cf. *JWJ.*I.415f. = *W.*I.72, where JW confesses himself "convinced of unbelief."

[32] *L.*I.262ff. = *W.*XII.33f.

[33] JW frequently records the fact, without comment, that his preaching proved unwelcome to the church authorities, and he was told he would not be allowed to preach there again. This happened even before Aldersgate, and before he preached salvation by faith. "It was for preaching the love of God and man that several of the Clergy forbade me their pulpits before that time," he says in *L.*II.65 = *W.*XII.70: to "John Smith" [30 Dec. 1745].

[34] *JWJ.*II.125-73 = *W.*I.170-85.

[35] *HPCM* 279; *MHB* 783; *WHB* 124. Johann Joseph Winckler (1670-1722), tr. by JW.

[36] *L.*III.308f. = *W.*IX.36: to Dr. Lavington, Bishop of Exeter [Dec. 1751].

[37] *L.*VI.153 = *W.*XII.284: to Miss March [9 June 1775].

[38] *L.*VII.319 = *W.*XIII.52: to Elizabeth Ritchie [24 Feb. 1786].

[39] *L.*V.15f.: to his brother Charles [27 June 1766]. The words in double brackets were written in shorthand, as intended only for Charles's eye.

[40] *HPCM* 189; *MHB* 375; *WHB* 31.

II. FULFILMENT OF A MISSION

[1] *W.*VIII.350.

[2] By "Primitive Church" JW means what to-day we more commonly call the "Early Church," particularly the Church of the first three centuries, the Church of the Ante-Nicene Fathers.

[3] *L.*VIII.224f = *W.*XIII.119: to Dr. Pretyman Tomline, Bishop of Lincoln [26 June 1790]. Cf. *L.*VIII.231 = *W.*XIII.126: to William Wilberforce, a Member of Parliament, [July 1790]. Had the Methodists applied for a licence as Dissenters, there would have been no trouble. They were refused it because they were members of the Church of England. Then they were threatened with starvation by the outrageously heavy fines imposed on them.

[4] *L.*III.192 = *W.*XIII.167: to Samuel Walker [3 Sept. 1756].

[5] *L.*II.289f. = *W.*XIII.493f.: to Dr. Gibson, Bishop of London [11 June 1747].

[6] *W.*XIII.195f. ("Reasons against a Separation from the Church of England," 1758).

[7] *W.*XIII.233: "Let them hold particular or general redemption, absolute or conditional decrees; let them be Churchmen or Dissenters, Presbyterians or Independents, it is no obstacle. Let them choose one mode of baptism or another, it is no bar to their admission. The Presbyterian may be a Presbyterian still; the Independent or Anabaptist uses his own mode of worship. So may the Quaker; and none will contend with him about it. They think and let think. One condition, and one only, is required—A real desire to save their soul" ("Thoughts upon a Late Phenomenon," 1788).

[8] *W.*VIII.352 ("Advice to the People Called Methodists," 1745).

[9] *L.*VIII.211: to Thomas Taylor [4 Apr. 1790].

[10] *W.*X.352 ("Remarks on a Defence of Aspasio Vindicated," 1766).

[11] *L.*V.155: to Professor John Liden [16 Nov. 1769].

[12] *L.*I.285f.: to James Hervey [20 Mar. 1739].

[13] *L.*III.150f. = *W.*XIII.176f.: to Thomas Adam [13 Oct. 1755].

[14] *L.*II.77f. = *W.*XII.79f.: to "John Smith" [25 June 1746].

[15] *L.*III.182 = *W.*XIII.179: to James Clark [3 July 1756].

[16] *L.*IV.110 and *JWJ.*IV.418f. = *W.*III.24f.: to the Editor of *Lloyd's Evening Post* [17 Nov. 1760].

[17] *W.*XIV.353; *MHB* (v).

[18] See his massive treatise on the subject, *W.*IX.191-464 ("The Doctrine of Original Sin according to Scripture, Reason and Experience," 1756-57). See also below, pp. 80-90.

[19] *HPCM* 93. JW also speaks of himself as having been a Pharisee—*JWU.*III.61 = *W.*I.409.

[20] *HPCM* 6; *MHB* 327; *AMH* 191.

[21] *HPCM* 6.

[22] *HPCM* 80.

[23] *HPCM* 400; *MHB* 87; *WHB* 69.

[24] *HPCM* 5; *MHB* 311.

[25] *HPCM* 10.

[26] Cf. *L.* VI.297f. = *W.*XII.33f; *W.*VII.336 and IX.194; and below, pp. 80-81, 88-90.

[27] *HPCM* 39; *MHB* 75. (Italics mine.)

[28] *HPCM*(S) 707; *MHB* 188; *WHB* 91.

[29] *HPCM* 105.

[30] See below, pp. 119-126.

[31] *HPCM* 96; *MHB* 377; *AMH* 208.

[32] *HPCM* 198; *MHB* 420.

[33] *HPCM* 205; *MHB* 406.

[34] *HPCM* 391; *MHB* 562; *WHB* 41.

[35] *HPCM* 363.

[36] *HPCM* 417; *MHB* 559.

[37] *HPCM* 186; *MHB* 346; *WHB* 20.

[38] *HPCM* 183.

[39] *HPCM* 401; *MHB* 548.

[40] *HPCM* 413.

[41] *HPCM*(S) 674; *MHB* 105.

[42] See below, pp. 157f.

[43] *W*.V.81 (S.7) = *SS*.I.155 (S.7: "The Way to the Kingdom").

[44] *HPCM* 11.

[45] *HPCM*(S) 745; *MHB* 787; *WHB* 122.

[46] *HPCM*(S) 744; *MHB* 791; *WHB* 121.

[47] *HLS* 8. On this whole subject see J. Ernest Rattenbury. *The Eucharistic Hymns of John and Charles Wesley,* in which the entire collection is reproduced, together with JW's Preface extracted from Brevint's *Christian Sacrament and Sacrifice.*

[48] *W*.VII.147-57 (S.101). When he reprinted this sermon in 1788 JW added a prefatory note, saying: "The following Discourse was written above five-and-fifty years ago, for the use of my pupils at Oxford. I have added very little, but retrenched much; as I then used more words than I do now. But, I thank God, I have not yet seen cause to alter my sentiments in any point which is therein delivered."

[49] *HLS* 43; *MHB* 760; *WHB* 142.

[50] *HLS* 57; *WHB* 147.

[51] We shall meet the distinction between "fact" and "manner" again, in connexion with Wesley's exposition of other doctrines of the Faith.

[52] *W*.VII.209 (S.107: "On God's Vineyard").

[53] *W*.VII.411 (S.131: "The Work of God in North America"); cf. *JWJ*.III.491 = *W*.II.204.

[54] *HPCM* 487.

[55] *HPCM* 485; *MHB* 718; *AMH* 25; *WHB* 5.

[56] *HPCM* 503; *MHB* 717; *AMH* 419. Concerning the origin of the Class Meeting, see *JWJ*.II.528 = *W*.I.357 [15 Feb. 1742]; *W*.VIII.252f. ("A Plain Account of the People Called Methodists"); *W*.XIII.226 ("Thoughts upon Methodism"); and *W*.XIII.276 ("A Short History of the People Called Methodists").

[57] *HPCM* 49; *MHB* 973.

[58] *HPCM*(S) 949; *MHB* 824; *AMH* 422; *WHB* 104.

[59] *HPCM* 279; *MHB* 783; *WHB* 124.

[60] *HPCM* 324; *MHB* 590; *AMH* 290; *WHB* 54.

[61] *HPCM* 470.

[62] *HPCM* 1; *MHB* 1; *AMH* 162; *WHB* 1.

[63] *L*.I.286—quoted above, p. 32.

64 *HPCM* 34; *MHB* 114.
65 *W*.XIII.195: "An the first message of all our Preachers is to the lost sheep of the Church of England" (Reasons against a Separation from the Church of England").
66 *HPCM*(S) 744; *MHB* 791; *WHB* 121.
67 *HPCM* 446.
68 *HPCM* 444-49 are for the Heathen, 450-52 for the Jews. *MHB* 794 and 814 are missionary hymns written by JW and CW respectively.
69 *HPCM* 526.
70 *W*.VIII.299 (Large Minutes).
71 *W*.V.296 (S.24) = *SS*.I.382 (S.19: "On the Sermon on the Mount, IV").
72 *W*.XIV.334 (Preface to Hymns and Sacred Poems, 1739).
73 *HPCM* 364; *MHB* 605.
74 *W*.XI.53-59 ("Thoughts on the Present Scarcity of Provisions").
75 Wesley would thoroughly have approved the idea of the Welfare State, with its policies of full employment, universal health and retirement insurance, and so forth.
76 *HPCM* 495.
77 *HPCM* 318; *MHB* 578; *AMH* 287; *WHB* 51.
78 *W*.V.492ff.(S.39) = *SS*.II.126ff.(S.34).
79 *W*.V.479ff.(S.38) = *SS*.II.104ff.(S.33).
80 *W*.VIII.43f. (where the entire hymn is appended to "An Earnest Appeal to Men of Reason and Religion") = *HPCM* 16 (which, however, omits the second of these two verses); and WHB 118.
81 *L*.IV.218 = *W*.XIII.209: to Henry Venn [22 June 1763].
82 *HPCM* 517.
83 *HPCM* 518; *HHB* 720; *WHB* 111.

PART ONE

Instruction in the Faith

* * *

I

The Mystery and Majesty of God

THE BLESSED TRINITY

Whatsoever the generality of people may think, it is certain that opinion is not religion; no, not right opinion, assent to one or to ten thousand truths. Persons may be quite right in their opinions, and yet have no religion at all; and on the other hand, persons may be truly religious who hold many wrong opinions. Can anyone possibly doubt of this, while there are Romanists in the world? For who can deny, not only that many of them formerly have been truly religious, but that many of them even at this day are real, inward Christians? And yet what a heap of erroneous opinions do they hold, delivered by tradition from their fathers! Nay, who can doubt of it while there are Calvinists in the world—assertors of absolute predestination? For who will dare to affirm that none of these are truly religious men? Not only many of them in the last century were burning and shining lights, but many of them are now real Christians, loving God and all mankind. And yet what are all the absurd opinions of all the Romanists in the world, compared to that one, that the God of love, the wise, just, merciful Father of the spirits of all flesh, has from all eternity fixed an absolute, unchangeable, irresistible decree, that part of mankind shall be saved, do what they will, and the rest damned, do what they can!

Hence we cannot but infer that there are ten thousand mistakes which may consist with real religion; with regard to which every candid, considerate man will think and let think. But there are some truths more important than others. It seems there are some which are of deep importance. I do not term them *fundamental* truths, because that is an ambiguous word; and hence there have been so many warm disputes about the number of *fundamentals*. But surely there are some which it nearly concerns us to know, as having a close connexion with vital religion. And doubtless we may rank among these that contained in the words: "There are three that bear record in heaven, the Father, the Word, and the Holy Ghost: and these three are one" [I John 5:7b].[1]

I do not mean that it is of importance to believe this or that *explication* of these words. I insist upon no explication at all; no, not even the best I ever saw; I mean that which is given us in the creed commonly ascribed to Athanasius. I am far from saying he who does not assent to this "shall without doubt perish everlastingly." For the sake of that and another clause, I for some time scrupled subscribing to that creed, till I considered (1) that these sentences only relate to *wilful,* not involuntary, unbelievers—to those who, having all the means of knowing the truth, nevertheless obstinately reject it; (2) that they relate only to the *substance* of the doctrine there delivered, not the philosophical illustrations of it.

I dare not insist upon anyone's using the word "Trinity" or "Person." I use them myself without any scruple, because I know of none better; but if any man has any scruple concerning them, who shall constrain him to use them? I cannot. Much less would I burn a man alive, and that with moist, green wood, for saying, "Though I believe the Father is God, the Son is God, and the Holy Ghost is God, yet I scruple using the words 'Trinity' and 'Persons,' because I do not find these terms in the Bible." These are the words which merciful John Calvin cites as wrote by Servetus in a letter to himself. I would insist only on the direct words, unexplained, just as they lie in the text: "There are three that bear record in heaven, the Father, the Word, and the Holy Ghost: and these three are one."[2]

> Three Persons there are
> Their record who bear,
> And Jehovah in heavenly places declare:
> But in Father and Son
> And Spirit made known,
> The Witnesses Three are essentially One.
>
> Full credence we give,
> And exult to believe
> What our reason in vain would aspire to conceive;
> Not *against* but *above*
> Our reason we prove,
> The Persons revealed in the essence of love.[3]

But it is objected: "We cannot believe what we cannot comprehend. When, therefore, you require us to believe mysteries, we pray you to have us excused."

Here is a twofold mistake: (1) We do not require you to believe any mystery in this, whereas you suppose the contrary. But (2) you do already believe many things which you cannot comprehend.

To begin with the latter: you do already believe many things which you cannot comprehend. For you believe there is a *sun* over your head. But whether he stands still in the midst of his system, or not only revolves on his own axis, but "rejoiceth as a giant to run his course," you cannot comprehend either the one or the other—*how* he moves, or *how* he rests.

You believe there is such a thing as *light,* whether flowing from the sun or any other luminous body; but you cannot comprehend either its nature or the manner wherein it flows. How does it move from Jupiter to earth in eight minutes—two hundred thousand miles in a moment? How do the rays of the candle, brought into the room, instantly disperse into every corner? Again: here are three candles, yet there is but one light. Explain this, and I will explain the Three-One God.

You believe there is such a thing as *earth.* Here you fix your foot upon it; you are supported by it. But do you comprehend what it is that supports the earth? "O, an elephant," says a Malabarian philosopher, "and a bull supports him." But what supports the bull? The Indian and the Briton are equally at loss for an answer. We know it is God that "spreadeth the north over empty space, and hangeth the earth upon nothing." This is the fact. But how? Who can account for this?

You believe you have a *soul.* "Hold there," says the Doctor, "I believe no such thing. If *you* have an immaterial soul, so have the brutes too." I will not quarrel with any that think they have; nay, I wish he could prove it. And surely I would rather allow *them* souls, than I would give up my own. Permit me then to go on. You believe you have a soul connected with this house of clay. But can you comprehend how? What are the ties that unite the heavenly flame with the earthly clod? You understand just nothing of the matter. So it is; but how, none can tell.

I bring but one instance more. At the command of your soul, your hand is lifted up. But who is able to account for this—for the connexion between the act of the mind and the outward actions? Nay, who can account for any muscular action at all, in any instance of it whatever?

But, secondly, strange as it may seem, in requiring you to believe "there are three that bear record in heaven, the Father, the Word, and the Holy Ghost: and these three are one," you are not required to believe any mystery. Nay, that great and good man, Dr. Peter Browne, sometime Bishop of Cork, has proved at large that the Bible does not require you to believe any mystery at all. The Bible barely requires you to believe such facts, not the manner of them. Now the mystery does not lie in the *fact,* but altogether in the *manner.*

For instance: "God said, Let there be light: and there was light." I believe it; I believe the plain *fact;* there is no mystery at all in this. The mystery lies in the *manner* of it. But of this I believe nothing at all, nor does God require it of me.

Again: "The Word was made flesh." I believe this *fact* also. There is no mystery in it. But as to the *manner how* he was made flesh, wherein the mystery lies, I know nothing about it; I believe nothing about it; it is no more the object of my faith than it is of my understanding.

To apply this to the case before us: "There are three that bear record in heaven: and these three are one." I believe this *fact* also (if I may use the expression) that God is Three and One. But the *manner how* I do not comprehend; and I do not believe it. Now in this, in the manner, lies the mystery; and so it may. I have no concern with it, it is no object of my faith. I believe just so much as God has revealed, and no more. But this, the manner, he has not revealed; therefore I believe nothing about it. But would it not be absurd in me to deny the fact because I do not understand the manner? That is, to reject *what God has revealed,* because I do not comprehend *what he has not revealed?*

Where is the wisdom of rejecting what is revealed, because we do not understand what is not revealed; of denying the *fact* which God has unveiled, because we cannot see the *manner,* which is veiled still? Especially when we consider that what God has been pleased to reveal upon this head is far from being a point of indifference, is a truth of the last importance. It enters into the very heart of Christianity. The knowledge of the Three-One God is interwoven with all true Christian faith, with all vital religion.

I do not say that every real Christian can say with the Marquis de Renty, "I bear about with me continually an experimental verity, and a plenitude of the presence of the ever-blessed Trinity." I apprehend this is not the experience of "babes," but rather "fathers in Christ."

But I know not how anyone can be a Christian believer till he "hath," as St. John speaks, "the witness in himself"; till "the Spirit of God witnesses with his spirit that he is a child of God"; that is, in effect, till God the Holy Ghost witnesses that God the Father has accepted him through the merits of God the Son; and having this witness, he honours the Son, and the blessed Spirit "even as he honours the Father."

Not that every Christian believer *adverts* to this; perhaps at first not one in twenty. But if you ask any of them a few questions, you will easily find it is implied in what he believes.

Therefore I do not see how it is possible for any to have vital religion, who denies that these Three are One. And all my hope for them is, not that they will be saved during their unbelief (unless on the footing of honest Heathens, upon the plea of invincible ignorance), but that God before they go hence will "bring them to the knowledge of the truth."[4]

Mr. Charles Perronet was the first person I was acquainted with who was favoured with the same experience as the Marquis de Renty with regard to the ever-blessed Trinity; Miss Ritchie was the second, Miss Roe (now Mrs. Rogers) the third. I have as yet found but a few instances; so that this is not, as I was at first apt to suppose, the common privilege of all that are "perfect in love."[5]

> Father, in whom we live,
> In whom we are and move,
> The glory, power, and praise receive
> Of thy creating love.
> Let all the angel-throng
> Give thanks to God on high;
> While earth repeats the joyful song,
> And echoes to the sky.
>
> Incarnate Deity,
> Let all the ransomed race
> Render in thanks their lives to thee
> For thy redeeming grace.
> The grace to sinners showed
> Ye heavenly choirs proclaim,
> And cry, "Salvation to our God,
> Salvation to the Lamb!"
>
> Spirit of Holiness,
> Let all thy saints adore
> Thy sacred energy, and bless
> Thine heart-renewing power.
> Not angel-tongues can tell
> Thy love's ecstatic height,
> The glorious joy unspeakable,
> The beatific sight.
>
> Eternal, Triune Lord!
> Let all the hosts above,
> Let all the sons of men record
> And dwell upon thy love.
> When heaven and earth are fled
> Before thy glorious face,
> Sing all the saints thy love hath made
> Thine everlasting praise![6]

HIS INESCAPABLE PRESENCE

I will endeavour, by the assistance of his Spirit, a little to explain the omnipresence of God; to show how we are to understand this glorious truth, "God is in this and every place." The Psalmist, you may remember, speaks strongly and beautifully upon it, in the 139th Psalm. He observes first, "Thou art about my bed, and about my path, and spiest out all my ways" (v.3), "Thou hast fashioned me behind and before, and laid thine hand upon me" (v.5); although the *manner* thereof he could not explain; *how* it was he could not tell. "Such knowledge," says he, "is too wonderful for me: I cannot attain unto it" (v.6). He next observes, in the most lively and affecting manner, that God is in every place. "Whither shall I go then from thy Spirit, or whither shall I go from thy presence? If I climb up into heaven, thou art there: if I go down to hell, thou art there also" (v.7f.). If I could ascend, speaking after the manner of men, to the highest part of the universe, or could I descend to the lowest point, thou art alike present both in one and the other. "If I should take the wings of the morning, and remain in the uttermost parts of the sea, even there thy hand would lead me"—thy power and thy presence would be before me—"and thy right hand hold me"; seeing thou art equally in the length and breadth, and in the height and depth, of the universe. In a word, there is no point of space, whether within or without the bounds of creation, where God is not.

Indeed, this subject is far too vast to be comprehended by the narrow limits of human understanding. We can only say, the great God, the eternal, the almighty Spirit, is as unbounded in his presence as in his duration and power. In condescension, indeed, to our weak understanding, he is said to dwell in heaven; but strictly speaking, the heaven of heavens cannot contain him, but he is in every part of his dominion. The universal God dwelleth in universal space; so that we may say:

> Hail, FATHER! whose creating call
> Unnumbered worlds attend!
> JEHOVAH, comprehending all,
> Whom none can comprehend!

God acts everywhere, and therefore is everywhere. God acts in heaven, in earth, and under the earth, throughout the whole compass of his creation; by sustaining all things, without which everything would in an instant sink into its primitive nothing; by governing all, every moment superintending everything he has made; strongly and sweetly influencing all, and yet without destroying the liberty of his rational creatures. And where no creature is, still God is there. The presence or absence of any or all creatures makes no difference with regard to him. He is equally in all or without all.

Many have been the disputes among philosophers, whether there be any such thing as empty space in the universe; and it is now generally supposed that all space is full. Perhaps it cannot be proved that all space is filled with matter. But the Heathen himself will bear us witness, *Jovis omnia plena,* "All things are full of God." Yea, and whatever space exists beyond the bounds of creation—for creation must have bounds, seeing nothing is boundless, nothing can be, but the great Creator—even that space cannot exclude Him who fills the heaven and the earth.

But to all that is or can be said of the omnipresence of God, the world has one grand objection: they cannot see him. And this is really the root of all their other objections. But is it not easy to reply, "Can you see the wind?" You cannot. But do you therefore deny its existence, or its presence? You say, "No; for I can perceive it by my other senses." But by which of your senses do you perceive your soul? Surely you do not deny either the existence or the presence of this! And yet it is not the object of your sight, or of any of your other senses. Suffice it then to consider that God is a Spirit, as is your soul also. Consequently, "Him no man hath seen or can see" with eyes of flesh and blood.

But allowing that God is here, as in every place, what inference should we draw from hence? What use should we make of this awful consideration? Is it not meet and right to humble ourselves before the eyes of his Majesty? Should we not labour continually to acknowledge his presence, "with reverence and godly fear"?

If you believe that God is about your bed and about your path, and spieth out all your ways, then take care not to do the least thing, not to speak the least word, not to indulge the least thought, which you have reason to think would offend him. Yea, if God sees our hearts as well as our hands, and in all places; if he understands our thoughts, long before they are clothed with words, how earnestly should we urge that petition, "Search me, O Lord, and prove me; try out my reins and my heart; look well if there be any way of wickedness in me, and lead me in the way everlasting!"

Spare no pains to preserve always a deep, a continual, a lively, and a joyful sense of his gracious presence. Cheerfully expect that He before whom you stand will ever guide you with his eye, will support you by his guardian hand, will keep you from all evil, and "when you have suffered a while, will make you perfect, will stablish, strengthen, and settle you," and then "preserve you unblameable unto the coming of our Lord Jesus Christ"![7]

> Far off we need not rove
> To find the God of love;
> In his providential care,
> Ever intimately near,
> All his various works declare,
> God, the bounteous God is here.
>
> We live, and move, and are,
> Through his preserving care;
> He doth still in life maintain
> Every soul that moves and lives;
> Gives us back our breath again,
> Being every moment gives.
>
> Who live O God in thee,
> Entirely thine should be:
> Thine we are, a heaven-born race,
> Only to thy glory move,
> Thee with all our powers we praise,
> Thee with all our being love.[8]

HIS ALL-EMBRACING PROVIDENCE

The Omnipresent God sees and knows all the properties of the beings that he has made. He knows all the connexions, dependencies, and relations, and all the ways wherein one of them can affect another. In particular, he sees all the inanimate parts of the creation, whether in heaven above or in the earth beneath. He knows all the animals of the lower world, whether beasts, birds, fishes, reptiles, or insects. He knows all the qualities and powers he has given them, from the highest to the lowest. He knows all the hearts of the sons of men, and understands all their thoughts. He sees what any angel, any devil, any man, either thinks or speaks or does; yea and all they feel. He sees all their sufferings, with every circumstance of them.

And is the Creator and Preserver of the world unconcerned for what he sees therein? Does he look upon these things either with a malignant or heedless eye? Is he an epicurean god? Does he sit at ease in the heaven, without regarding the poor inhabitants of earth? It cannot be. He hath made us, not we ourselves, and he cannot despise the work of his own hands. We are his children. And can a mother forget the children of her womb? Yea, she may forget; yet will not God forget us! On the contrary, he has expressly declared that as his "eyes are over all the earth," so he "is loving to every man, and his mercy is over all his works." Consequently, he is concerned every moment for what befalls every creature upon earth, and more especially for everything that befalls any of the children of men. It is hard indeed to comprehend this; nay it is hard to believe it, considering the complicated wickedness and the complicated misery which we see on every side. But believe it we must, unless we will make God a liar; although it is sure no man can comprehend it. It behooves us, then, to humble ourselves before God, and to acknowledge our ignorance. Indeed, how can we expect that a man should be able to comprehend the ways of God? "For how can finite measure infinite?"

He is infinite in wisdom as well as in power, and all his wisdom is continually employed in managing all the affairs of his creation for the good of all his creatures. For his wisdom and goodness go hand in hand. They are inseparably united, and continually act in concert with almighty power. And to him all things are possible. He doeth whatsoever pleaseth him. And we cannot doubt of his exerting all his power, as in sustaining, so in governing, all that he has made.

Only, He that can do all things else, cannot deny himself. He cannot counteract himself, or oppose his own work. Were it not for this, he would destroy all sin, with its attendant pain, in a moment. He would abolish wickedness out of his whole creation, and suffer no trace of it to remain. But in so doing, he would altogether overturn his own work, and undo all that he has been doing since he created man upon the earth. For he created man in his own image, a spirit like himself; a spirit endued with understanding, with will or affections, and liberty—without which neither his understanding nor his affections could have been of any use, neither would he have been capable either of vice or virtue. He could not be a moral agent, any more than a tree or a stone.

Therefore (with reverence be it spoken), the Almighty himself cannot do this thing. He cannot destroy out of the soul of man that image of himself wherein he made him. And without doing this, he cannot abolish sin and pain out of the world. But were it to be done, it would imply no wisdom at all, but barely a stroke of omnipotence.

All the manifold wisdom of God (as well as his power and goodness) is displayed in governing man as man, not as a stock or stone, but as an intelligent and free spirit, capable of choosing either good or evil. He commands all things, both in heaven and earth, to assist man in attaining the end of his being, in working out his own salvation, so far as it can be done without compulsion, without overruling his liberty. The whole frame of divine providence is so constituted as to afford every man every possible help, in order to his doing good and eschewing evil, which can be done without turning man into a machine.

But what say the wise men of the world to this? They answer with all readiness, "Who doubts of this? We are not atheists. We all acknowledge a providence; that is, a general providence; for indeed, the particular providence of which some talk, we know not what to make of. Surely the little affairs of men are far beneath the regard of the great Creator and Governor of the universe! Accordingly,

> He sees with equal eyes, as Lord of all,
> A hero perish, or a sparrow fall.

Does he indeed? I cannot think it; because (whatever that fine poet did) I believe the Bible, wherein the great Creator and Governor of the world himself tells me quite the contrary.

But in support of a general, in contradiction to a particular providence, the same elegant poet lays it down as an unquestionable maxim,

> The Universal Cause
> Acts not by partial, but by general laws;

plainly meaning that he never deviates from these general laws in favour of any particular person. This is a common supposition, but which is altogether inconsistent with the whole tenor of Scripture. For if God never deviates from these general laws, then there never was a miracle in the world, seeing every miracle is a deviation from the general laws of nature. "What! you expect miracles then?" Certainly I do if I believe the Bible; for the Bible teaches me that God hears and answers prayer. But every answer to prayer is, properly, a miracle. For if natural causes take their course, if things go on in their natural way, it is no answer at all. Gravitation therefore shall cease, that is, cease to operate, whenever the Author of it pleases. Cannot the men of the world understand these things?

You say you "allow a *general* providence, but deny a *particular* one." And what is a general, of whatever kind it be, that includes no particulars? Tell me any genus, if you can, that contains no species. What is it that constitutes a genus, but so many species added together? What, I pray, is a whole that contains no parts? Mere nonsense and contradiction!

What do you mean by a general providence contradistinguished from a particular? Do you mean a providence which superintends only the larger parts of the universe? Suppose the sun, moon, and stars.

Does it not regard the earth, too? You allow it does. But does it not likewise regard the inhabitants of it? Or do you mean that God regards only some parts of the world, and does not regard others? What parts of it does he regard? Those without, or those within, the solar system? Or does he regard some parts of the earth, and not others? Which parts?

Do you mean that the providence of God does indeed extend to all parts of the earth, with regard to great and singular events, such as the rise and fall of empires, but that the little concerns of this or that man are beneath the notice of the Almighty? Then you do not consider that *great* and *little* are merely relative terms, which have place only with respect to men. With regard to the Most High, man and all the concerns of men are nothing, less than nothing, before him. And nothing is small in his sight that in any degree affects the welfare of any that fear God and work righteousness. What becomes, then, of your general providence, exclusive of a particular? Let it be forever rejected by all rational men, as absurd, self-contradictory nonsense. We may then sum up the whole scriptural doctrine of providence in that fine saying of St. Austin, *Ita praesidet singulis sicut universis, et universis sicut singulis!* ["He presides over each creature as if it were the universe, and over the universe as over each individual creature."][9]

> Happy man whom God doth aid!
> God our souls and bodies made;
> God on us in gracious showers,
> Blessings every moment pours;
> Compasses with angel-bands,
> Bids them bear us in their hands;
> Parents, friends, 'twas God bestowed,
> Life, and all, descend from God.
>
> He this flowery carpet spread,
> Made this earth on which we tread;
> God refreshes in the air,
> Covers with the clothes we wear,
> Feeds us with the food we eat,
> Cheers us by his light and heat,
> Makes his sun on us to shine;
> All our blessings are divine.
>
> Give him, then, and ever give,
> Thanks for all that we receive!
> Man we for his kindness love,
> How much more our God above!
> Worthy thou, our heavenly Lord,

To be honoured and adored;
God of all-creating grace,
Take the everlasting praise![10]

OUR KNOWLEDGE OF HIS NATURE

Some great truths, as the being and attributes of God, and the difference between moral good and evil, were known in some measure to the heathen world. The traces of them are to be found in all nations. So that in some sense it may be said to every child of man, "He hath showed thee, O man, what is good; even to do justly, to love mercy, and to walk humbly with thy God." With this truth he has in some measure "enlightened everyone that cometh into the world." And hereby they that "have not the law," that have no written law, "are a law unto themselves." They show "the work of the law"—the substance of it, though not the letter—"written in their hearts," by the same hand which wrote the commandments on the tables of stone; "their conscience also bearing them witness," whether they act suitably thereto or not.

But there are two grand heads of doctrine, which contain many truths of the most important nature, of which the most enlightened Heathens in the ancient world were totally ignorant; as are also the most intelligent Heathens that are now on the face of the earth. I mean those which relate to the eternal Son of God, and the Spirit of God: to the Son, giving himself to be "a propitiation for the sins of the world"; and to the Spirit of God, renewing men in that image of God wherein they were created. For after all the pains which ingenious and learned men have taken to find some resemblance of these truths in the immense rubbish of heathen authors, the resemblance is so exceeding faint, as not to be discerned but by a very lively imagination. Beside that, even this resemblance, faint as it was, is only to be found in the discourses of a very few; and those were the most improved and deeply-thinking men in their several generations; while the innumerable multitudes that surrounded them were little better for the knowledge of the philosophers, but remained as totally ignorant even of these capital truths as were the beasts that perish.

Certain it is that these truths were never known to the vulgar, the bulk of mankind, to the generality of men in any nation, till they were brought to light by the gospel. Notwithstanding a spark of knowledge glimmering here and there, the whole earth was covered with darkness, till the Sun of righteousness arose and scattered the shades of night. Since this day-spring from on high has appeared, a great light hath shined unto those who, till then, sat in darkness and in the shadow of death. And thousands of them in every age have known that "God so loved the world, as to give his only Son, to the end that whosoever believeth on him should not perish, but have everlasting life." And being entrusted with the oracles of God, they have known that God hath also given us his Holy Spirit, who "worketh in us both to will and to do of his good pleasure."[11]

> The people that in darkness lay,
> The confines of eternal night,
> We, we have seen a gospel day,
> The glorious beams of heavenly light,
> His Spirit in our hearts hath shone,
> And showed the Father in the Son.
>
> Father of everlasting love,
> To every soul thy Son reveal,
> Our guilt and sufferings to remove,
> Our deep, original wound to heal;
> And bid the fallen race arise,
> And turn our earth to paradise.[12]

OUR IGNORANCE OF HIS WAYS

It is a childish conceit to suppose chance governs the world, or has any part in the government of it: no, not even in those things that, to a vulgar eye, appear to be perfectly casual. Our blessed Master himself has put this matter beyond all possible doubt: "Not a sparrow," saith he, "falleth to the ground without the will of your Father which is in heaven. Yea" (to express the thing more strongly still) "even the very hairs of your head are all numbered."

But although we are well apprised of this general truth, that all things are governed by the providence of God (the very language of the heathen orator, *Deorum moderamine cuncta geri*), yet how amazingly little do we know of the particulars contained under this general! How little do we understand of his providential dealings, either with regard to nations, or families, or individuals! There are heights and depths in all these which our understanding can in no wise fathom. We can comprehend but a small part of his ways now; the rest we shall know hereafter.

Even with regard to entire nations, how little do we comprehend of God's providential dealings with them! What innumerable nations once flourished and are now swept away from the face of the earth! But it is not only with regard to ancient nations that the providential dispensations of God are utterly incomprehensible to us. The same difficulties occur now. We know "the Lord is loving unto every man, and his mercy is over all his works." But we know not how to reconcile this with the present dispensations of his providence.

At this day, is not almost every part of the earth full of darkness and cruel habitations? In what a condition, in particular, is the large and populous empire of Indostan [India]! How many hundred thousands of the poor, quiet people have been destroyed, and their carcases left as the dung of the earth! And who cares for thousands, myriads, if not millions, of the wretched Africans? Are not whole droves of these poor sheep (human, if not rational beings!) continually driven to market, and sold like cattle into the vilest bondage, without any hope of deliverance but by death? How little better is either the civil or religious state of the poor American Indians! That is, the miserable remains of them. For in some provinces, not one of them is left to breathe. Add to these, myriads of human savages that are freezing among the snows of Siberia, and as many, if not more, who are wandering up and down in the deserts of Tartary. And did "God so love" these,"that he gave his Son, his only begotten Son, to the end they might not perish, but have everlasting life"? Then why are they thus?

Is there not something equally mysterious in the divine dispensation with regard to Christianity itself? Who can explain why Christianity is not spread as far as sin? Why is not the medicine sent to every place where the disease is found? But, alas! it is not. The poison is diffused over the whole globe; the antidote is not known in a sixth part of it. Nay, and how is it that the wisdom and goodness of God suffer the antidote itself to be so grievously adulterated, not only in Roman Catholic countries, but in almost every part of the Christian world? So adulterated, that it retains none, or at least a very small part, of its original virtue. In consequence of this, there is little more mercy or truth to be found among Christians than among Pagans.

Equally incomprehensible to us are many of the divine dispensations with regard to particular families. We cannot at all comprehend why he raises some to wealth, honour, power; and why, in the meantime, he depresses others with poverty and various afflictions. As little can we account for the divine dispensations with regard to individuals. We know not why the lot of this man is cast in Europe, the lot of that man in the wilds of America; why one is born of rich or noble, the other of poor, parents; why the father and mother of one are strong and healthy, those of another weak and diseased, in consequence of which he drags a miserable being all the days of his life. How many are, from their very infancy, hedged in with such relations that they seem to have no chance (as some speak), no possibility, of being useful to themselves or others? Why are they, antecedent to their own choice, entangled in such connexions?

Are we able to search out his works of grace, any more than his works of providence? Nothing is more sure than that "without holiness no man shall see the Lord." Why is it, then, that so vast a majority of mankind are, so far as we can judge, cut off from all means, all possibility, of holiness, even from their mother's womb? For instance: what possibility is there that a Hottentot, a New-Zealander, or an inhabitant of Nova Zembla, if he lives and dies there, should ever know what holiness means, or, consequently, ever attain it? Yea, but one may say, "He sinned before he was born, in a pre-existent state; therefore, he was placed here in so unfavourable a situation; and it is mere mercy that he should have a second trial." I answer: supposing such a pre-existent state, this, which you call a second trial, is really no trial at all. As soon as he is born into the world, he is absolutely in the Power of his savage parents and relations, who, from the first dawn of reason, train him up in the same ignorance, atheism, and barbarity with themselves. He has no possibility of any better education.

I desire it may be observed, that if this be improved into an objection against revelation, it is an objection that lies full as much against natural as revealed religion. If it were conclusive, it would not drive us into Deism, but into flat Atheism. And yet I see not how we can avoid the force of it, but by resolving all into the unsearchable wisdom of God; together with a deep conviction of our own ignorance, and inability to fathom his counsels.

Several valuable lessons we may learn from a deep consciousness of our own ignorance. First, we may learn hence a lesson of humility; not "to think of ourselves," particularly with regard to our understanding, "more highly than we ought to think"; but "to think soberly." From hence we may learn, secondly, a lesson of faith, of confidence in God. A full conviction of our own ignorance may teach us a full trust in his wisdom. It may teach us (what is not always so easy as one would conceive it to be) to trust the invisible God, farther than we can see him. There are at present two grand obstructions to our forming a right judgment of the dealings of God with respect to men. The one is, there are innumerable *facts* relating to every man, which we do not and cannot know. The other is, we cannot see *the thoughts* of men, even when we know their actions. Conscious of this, "judge nothing before the time," concerning his providential dispensations.

From a consciousness of our own ignorance we may learn, thirdly, a lesson of resignation. We may be instructed to say, at all times, and in all instances, "Father, not as I will, but as thou wilt." This was the last lesson which our blessed Lord, as man, learned while he was upon earth. He could go no higher than, "Not as I will, but as thou wilt," till he bowed his head and gave up the ghost. Let us also herein be made conformable to his death, that we may know the full "power of his resurrection"![13]

O God, thou bottomless abyss!
   Thee to perfection who can know?
O height immense! What words suffice
   Thy countless attributes to show?
Eternity thy fountain was,
   Which, like thee, no beginning knew;
Thou wast ere time began his race,
   Ere glowed with stars the ethereal blue.

Unchangeable, all-perfect Lord,
   Essential life's unbounded sea,
What lives and moves, lives by thy word;
   It lives, and moves, and is from thee.
High is thy power above all height,
   Whate'er thy will decrees is done;
Thy wisdom, equal to thy might,
   Only to thee, O God, is known![14]

II

The Greatness and Littleness of Man

EXISTENTIAL ANXIETY

Consider we, first, what is man with regard to his magnitude? And in this respect, what is any one individual compared to all the inhabitants of the earth? These, we may easily suppose, amount to four thousand millions. And what is any single individual in comparison of this number?

But what is the magnitude of the earth itself, compared to that of the solar system—including, beside that vast body the sun, so immensely larger than the earth, the whole train of primary and secondary planets, several of which are abundantly larger than the whole earth?

And yet, what is the whole quantity of matter, with all the spaces comprised in the solar system, in comparison of that which is pervaded by those amazing bodies, the comets? Yet what is even the orbit of a comet, and the space contained therein, to the space which is occupied by the fixed stars?

Whether the bounds of the creation do or do not extend beyond the region of the fixed stars, who can tell? But that it is finite, that the bounds of it are fixed, we have no reason to doubt. [And] what is all finite space that is, or can be conceived in comparison of infinite? What is it but a point, a cypher, compared to that which is filled by Him that is All in all? Think of this, and then ask "What is man?"

What is man, that the great God, who filleth heaven and earth, "the high and lofty One that inhabiteth eternity," should stoop so inconceivably low as to be "mindful of him"? Would not reason suggest to us that so diminutive a creature would be overlooked by him in the immensity of his works?—especially when we consider:

Secondly, what is man with regard to his duration? The days of man "are threescore years and ten." "And if men be so strong," perhaps one in a hundred "that they come to fourscore years, yet then is their strength but labour and sorrow: so soon it passeth away, and we are gone!"

Now, what a poor pittance of duration is this, compared to the life of Methuselah! But what are [Methuselah's] nine hundred and sixty and nine years to the duration of an angel, which began "or ever the mountains were brought forth," or the foundations of the earth were laid? And what is the duration which has passed since the creation of angels, to that which passed before they were created, to unbeginning eternity?

Indeed, what proportion can there possibly be between any finite and infinite duration? What proportion is there between a thousand or ten thousand years, or ten thousand times ten thousand ages, and eternity? In what terms can the proportion between these be expressed? It is nothing, yea infinitely less than nothing!

If then we add to the littleness of man the inexpressible shortness of his duration, is it any wonder that a man of reflection should sometimes feel a kind of fear, lest the great, eternal, infinite Governor of the universe should disregard so diminutive a creature as man—a creature so every way inconsiderable, when compared either with immensity or eternity? Did not both these reflections glance through, if not dwell upon, the mind of the royal Psalmist [Ps. 8:3f.; 144:3f.]? And it is natural for us to make the same reflections, and to entertain the same fear.

But how may we prevent this uneasy reflection, and effectually cure this fear? First by considering that the body is not the man; that man is not only a house of clay, but an immortal spirit; a spirit made in the image of God; a spirit that is of infinitely more value than the whole earth; of more value than the sun, moon and stars put together; yea, than the whole material creation. Consider that the spirit of man is not only of a higher order, of a more excellent nature, than any part of the visible world, but also more durable; not liable either to dissolution or decay.

Consider, secondly, that declaration which the Father of spirits hath made to us by the prophet Hosea: "I am God, and not man: therefore my compassions fail not." As if he had said: "If I were only a man, or an angel, or any finite being, my knowledge might admit of bounds, and my mercy might be limited. But 'my thoughts are not as your thoughts,' and my mercy is not as your mercy. 'As the heavens are higher than the earth, so are my thoughts higher than your thoughts'; and my mercy, my compassion, 'my ways' of showing it, 'higher than your ways.'"

That no shadow of fear might remain, no possibility of doubting, to show what manner of regard the great eternal God bears to little, short-lived man, God gave his Son, "his only Son, to the end that whosoever believeth in him should not perish, but have everlasting life." See how God loved the world! The Son of God, that was "God of God, Light of Light, very God of very God," in glory equal with the Father, in majesty co-eternal, "emptied himself, took upon him the form of a servant; and being found in fashion as a man, was obedient unto death, even the death of the cross." And all this he suffered, not for himself, but "for us men and for our salvation."

After this demonstration of his love, is it possible to doubt any longer of God's tender regard for man; even though he was "dead in trespasses and sins"? Even when he saw us in our sins and in our blood, he said unto us, "Live!" Let us then fear no more! Let us doubt no more! "He that spared not his own Son, but delivered him up for us all, shall he not With him freely give us all things?"[1]

COSMIC INSECURITY

But supposing the earthquake which made such havoc at Lisbon [in 1755] should never travel so far as London, is there nothing else which can reach us? What think you of a comet? Are we absolutely out of the reach of this? And would the approach of one of these amazing spheres be of no importance to us—especially in its return from the sun; when that immense body is (according to Sir Isaac Newton's calculation) heated two thousand times hotter than a red-hot cannon ball? The late ingenious and accurate Dr. Halley (never yet suspected of enthusiasm) fixes the return of the great comet in the year 1758; and he observes that in this revolution it will move, not only in the same line, but in the same part of that line, wherein the earth moves. And "who can tell," says that great man, "what the consequences of such a contact may be?"

Who can tell! Any man of common understanding, who knows the very first elements of astronomy. The immediate consequence of such a body of solid fire touching the earth must necessarily be that it will set the earth on fire and burn it to a coal, if it do not likewise strike it out of its course; in which case (so far as we can judge) it must drop down directly into the sun.

But what if this vast body is already on the way—if it is nearer than we are aware of? We cannot be certain that it will be visible to the inhabitants of our globe, till it has imbibed the solar fire. But possibly we may see it sooner than we desire.

Probably it will be seen first drawing nearer and nearer, till it appears as another moon in magnitude, though not in colour, being of a deep fiery red; then scorching and burning up all the produce of the earth, drying up every fountain, stream and river, causing all faces to gather blackness, and all men's hearts to fail; then executing its grand commission on the globe itself, and causing the stars to fall from heaven.[2] O, who may abide when this is done? Who will then be able to stand?

What shall we do—do now—that none of these things may come upon us unawares? If our own wisdom and strength be not sufficient to defend us, let us not be ashamed to seek farther help. Let us even dare to own we believe there is a God; nay, and not a lazy, indolent, epicurean deity, who sits at ease upon the circle of the heavens, and neither knows nor cares what is done below; but one who, as he created heaven and earth and all the armies of them, as he sustains them all by the word of his power, so cannot neglect the work of his own hands. With pleasure we own there is such a God whose eye pervades the whole sphere of created beings, who knoweth the number of the stars, and calleth them all by their names; a God whose wisdom is as the great abyss, deep and wide as eternity. Yet more: whose mercy riseth above the heavens, and his faithfulness above the clouds; who is loving to every man, and his mercy over all his works. Let us secure him on our side; let us make this wise, this powerful, this gracious God our friend. Then need we not fear, though the earth be moved, and the hills be carried into the midst of the sea; no, not though the heavens being on fire are dissolved, and the very elements melt with fervent heat. It is enough that the Lord of Hosts is with us, the God of love is our everlasting refuge.[3]

THE PRIVILEGE OF HUMANITY

[God] "made all things," as the wise man observes, "for himself; for his glory they were created." Not "as if he needed anything," seeing "he giveth to all life, and breath, and all things." He made all things to be happy. He made man to be happy in himself. He is the proper centre of spirits; for whom every created spirit was made. So true is the well-known saying of the ancient Fathers: *Fecisti nos ad te; et inquietum est cor nostrum, donec requiescat in te* [Augustine]. "Thou hast made us for thyself; and our heart cannot rest till it resteth in thee."

This observation gives us a clear answer to that question in the [Westminster] Assembly's Catechism: "For what end did God create man?" The answer is, "To glorify and enjoy him for ever." This is undoubtedly true; but is it quite clear, especially to men of ordinary capacities? Do the generality of common people understand that expression, "to glorify God"? No; no more than they understand Greek. And it is altogether above the capacity of children, to whom we, can scarce ever speak plain enough. Now, is not this the very principle that should be inculcated upon every human creature—"You are made to be happy in God"—as soon as ever reason dawns? Should not every parent, as soon as a child begins to talk or to run alone, say something of this kind: "See! what is that which shines so over your head? That we call the sun. See how bright it is! Feel how it warms you! It makes the grass to spring, and everything to grow. But God made the sun. The sun could not shine, nor warm, nor do any good without him." In this plain and familiar way a wise parent might, many times in a day, say something of God; particularly insisting, "He made you; and he made you to be happy in him; and nothing else can make you happy." We cannot press this too soon. If you say, "Nay, but they cannot understand you when they are so young"; I answer, No, nor when they are fifty years old, unless God opens their understanding. And can he not do this at any age?[4]

What then is the barrier between men and brutes, the line which they cannot pass? It is not reason. Set aside that ambiguous term; exchange it for the plain word, understanding; and who can deny that brutes have this? We may as well deny that they have sight or hearing. But it is this: man is capable of God; the inferior creatures are not. We have no ground to believe that they are in any degree capable of knowing, loving, or obeying God. This is the specific difference between man and brute, the great gulf which they cannot pass over.

From what has been said, I cannot but draw one inference which no man of reason can deny. If it is this which distinguishes men from beasts—that they are creatures capable of God, capable of knowing and loving and enjoying him—then whoever is "without God in the world," whoever does not know or love or enjoy God and is not careful about the matter, does in effect disclaim the nature of man, and degrade himself into a beast! Let such vouchsafe a little attention to those remarkable words of Solomon: "I said in my heart concerning the estate of the sons of men, . . . they might see that they themselves are beasts" (Eccles. 3:18). These sons of men are undoubtedly beasts; and that by their own act and deed; for they deliberately and wilfully disclaim the sole characteristic of human nature. It is true, they may have a share of reason; they have speech, and they walk erect; but they have not the mark, the only mark, which totally separates man from the brute creation. "That which befalleth beasts, the same thing befalleth them." They are equally without God in the world; "so that a man" of this kind "hath no pre-eminence above a beast."

So much more let all those who are of a nobler turn of mind assert the distinguishing dignity of their nature. Let all who are of a more generous spirit know and maintain their rank in the scale of beings. Rest not till you enjoy the privilege of humanity—the knowledge and love of God. Lift up your heads, ye creatures capable of God! Lift up your hearts to the Source of your being!

> Know God, and teach your souls to know
> The joys that from religion flow.

Give your hearts to Him who, together with ten thousand blessings, has given you his Son, his only Son! Let your continual "fellowship be with the Father, and with his Son Jesus Christ"! Let God be in all your thoughts, and ye will be men indeed.[5]

And let it be observed, as this is the end, so it is the whole and sole end, for which every man upon the face of the earth, for which every one of *you,* were brought into the world and endued with a living soul. Remember! You are born for nothing else. Your life is continued to you upon earth for no other purpose than this, that you may know, love and serve God on earth, and enjoy him to all eternity. Consider! You were not created to please your senses, to gratify your imagination, to gain money, or the praise of men; to seek happiness in any created good, in anything under the sun. All this is "walking in a vain shadow"; it is leading a restless, miserable life, in order to a miserable eternity. On the contrary, you were created for this and for no other purpose, by seeking and finding happiness in God on earth, to secure the glory of God in heaven. Therefore let your heart continually say, "This one thing I do"—having one thing in view, remembering why I was born, and why I am continued in life—"I press on to the mark." I aim at the one end of my being, God; even at "God in Christ reconciling the world to himself." He shall be my God for ever and ever, and my guide even unto death![6]

OUR FALLEN STATE

The writings of many of the ancients abound with gay descriptions of the dignity of man; whom some of them paint as having all virtue and happiness in his composition, or at least, entirely in his power, without being beholden to any other being; yea, as self-sufficient, able to live on his own stock, and little inferior to God himself.

Nor have Heathens alone, men who are guided in their researches by little more than the dim light of reason, but many likewise of them that bear the name of Christ, and to whom are entrusted the oracles of God, spoken as magnificently concerning the nature of man, as if it were all innocence and perfection. Accounts of this kind have particularly abounded in the present century; and perhaps in no part of the world more than in our own country. Here not a few persons of strong understanding, as well as extensive learning, have employed their utmost abilities to show what they termed "the fair side of human nature." And it must be acknowledged that if their accounts of him be just, man is still but "a little lower than the angels"; or, as the words may be more literally rendered, "a little less than God."

Is it any wonder that these accounts are very readily received by the generality of men? For who is not easily persuaded to think favourably of himself? Accordingly, writers of this kind are most universally read, admired, applauded. And innumerable are the converts they have made, not only in the gay, but the learned world. So that it is now quite unfashionable to talk otherwise, to say anything to the disparagement of human nature; which is generally allowed, not withstanding a few infirmities, to be very innocent, and wise, and virtuous!

But in the meantime, what must we do with our Bibles? For they will never agree with this. These accounts, however pleasing to flesh and blood, are utterly irreconcilable with the scriptural. The Scripture avers that "by one man's disobedience all men were constituted sinners"; that "in Adam all died," spiritually died, lost the life and image of God; that fallen, sinful Adam then "begat a son in his own likeness"; that consequently we, as well as other men, were by nature "dead in trespasses and sins," "without hope, without God in the world," and therefore "children of wrath"; that "there is no difference," in that "all have sinned and come short of the glory of God," of that glorious image of God wherein man was originally created. And hence, when "the Lord looked down from heaven upon the children of men, he saw they were all gone out of the way; they were altogether become abominable, there was none righteous, no, not one," none that truly sought after God. "God saw that the wickedness of man was great in the earth"; so great, that "every imagination of the thoughts of his heart was only evil continually." This is God's account of man.

And this account of the present state of man is confirmed by daily experience. It is true, the natural man discerns it not; and this is not to be wondered at. So long as a man born blind continues so, he is scarce sensible of his want; much less, could we suppose a place where all were born without sight, would they be sensible of the want of it. In like manner, so long as men remain in their natural blindness of understanding, they are not sensible of their spiritual wants, and of this in particular. But as soon as God opens the eyes of their understanding, they see the state they were in before; they are then deeply convinced that "every man living," themselves especially, are by nature "altogether vanity"; that is, folly and ignorance, sin and wickedness.[7]

Let everyone, then, speak as he finds. As for me, I cannot admire either the wisdom or virtue or happiness of mankind. Wherever I have been, I have found the bulk of mankind, Christian as well as heathen, deplorably ignorant, vicious, and miserable. And who can account for this, but on the supposition that we are in a fallen state?[8]

"There are but three opinions concerning the transmission of original sin." That is, there are but three ways of accounting how it is transmitted. I care not if there were none. The *fact* I know, both by Scripture and by experience. I know it is transmitted; but *how* it is transmitted I neither know nor desire to know.[9]

THE DISEASES OF HUMAN NATURE

What are those spiritual diseases which everyone that is born of a woman brings with him into the world?

Is not the first of these *atheism?* After all that has been so plausibly written concerning "the innate idea of God"; after all that has been said of its being common to all men, in all ages and nations; it does not appear that man naturally has any more idea of God than any of the beasts of the field; he has no knowledge of God at all; no fear of God at all, neither is God in all his thoughts. Whatever change may afterwards be wrought (whether by the grace of God, or by his own reflection, or by education), he is by nature a mere atheist.

Indeed it may be said that every man is by nature, as it were, his own god. He worships himself. He is, in his own conception, absolute Lord of himself. Dryden's hero speaks only according to nature when he says, "Myself am king of *me."* He seeks himself in all things. He pleases himself. And why not? Who is Lord over him? *His own will* is his only law; he does this or that because it is his good pleasure. In the same spirit as the "son of the morning" said in old time, "I will sit upon the sides of the north," he says, "I *will* do thus or thus." And do we not find sensible men on every side who are of the self-same spirit—who if asked, "Why did you do this?" will readily answer, "Because I had a mind to it"?

Another evil disease which every human soul brings into the world with him, is *pride,* a continual proneness to think of himself more highly than he ought to think. Every man can discern more or less of this disease in everyone—but himself. And indeed if he could discern it in himself, it would subsist no longer; for he would then in consequence think of himself just as he ought to think.

The next disease natural to every human soul, born with every man, is *love of the world.* Every man is, by nature, a lover of the creature instead of the Creator, a "lover of pleasure" in every kind, "more than a lover of God." He is a slave to foolish and hurtful desires, in one kind or another; either to the "desire of the flesh, the desire of the eyes, or the pride of life." The "desire of the flesh" is a propensity to seek happiness in what gratifies one or more of the outward senses. The "desire of the eyes" is a propensity to seek happiness in what gratifies the internal sense, the imagination, either by things grand, or new, or beautiful. The "pride of life" seems to mean a propensity to seek happiness in what gratifies the sense of honour. To this head is usually referred "the love of money," one of the basest passions that can have place in the human heart. But it may be doubted whether this be not an acquired rather than a natural distemper.

Whether this be a natural disease or not, it is certain *anger* is. The ancient philosopher defines it, "A sense of injury received, with a desire of revenge." Now, was there ever anyone born of a woman, who did not labour under this? Indeed, like other diseases of the mind, it is far more violent in some than in others. But it is *furor brevis,* as the poet speaks; it is a real, though short, madness wherever it is.

A *deviation from truth* is equally natural to all the children of men. One said in his haste, "All men are liars"; but we may say upon cool reflection, All natural men will, upon a close temptation, vary from or disguise the truth. If they do not offend against veracity, if they do not say what is false, yet they frequently offend against simplicity. They use art; they hang out false colours; they practice either simulation or dissimulation. So that you cannot say truly of any person living, till grace has altered nature, "Behold an Israelite indeed, in whom is no guile!"

Everyone is likewise prone, by nature, to speak or act *contrary to justice.* This is another of the diseases which we bring with us into the world. All human creatures are naturally partial to themselves, and when opportunity offers, have more regard to their own interest or pleasure than strict justice allows. Neither is any man, by nature, merciful as our heavenly Father is merciful; but all more or less transgress that glorious rule of mercy as well as justice, "Whatsoever ye would that men should do unto you, the same do unto them."[10]

THE DECEITFULNESS OF MAN'S HEART

It would be endless to enumerate all the species of wickedness, whether in thought, word, or action, that now overspread the earth, in every nation, and city, and family. They all centre in this: atheism, or idolatry—pride, either thinking of themselves more highly than they ought to think, or glorying in something which they have received, as though they had not received it; independence and self-will, doing their own will, not the will of Him that made them. Add to this, seeking happiness out of God, in gratifying the desire of the flesh, the desire of the eye, and the pride of life. Hence it is a melancholy truth, that (unless when the Spirit of God has made the difference) all mankind now, as well as four thousand years ago, "have corrupted their ways before the Lord; and every imagination of the thought of man's heart is evil, only evil, and that continually." However therefore men may differ in their outward ways (in which undoubtedly there are a thousand differences), yet in the inward root, the enmity against God, atheism, pride, self-will, and idolatry, it is true of all, that "the heart of man," of every natural man, "is desperately wicked."

But if this be the case, how is it that not everyone is conscious of it? Why is it that so few know themselves? For this plain reason: because the heart is not only "desperately wicked" but "deceitful above all things." So deceitful, that the generality of men are continually deceiving both themselves and others. How strangely do they deceive themselves, not knowing either their own tempers or characters, imagining themselves to be abundantly better and wiser than they are! And if men thus deceive themselves, is it any wonder that they deceive others also, and that we so seldom find "an Israelite indeed, in whom is no guile"?

This is one of the sorts of desperate wickedness which cleaves to the nature of every man, proceeding from those fruitful roots, self-will, pride, and independence on God. Hence springs every species of vice and wickedness; hence every sin against God, our neighbour, and ourselves. Hence there is, in the heart of every child of man, an inexhaustible fund of ungodliness and unrighteousness, so deeply and strongly rooted in the soul, that nothing less than almighty grace can cure it. From hence naturally arises a plentiful harvest of all evil words and works; and to complete the whole, that complex of all evils, "that foul monster, War." In the train of this fell monster are murder, adultery, rape, violence, and cruelty of every kind. And all these abominations are not only found in Mahometan or pagan countries, where their horrid practice may seem to be the natural result of equally horrid principles, but in those that are called Christian countries, yea, in the most civilised states and kingdoms.

But is there no exception as to the wickedness of man's heart? Yea, in those that are born of God. "He that is born of God keepeth himself, and that wicked one toucheth him not." God has "purified his heart by faith," so that his wickedness is departed from him. "Old things are passed away, and all things" in him "are become new." So that his heart is no longer desperately wicked, but "renewed in righteousness and true holiness." Only let it be remembered that the heart even of a believer is not wholly purified when he is justified. Sin is then overcome, but it is not rooted out; it is conquered, but not destroyed. Experience shows him, first, that the root of sin, self-will, pride, and idolatry remain still in his heart. But as long as he continues to watch and pray, none of them can prevail against him. Experience teaches him, secondly, that sin (generally pride or self-will) cleaves to his best actions; so that, even with regard to these, he finds an absolute necessity for the blood of atonement.

But how artfully does this conceal itself, not only from others, but even from ourselves! Who can discover it in all the disguise it assumes, or trace it through all its latent mazes? And if it be so difficult to know the heart of a good man, who can know the heart of a wicked one, which is far more deceitful? No unregenerate man, however sensible, ever so experienced, ever so wise in his generation. And yet these are they who pique themselves upon "knowing the world," and imagine they see through all men.[11]

THE INHUMAN FOLLY OF WAR

But there is a still greater and more undeniable proof that the very foundations of all things are utterly out of course in the Christian as well as the heathen world. There is a still more horrid reproach to the Christian name, yea, to the name of man, to all reason and humanity. There is war in the world! War between men! War between Christians! I mean, between those that bear the name of Christ, and profess to "walk as he also walked." Now, who can reconcile war, I will not say to religion, but to any degree of reason or common sense?

Here are thirty or forty thousand men gathered together on this plain. What are they going to do? See, there are thirty or forty thousand more at a little distance. And these are going to shoot them through the head or body, to stab them, or split their skulls, and send most of their souls into everlasting fire, as fast as they possibly can. Why so? What harm have they done to them? O, none at all! They do not so much as know them. But a man, who is King of France, has a quarrel with another man, who is King of England. So these Frenchmen are to kill as many of these Englishmen as they can, to prove the King of France is in the right. Now, what an argument is this! What a method of proof! What an amazing way of deciding controversies! What must mankind be, before such a thing as war could ever be known or thought of upon earth? How shocking, how inconceivable a want must there have been of common understanding, as well as common humanity, before any two Governors, or any two nations in the universe, could once think of such a method of decision! If, then, all nations, Pagan, Mahometan, and Christian, do in fact make this their last resort, what farther proof do we need of the utter degeneracy of all nations from the plainest principles of reason and virtue; of the absolute want both of common sense and common humanity, which runs through the whole race of mankind?

In how just and strong a light is this placed by the writer cited before [Cowley]—"I gave him a description of cannons, muskets, pistols, swords, bayonets; of sieges, attacks, mines, countermines, bombardments; of engagements by sea and land; ships sunk with a thousand men, twenty thousand killed on each side, dying groans, limbs flying in the air; smoke, noise, trampling to death under horses' feet, flight, pursuit, victory; fields strewed with carcases, left for food to dogs and beasts of prey; and farther, of plundering, stripping, ravishing, burning, and destroying. I assured him I had seen a hundred enemies blown up at once in a siege, and as many in a ship, and beheld the dead bodies drop down in pieces from the clouds, to the great diversion of the spectators."

Is it not astonishing beyond all expression that this is the naked truth—that within a short term of years, this has been the real case in almost every part of even the Christian world? And meanwhile we gravely talk of the "dignity of our nature" in its present state! This is really surprising, and might easily drive even a well-tempered man to say, "One might bear with men, if they would be content with those vices and follies to which nature has entitled them. I am not provoked at the sight of a pickpocket, a gamester, a politician, a suborner, a traitor, or the like. But when I behold a lump of deformity and diseases, both in body and mind, smitten with pride, it breaks all the measures of my patience; neither shall I ever be able to comprehend how such an animal and such a vice can tally together.

And surely all our declamations on the strength of human reason, and the eminence of our virtues, are no more than the cant and jargon of pride and ignorance, so long as there is such a thing as war in the world. Men in general can never be allowed to be reasonable creatures, till they know not war any more. So long as this monster stalks uncontrolled, where is reason, virtue, humanity? They are utterly excluded; they have no place; they are a name, and nothing more.[12]

THE MISERY OF MANKIND

Universal misery is at once a consequence and a proof of this universal corruption. Men are unhappy (how very few are the exceptions!) because they are unholy. Why is the earth so full of complicated distress? Because it is full of complicated wickedness. Why are not you happy? Other circumstances may concur, but the main reason is because you are not holy. If you are not guilty of any gross outward vice, yet you have vicious tempers; and as long as these have power in your heart, true peace has no place. You are proud; you think too highly of yourself. You are passionate; often angry without reason. You are self-willed; you would have your own will, your own way, in everything; that is, plainly, you would rule over God and man; you would be the governor of the world. You are daily liable to unreasonable desires. Some things you desire that are no way desirable; others which ought to be avoided, yea abhorred, at least as they are now circumstanced. And can a proud or a passionate man be happy? O no! Experience shows it is impossible. Can a man be happy who is full of self-will? Not unless he can dethrone the Most High. Can a man of unreasonable desires be happy? Nay, they "pierce" him "through with many sorrows."

You think, however, you could bear yourself pretty well, but you have such a husband or wife, such parents and children, as are intolerable! One has such a tongue, the other so perverse a temper! The language of these, the carriage of those, is so provoking; otherwise you should be happy enough. True, if both you and they were wise and virtuous. Meanwhile, neither the vices of your family nor your own will suffer you to rest.

Look out of your own doors. Why is it that the friend or relation for whom you are so tenderly concerned is involved in so many troubles? Have you not done your part towards making them happy? Yes, but they will not do their own. One has no management, no frugality, or no industry; another is too fond of pleasure. If he is not what is called scandalously vicious, he loves wine, women, or gaming. And to what does all this amount? He might be happy, but sin will not suffer it.

Perhaps you will say, "Nay, he is not at fault; he is both frugal and diligent; but he has fallen into the hands of those who have imposed upon his good nature." Very well; but sin is still the cause of his misfortunes; only it is another's, not his own.

If you inquire into the troubles under which your neighbour, your acquaintance, or one you casually talk with, labours, still you will find the far greater part of them arise from some fault, either of the sufferer or of others; so that still sin is at the root of the trouble, and it is unholiness which causes unhappiness.

And this holds as well with regard to families as with regard to individuals. Many families are miserable through want. They have not the conveniences, if the necessaries, of life. Why have they not? Because they will not work. Were they diligent, they would want nothing. Or if not idle, they are wasteful. They squander away in a short time what might have served for many years. Others, indeed, are diligent and frugal too; but a treacherous friend, or a malicious enemy, has ruined them; or they groan under the hand of the oppressor. You see, then, in all these cases, want (though in various ways) is the effect of sin. But is there no rich man near? None that could relieve these innocent sufferers, without impairing his own fortune? Yea; but he thinks of nothing less. They may rot and perish for him. See, more sin is implied in their suffering.

But is not the family of the rich man himself happy? No, far from it; perhaps farther than his poor neighbours. For they are not content; their "eye is not satisfied with seeing, nor" their "ear with hearing." Endeavouring to fill their souls with the pleasures of sense and imagination, they are only pouring water into a sieve. Is not this the case with the wealthiest families you know? But it is not the whole case with some of them. There is a debauched, a jealous, or an ill-natured husband; a gaming, passionate, or imperious wife; an undutiful son; or an imprudent daughter—who banishes happiness from the house. And what is all this but sin in various shapes, with its sure attendant, misery?

In a town, a corporation, a city, a kingdom, is it not the same thing still? From whence comes that complication of all the miseries incident to human nature—war? Is it not from the tempers "which war in the soul"? When nation rises up against nation, and kingdom against kingdom, does it not necessarily imply pride, ambition, coveting what is another's; or envy, or malice, or revenge, on one side if not on both? Still, then, sin is the baleful source of affliction; and consequently, the flood of miseries which covers the face of the earth—which overwhelms not only single persons, but whole families, towns, cities, kingdoms—is a demonstrative proof of the overflowing of ungodliness in every nation under heaven.[13]

ORIGINAL SIN

The fact, then, being undeniable, I would ask, how is it to be accounted for? Will you resolve it into the prevalence of custom, and say, "Men are guided more by example than reason"? It is true; they run after one another like a flock of sheep. But I gain no ground by this;

I am equally at a loss to account for this custom. How is it (seeing men are reasonable creatures, and nothing is so agreeable to reason as virtue) that the custom of all ages and nations is not on the side of virtue rather than vice? If you say, "This is owing to bad education, which propagates ill customs"; I own, education has an amazing force, far beyond what is commonly imagined. I own, too, that as bad education is found among Christians as ever obtained among the Heathens. But I am no nearer still; I am not advanced a hair's breadth towards the conclusion. For how am I to account for the almost universal prevalence of this bad education? I want to know when this prevailed first, and how it came to prevail. How came wise and good men (for such they must have been before bad education commenced) not to train up their children in wisdom and goodness? They had then no ill precedent before them. How came they to make such a precedent? And how came all the wisdom of after-ages never to correct such a precedent?[14]

Do we not derive from Adam a moral taint and infection, whereby we have a natural propensity to sin? [You may reply:] "We have many natural appetites and passions which, if they grow irregular, become sinful. But this does not amount to a natural propensity to sin." But is not pride sin? Is not idolatry sin? And is it not idolatry to "love the creature more than the Creator"? Is not revenge sin? Is it not sin to "look upon a woman" so as "to lust after her"? And have not all men a natural propensity to these things? They have all, then, a natural propensity to sin. Nevertheless, this propensity is not necessary, if by necessary you mean irresistible. We can resist and conquer it too, by the grace which is ever at hand.

"But nature cannot be morally corrupted, but by the choice of a moral agent." You may play upon words as long as you please; but still I hold this fast: I (and you too, whether you will own it or no) am inclined, and was ever since I can remember, antecedently to any choice of my own, to pride, revenge, idolatry. If you will not call these moral corruptions, call them just what you will; but the fact I am as well assured of, as that I have any memory or understanding.

"But to disparage our nature is to disparage the work and gifts of God." True; but to describe the corruption of our nature as it is, is not disparaging the work of God. For that corruption is not his work. On the other hand, to say it is, to say God created us as corrupt as we are now, with as weak an understanding and as perverse a will—this is disparaging the work of God, and God himself, to some purpose!

"But doth not this doctrine teach you to transfer your wickedness and sin to a wrong cause? Whereas you ought to blame yourself alone, you lay the whole blame upon Adam." I do not. I know God is willing to save me from all sin, both original and actual. Therefore, if I am not saved I must lay the whole blame upon myself.

"But what good end does this doctrine promote?" The doctrine that we are by nature "dead in sin," and therefore "children of wrath," promotes repentance, a true knowledge of ourselves, and thereby leads to faith in Christ, to a true knowledge of Christ crucified. And faith worketh love; and by love, all holiness both of heart and life. Consequently, this doctrine promotes (nay, and is absolutely, indispensably necessary to promote) the whole of that religion which the Son of God lived and died to establish.

This doctrine, therefore, is the "most proper" of all others "to be instilled into a child"—that it is by nature a "child of wrath," under the guilt and power of sin; that it can be saved from wrath only by the merits and sufferings and love of the Son of God; that it can be delivered from the power of sin only by the inspiration of his Holy Spirit; but that by his grace it may be renewed in the image of God, perfected in love, and made meet for glory.

But "must it not lessen the due love of parents to children to believe they are the vilest creatures in the world?" Far from it, if they know how God loves both them and theirs, vile and sinful as they are. And it is a certain fact that no parents love their children more tenderly than those who firmly believe this doctrine; and that none are more careful to "bring them up in the nurture and admonition of the Lord."

But "how can young people 'remember their Creator' without horror, if he has given them life under such deplorable circumstances?" They can remember him with pleasure, with earnest thankfulness, when they reflect out of what a "pit" he hath "brought them up"; and that if "sin abounded," both by nature and habit, "grace" did "much more abound."[15]

III

The Mystery of Godliness

FOR SINNERS ONLY

"Indeed my L[ady]," said an eminent man to a person of quality, "I cannot see that we have much need of Jesus Christ." And who might not say, upon this supposition, "I cannot see that we have much need of Christianity"? Nay, not any at all; for "they that are whole have no need of a Physician"; and the Christian Revelation speaks of nothing else but the great "Physician" of our souls; nor can Christian philosophy, whatever be thought of the Pagan, be more properly defined than in Plato's word. It is θεραπεία ψυχῆς, "the only true method of healing a distempered soul." But what need of this, if we are in perfect health? If we are not diseased, we do not want a cure. If we are not sick, why should we seek for a medicine to heal our sickness? What room is there to talk of our being renewed in "knowledge" or "holiness, after the image wherein we were created," if we never have lost that image—if we are as knowing and holy now, nay, far more so, than Adam was immediately after his creation? If, therefore, we take away this foundation, that man is by nature foolish and sinful, "fallen short of the glorious image of God," the Christian system falls at once; nor will it deserve so honourable an appellation, as that of a "cunningly devised fable."[1]

[Yet] an ingenious gentleman being asked, "My Lord, what do you think of the Bible?" answered, "I think it is the finest book I ever read in my life. Only that part of it which indicates the mediatorial scheme, I do not understand; for I do not conceive there is any need of a Mediator between God and man. If indeed," continued he, "I was a sinner, then I should need a Mediator; but I do not conceive I am. It is true, I often act wrong, for want of more understanding. And I frequently *feel* wrong tempers, particularly proneness to anger; but I cannot allow this to be a sin; for it depends on the motion of my blood

91

and spirits, which I cannot help.Therefore it cannot be a sin; or if it be, the blame must fall not on *me,* but on Him that made me." The very sentiments of pious Lord Kames, and modest Mr. Hume!

Some years ago, a charitable woman discovered that there was no sinner in the world but the devil. "For," said she, "he *forces* men to act as they do; therefore they are unaccountable; the blame lights on Satan." But these more enlightened gentlemen have discovered that there is no sinner in the world but God! For he *forces* men to think, speak and act as they do; therefore the blame lights on God alone. Satan, avaunt! It may be doubted whether he himself ever uttered so foul a blasphemy as this![2]

> Come, O thou all-victorious Lord!
> Thy power to us make known;
> Strike with the hammer of thy word,
> And break these hearts of stone.
>
> Give us ourselves and thee to know,
> In this our gracious day;
> Repentance unto life bestow,
> And take our sins away.
>
> Impoverish, Lord, and then relieve,
> And then enrich the poor;
> The knowledge of our sickness give,
> The knowledge of our cure.[3]

THE GOSPEL OF THE KINGDOM

We are first to consider the nature of true religion, here termed by our Lord "the kingdom of God" [Mark 1:15]. The same expression the great Apostle uses in his Epistle to the Romans, where he likewise explains his Lord's words, saying, "The kingdom of God is not meat and drink; but righteousness, and peace, and joy in the Holy Ghost" (Rom. 14:17).

"The kingdom of God " or true religion, "is not meat and drink." It is well known that not only the unconverted Jews, but great numbers of those who had received the faith of Christ, were, notwithstanding, "zealous of the law" (Acts 21:20), even the ceremonial law of Moses. Whatsoever, therefore, they found written therein, either concerning meat and drink offerings, or the distinction between clean and unclean meats, they not only observed themselves, but vehemently pressed the same even on those "among the Gentiles"(or Heathens) "who were turned to God."

In opposition to these, the Apostle declares, both here and in many other places, that true religion does not consist in *meat* and *drink,* or in any ritual observances; nor indeed in any outward thing whatsoever, in anything exterior to the heart; the whole substance thereof lying in "righteousness, peace, and joy in the Holy Ghost."

And first, *righteousness.* We cannot be at a loss concerning this, if we remember the words of our Lord describing the two grand branches thereof, on which "hang all the Law and the Prophets." "Thou shalt love the Lord thy God with all thy heart, and with all thy mind, and with all thy soul, and with all thy strength: this is the first and great commandment" (Mark 12:30); the first and great branch of Christian righteousness. Thou shalt delight thyself in the Lord thy God; thou shalt seek and find all happiness in him. He shall be "thy shield and thy exceeding great reward," in time and in eternity.

And the second commandment is like unto this; the second great branch of Christian righteousness is closely and inseparably connected therewith; even "Thou shalt love thy neighbour as thyself." *Thou shalt love*—thou shalt embrace with the most tender good-will, the most earnest and cordial affection, the most inflamed desires of preventing or removing all evil, and of procuring for him every possible good. *Thy neighbour*—that is, not only thy friend, thy kinsman, or thy acquaintance; not only the virtuous, the friendly, him that loves thee, that prevents [anticipates] or returns thy kindness; but every child of man, not excepting him whom thou knowest to be evil and unthankful, him that still despitefully uses and persecutes thee. Him thou shalt love *as thyself;* with the same invariable thirst after his happiness in every kind; the same unwearied care to screen him from whatever might grieve or hurt either his soul or body.

But true religion, or a heart right towards God and man, implies happiness as well as holiness. For it is not only "righteousness," but also "peace, and joy in the Holy Ghost." What peace? "The peace of God," which God only can give, and the world cannot take away; the peace which "passeth all understanding," all barely rational conception; being a supernatural sensation, a divine taste, of "the powers of the world to come." It is a peace that banishes all doubt, all painful uncertainty; the Spirit of God bearing witness with the spirit of a Christian, that he is "a child of God." And it banishes fear, all such fear as "hath torment": the fear of the wrath of God; the fear of hell; the fear of death.

With this peace of God, wherever it is fixed in the soul, there is also "joy in the Holy Ghost"; joy wrought in the heart by the Holy Ghost, by the ever-blessed Spirit of God. He it is that worketh in us that calm, humble rejoicing in God, through Christ Jesus, "by whom we have now received the atonement," the reconciliation with God; and that enables us boldly to confirm the truth of the royal Psalmist's declaration, "Blessed is the man" (or rather, *happy*) "whose unrighteousness is forgiven, and whose sin is covered." He it is that inspires the Christian soul with that even, solid joy, which arises from the testimony of the Spirit that he is a child of God; and that gives him to "rejoice with joy unspeakable, in hope of the glory of God"; hope both of the glorious image of God, which is in part, and shall be fully, "revealed in him"; and of that crown of glory which fadeth not away, reserved in heaven for him.

This holiness and happiness, joined in one, are sometimes styled, in the inspired writings, "the kingdom of God" and sometimes "the kingdom of heaven." It is termed "the kingdom of God," because it is the immediate fruit of God's reigning in the soul. It is called "the kingdom of heaven," because it is (in a degree) heaven opened in the soul. For whosoever they are that experience this, they can aver before angels and men,

> Everlasting life is won,
> Glory is on earth begun.

And this "kingdom of God," or of heaven, "is at hand."As these words were originally spoken, they implied that "the time" was then fulfilled, God being "made manifest in the flesh," when he would set up his kingdom among men, and reign in the hearts of his people. And is not the time now fulfilled? For "Lo," (saith he), "I am with you always," you who preach remission of sins in my name, "even unto the end of the world" (Matt. 28:20). Wheresoever, therefore, the gospel of Christ is preached, this his "kingdom is nigh at hand." It is not far from every one of you. Ye may this hour enter there into, if so be ye hearken to his voice, "Repent ye, and believe the gospel."[4]

The gospel (that is, good tidings, good news for guilty, helpless sinners), in the largest sense of the word, means the whole revelation made to men by Jesus Christ; and sometimes the whole account of what our Lord did and suffered while he tabernacled among men. The substance of all is, "Jesus Christ came into the world to save sinners"; or, "God so loved the world, that he gave his only-begotten Son, to the end we might not perish, but have everlasting life"; or, "He was bruised for our transgressions, he was wounded for our iniquities; the chastisement of our peace was upon him; and with his stripes we are healed."

Believe this, and the kingdom of God is thine. By faith thou attainest the promise. "He pardoneth and absolveth all that truly repent, and unfeignedly believe his holy gospel." As soon as ever God hath spoken to thy heart, "Be of good cheer, thy sins are forgiven thee," his kingdom comes: thou hast "righteousness, and peace, and joy in the Holy Ghost."[5]

> Jesu, if still the same thou art,
> If all thy promises are sure,
> Set up thy kingdom in my heart,
> And make me rich, for I am poor:
> To me be all thy treasures given,
> The kingdom of an inward heaven.
>
> Where is the blessedness bestowed
> On all that hunger after thee?
> I hunger now, I thirst for God;
> See the poor fainting sinner, see,
> And satisfy with endless peace,
> And fill me with thy righteousness.
>
> Lord, I believe the promise sure,
> And trust thou wilt not long delay:
> Hungry, and sorrowful, and poor,
> Upon thy word myself I stay;
> Into thine hands my all resign,
> And wait till all thou art is mine.[6]

THE MANIFESTATION OF THE SON OF GOD

It is certain that "God made man upright," perfectly holy and perfectly happy; but by rebelling against God he destroyed himself, lost the favour and image of God, and entailed sin, with its attendant pain, on himself and all his posterity. Yet his merciful Creator did not leave him in this helpless, hopeless state. He immediately appointed His Son, his well-beloved Son, to be the Saviour of men, "the propitiation for the sins of the whole world," the great Physician who, by his almighty Spirit, should heal the sicknesses of their souls and restore them not only to the favour but to the "image of God wherein they were created."

This great mystery of godliness began to work from the very time of the original promise. Accordingly, the Lamb being in the purpose of God "slain from the beginning of the world," from the same period his sanctifying Spirit began to renew the souls of men. We have an undeniable instance of this in Abel, who "obtained a testimony" from God "that he was righteous" (Heb. 11:4). And from that very time, all that were partakers of the same faith were partakers of the same salvation; were not only reinstated in the favour, but likewise restored to the image, of God.[7]

How the Son of God was manifested to our first parents in Paradise it is not easy to determine. It is generally, and not improbably, supposed that he appeared to them in the form of a man, and conversed with them face to face.

May we not reasonably believe it was by similar appearances that he was manifested in succeeding ages to Enoch . . . to Noah . . . to Abraham, Isaac and Jacob . . . and, to mention no more, to Moses?

But all these were only types of his grand manifestation. It was in the fulness of time that God "brought his first-begotten into the world, made of a woman" by the power of the Most High overshadowing her. He was afterwards manifested to the shepherds, to devout Simeon, to Anna the prophetess, and to "all that waited for redemption in Jerusalem."[8]

> Glory be to God on high,
>   And peace on earth descend!
> God comes down, he bows the sky,
>   And shows himself our Friend:
> God the invisible appears!
>   God, the blest, the great I AM,
> Sojourns in this vale of tears,
>   And Jesus is his name.
>
> Him the angels all adored,
>   Their Maker and their King;
> Tidings of their humbled Lord
>   They now to mortals bring.
> Emptied of his majesty,
>   Of his dazzling glories shorn,
> Being's Source begins to be,
>   And God himself is born!
>
> See the eternal Son of God
>   A mortal Son of Man;
> Dwelling in an earthly clod,
>   Whom heaven cannot contain.
> Stand amazed, ye heavens, at this:
>   See the Lord of earth and skies;
> Humbled to the dust he is,
>   And in a manger lies.

We, the sons of men, rejoice,
The Prince of Peace proclaim;
With heaven's host lift up our voice,
And shout Immanuel's name:
Knees and hearts to him we bow;
Of our flesh and of our bone,
Jesus is our brother now,
And God is all our own.[9]

When he was of due age for executing his priestly office, he was manifested to Israel; preaching the gospel of the kingdom of God in every town and in every city. He was manifested by numberless "signs and wonders and mighty works which he did," as well as by his whole life; being the only one born of a woman "who knew no sin," who from his birth to his death did "all things well"; doing continually "not his own will, but the will of him that sent him."[10]

How remarkable are those words of the Apostle: "Let this mind be in you, which was also in Christ Jesus; who, being in the form of God"—the incommunicable nature of God from eternity—"counted it no act of robbery" (that is the precise meaning of the word)—no invasion of any other's prerogative, but his own unquestionable right—"to be equal with God." The word implies both the *fulness* and the supreme *height* of the Godhead; to which are opposed the two words, he *emptied* and he *humbled himself*. He "emptied himself" of that divine fulness, veiled his fulness from the eyes of men and angels; "taking," and by that very act emptying himself, "the form of a servant; being made in the likeness of man," a real man, like other men. "And being found in fashion as a man"—a common man, without any peculiar beauty or excellency—"he humbled himself" to a still greater degree, "becoming obedient" to God, though equal with him, "even unto death; yea, the death of the cross"—the greatest instance both of humiliation and obedience.[11]

After all, "behold the Lamb of God, taking away the sin of the world!" This was a more glorious manifestation of himself than any he had made before. How wonderfully was he manifested to angels and men, when he "was wounded for our transgressions"; when he "bare all our sins in his own body on the tree"; when he cried out, "It is finished; and bowed his head, and gave up the ghost"![12]

O God of all grace,
Thy goodness we praise;
Thy Son thou hast given to die in our place.

He came from above
Our curse to remove,
He hath loved, he hath loved us, because
he would love,

Love moved him to die,
And on this we rely,
He hath loved, he hath loved us, we cannot tell why.
But this we can tell,
He hath loved us so well,
As to lay down his life to redeem us from hell.

He hath ransomed our race;
O how shall we praise
Or worthily sing thy unspeakable grace?
Nothing else will we know
On our journey below
But singing thy grace to thy paradise go.[13]

We need but just mention those farther manifestations—his resurrection from the dead, his ascension into heaven, and his pouring out the Holy Ghost; both of which are beautifully described in those words of the Psalmist: "Thou art gone up on high, thou hast led captivity captive, and hast received gifts for men; yea, even for thine enemies, that the Lord God might dwell among" or in "them."[14]

Our Lord is risen from the dead!
Our Jesus is gone up on high!
The powers of hell are captive led,
Dragged to the portals of the sky.

There his triumphal chariot waits,
And angels chant the solemn lay:
Lift up your heads, ye heavenly gates;
Ye everlasting doors, give way!

Loose all your bars of massy light,
And wide unfold the ethereal scene;
He claims these mansions as his right;
Receive the King of Glory in!

Who is this King of Glory? Who?
The Lord that all our foes o'ercame,
The world, sin, death, and hell o'erthrew;
And Jesus is the Conqueror's name.[15]

"That the Lord God might dwell in them"—this refers to a yet farther manifestation of the Son of God; even his inward manifestation of himself. When he spoke of this to his Apostles but a little before his death, one of them immediately asked, "Lord, how is it that thou wilt manifest thyself to us, and not unto the world?" By enabling us to believe in his name. For he is then inwardly manifested to us when we are enabled to say with confidence, "My Lord, and my God!" Then each of us can boldly say, "The life which I now live, I live by faith in the Son of God, who loved me and gave himself for me."[16]

THE CENTRALITY OF THE ATONEMENT

Nothing in the Christian system is of greater consequence than the doctrine of the Atonement. It is properly the distinguishing point between Deism and Christianity. "The scriptural scheme of morality," said Lord Huntingdon,[17] "is what everyone must admire; but the doctrine of the Atonement I cannot comprehend." Here, then, we divide. Give up the Atonement, and the Deists are agreed with us.

This point, therefore, deserves to be more largely considered than my time will permit. But it is the less needful now because I have done it already in my letter to Mr. Law,[18] to which I beg you will give a serious reading, whether you have read it before or no. But it is true I can no more *comprehend* it than his lordship; perhaps I might say than the angels of God, than the highest created understanding. Our *reason* is here quickly bewildered. If we attempt to expatiate in this field, we "find no end, in wandering mazes lost." But the question is (the only question with me; I regard nothing else), What saith the Scripture? It says, "God was in Christ, reconciling the world unto himself"; that "He made him, who knew no sin, to be a sin-offering for us." It says, "He was wounded for our transgressions and bruised for our iniquities." It says, "We have an Advocate with the Father, Jesus Christ the righteous; and he is the atonement for our sins."

But it is certain had God never been angry, he could never have been reconciled. So that, in affirming this, Mr. Law strikes at the very root of the Atonement, and finds a very short method of converting Deists.[19] Although, therefore, I do not term God, as Mr. Law supposes, "a wrathful Being," which conveys the wrong idea; yet I firmly believe he was angry with all mankind, and that he was reconciled to them by the death of his Son. And I know he was angry with me till I believed in the Son of his love; and yet this is no impeachment to his mercy, that he is just as well as merciful.

But undoubtedly, as long as the world stands, there will be a thousand objections to this scriptural doctrine. For still the preaching of Christ crucified will be foolishness to the wise men of the world. However, let us hold the precious truth fast in our heart as well as in our understanding; and we shall find by happy experience that this is to us the wisdom of God and the power of God.[20]

> And can it be that I should gain
>   An interest in the Saviour's blood?
> Died he for me, who caused his pain?
>   For me, who him to death pursued?
> Amazing love! how can it be
> That thou, my God, shouldst die for me!
>
> 'Tis mystery all! The Immortal dies!
>   Who can explore his strange design?
> In vain the first-born seraph tries
>   To sound the depths of love divine.
> Tis mercy all! let earth adore,
> Let angel minds inquire no more.
>
> He left his Father's throne above—
>   So free, so infinite his grace—
> Emptied himself of all but love,
>   And bled for Adam's helpless race.
> 'Tis mercy all, immense and free;
> For, O my God, it found out me!
>
> No condemnation now I dread;
>   Jesus, and all in him, is mine!
> Alive in him, my living Head,
>   And clothed in righteousness divine,
> Bold I approach the eternal throne,
> And claim the crown, through Christ, my own.[21]

THE LIBERATING WORK OF CHRIST

As Satan began his work in Eve by tainting her with unbelief, so the Son of God begins his work in man by enabling us to believe in him. He both opens and enlightens the eyes of our understanding. Out of darkness he commands the light to shine, and takes away the veil which "the god of this world" had spread over our hearts. And we then see, not by a chain of *reasoning,* but by a kind of *intuition,* by a direct view, that "God was in Christ reconciling the world to himself, not imputing to them their (former) trespasses"; not imputing them to me. In that day "we know that we are of God," children of God by faith; "having redemption through the blood of Christ, even the forgiveness of sins." "Being justified by faith, we have peace with God through our Lord Jesus Christ"—that peace which enables us in every state therewith to be content; which delivers us from all perplexing doubts, from all tormenting fears; and in particular, from that "fear of death whereby we were all our life-time subject to bondage."

At the same time the Son of God strikes at the root of that grand work of the devil, pride; causing the sinner to humble himself before the Lord, to abhor himself, as it were, in dust and ashes. He strikes at the root of self-will; enabling the humbled sinner to say in all things, "Not as I will, but as thou wilt." He destroys the love of the world, delivering them that believe in him from "every foolish and hurtful desire"; from the "desire of the flesh, the desire of the eyes, and the pride of life." He saves them from seeking, or expecting to find, happiness in any creature. As Satan turned the heart of man from the Creator to the creature, so the Son of God turns his heart back again from the creature to the Creator. Thus it is, by manifesting himself, he destroys the works of the devil; restoring the guilty outcast from God, to his favour, to pardon and peace; the sinner in whom dwelleth no good thing, to love and holiness; the burdened, miserable sinner, to joy unspeakable, to real, substantial happiness.

But it may be observed that the Son of God does not destroy the whole work of the devil in man, as long as he remains in this life. He does not yet destroy bodily weakness, sickness, pain, and a thousand infirmities incident to flesh and blood. He does not destroy all that weakness of understanding which is the natural consequence of the soul's dwelling in a corruptible body; so that still *humanum est errare et nescire*—"both ignorance and error belong to humanity." He entrusts us with only an exceeding small share of knowledge in our present state, lest our knowledge should interfere with our humility, and we should again affect to be as gods. It is to remove from us all temptation to pride, and all thought of independency (which is the very thing that men in general so earnestly covet under the name of *liberty),* that he leaves us encompassed with all these infirmities, particularly weakness of understanding; till the sentence takes place, "Dust thou art, and unto dust thou shalt return!"

Then error, pain, and all bodily infirmities cease: all these are destroyed by death. And death itself, "the last enemy" of man, shall be destroyed at the resurrection. The moment that we hear the voice of the archangel and the trump of God, "then shall be fulfilled the saying that is written, Death is swallowed up in victory." "This corruptible" body "shall put on incorruption; this mortal" body "shall put on immortality"; and the Son of God, manifested in the clouds of heaven, shall destroy this last work of the devil!

Here then we see in the clearest, strongest light, what is real religion: a restoration of man by Him that bruises the serpent's head to all that the old serpent deprived him of: a restoration not only to the favour but likewise to the image of God, implying not barely deliverance from sin, but the being filled with the fulness of God.[22]

> Surrounded by a host of foes,
>   Stormed by a host of foes within,
> Nor swift to flee, nor strong to oppose,
>   Single, against hell, earth, and sin,
> Single, yet undismayed, I am;
> I dare believe in Jesu's name.
>
> What though a thousand hosts engage,
>   A thousand worlds, my soul to shake?
> I have a shield shall quell their rage,
>   And drive the alien armies back;
> Portrayed it bears a bleeding Lamb:
> I dare believe in Jesu's name.
>
> Me to retrieve from Satan's hands,
>   Me from this evil world to free,
> To purge my sins, and loose my bands,
>   And save from all iniquity,
> My Lord and God from heaven he came;
> I dare believe in Jesu's name.
>
> Salvation in his name there is,
>   Salvation from sin, death, and hell,
> Salvation into glorious bliss,
>   How great salvation, who can tell!
> But all he hath for mine I claim;
> I dare believe in Jesu's name.[23]

THE RENEWING POWER OF THE SPIRIT

The moment the Spirit of the Almighty strikes the heart of him that was till then without God in the world, it breaks the hardness of his heart, and creates all things new. The Sun of Righteousness appears, and shines upon his soul, showing him the light of the glory of God in the face of Jesus Christ. He is in a new world. All things around him are become new, such as it never before entered into his heart to conceive. He *sees,* so far as his newly opened eyes can bear the sight,

> The opening heavens around him shine,
> With beams of sacred bliss.

He sees that he has "an Advocate with the Father, Jesus Christ the righteous"; and that he has "redemption in his blood, the remission of sins." He sees "a new way that is opened into the holiest by the blood of Jesus"; and his light "shineth more and more unto the perfect day."

By the same gracious stroke, he that before had ears, but heard not, is now made capable of *hearing.* He hears the voice that raiseth the dead—the voice of Him that is "the resurrection and the life." He is no longer deaf to his invitations or commands, to his promises or threatenings; but gladly hears every word that proceeds out of his mouth, and governs thereby all his thoughts, words, and actions.

At the same time, he receives other spiritual senses, capable of discerning spiritual good and evil. He is enabled to *taste,* as well as to see, how gracious the Lord is. He enters into the holiest by the blood of Jesus, and tastes of the powers of the world to come. He *feels* the love of God shed abroad in his heart by the Holy Ghost which is given unto him; or, as our Church expresses it "feels the working of the Spirit of God in his heart." Meantime, it may easily be observed that the substance of all these figurative expressions is comprised in that one word *faith,* taken in its widest sense; being enjoyed, more or less, by everyone that believes in the name of the Son of God. This change, from spiritual death to spiritual life, is properly the new birth; all the particulars whereof are admirably well expressed by Dr. Watts in one verse:

> Renew my eyes, open my ears,
> And form my soul afresh;
> Give me new passions, joys, and fears,
> And turn the stone to flesh!

But before this universal change, there may be many partial changes in a natural man, which are frequently mistaken for it; whereby many say, "peace, peace!" to their souls, when there is no peace. There may be not only a considerable change in the life, so as to refrain from open sin, yea, the easily besetting sin; but also a considerable change of tempers, conviction of sin, strong desires, and good resolutions. And here we have need to take great care not, on the one hand, to despise the day of small things; nor, on the other, to mistake any of these partial changes for that entire, general change, the new birth; that total change, from the image of the earthly Adam into the image of the heavenly; from an earthly, sensual, devilish mind, into the mind that was in Christ.

Settle it therefore in your hearts, that however you may be changed in many other respects, yet in Christ Jesus, that is, according to the Christian Institution, nothing will avail without the whole mind that was in Christ, enabling you to walk as Christ walked. Nothing is more sure than this: "If any man be in Christ," a true believer in him, "he is a new creature. Old things" in him "are passed away; all things are become new."[24]

> Spirit of faith, come down,
> Reveal the things of God;
> And make to us the Godhead known,
> And witness with the blood.
>
> 'Tis thine the blood to apply,
> And give us eyes to see
> Who did for every sinner die
> Hath surely died for me.
>
> No man can truly say
> That Jesus is the Lord
> Unless Thou take the veil away,
> And breathe the living word;
> Then, only then, we feel
> Our interest in his blood,
> And cry, with joy unspeakable;
> Thou art my Lord, my God!
>
> O that the world might know
> The all-atoning Lamb!
> Spirit of faith, descend, and show
> The virtue of his name;
> The grace which all may find,
> The saving power impart;
> And testify to all mankind,
> And speak in every heart.[25]

WHY GOD LET ADAM FALL

"Did not God foresee that Adam would abuse his liberty? And did he not know the baneful consequences which this must naturally have on all his posterity? And why, then, did he permit that disobedience? Was it not easy for the Almighty to have prevented it?" He certainly did foresee the whole. This cannot be denied. And it was undoubtedly in his power to prevent it; for he hath all power both in heaven and earth. But it was known to him at the same time that it was best upon the whole not to prevent it. He knew that "not as the transgression, so is the free gift"; that the evil resulting from the former was not as the good resulting from the latter—not worthy to be compared with it. He saw that to permit the fall of the first man was far best for mankind in general; that if "sin abounded" thereby over all the earth, yet grace "would much more abound"; yea, and that to every individual of the human race, unless it was by his own choice.

First, mankind in general have gained by the fall of Adam a capacity of attaining more holiness and happiness on earth than it would have been possible for them to attain if Adam had not fallen. For if Adam had not fallen, Christ had not died. So there would have been no room for that amazing display of the Son of God's love to mankind. It could not then have been said, to the astonishment of all the hosts of heaven, "God so loved the world," yea the ungodly world, which had no thought or desire of returning to him, "that he gave his Son, his only begotten Son, to the end that whosoever believeth on him should not perish, but have everlasting life."

What is the necessary consequence of this? It is this: there could then have been no such thing as faith in God thus loving the world, giving his only Son for us men and our salvation. There could have been no such thing as faith in the Son of God, as "loving us and giving himself for us." There could have been no faith in the Spirit of God, as renewing the image of God in our hearts, as raising us from the death of sin to the life of righteousness.

And the same grand blank which was in our faith must likewise have been in our love. We might have loved the Author of our being, the Father of angels and men, as our Creator and Preserver. But we could not have loved him under the nearest and dearest relation—as delivering up his Son for us all. We might have loved the Son of God, as being "the brightness of His Father's glory, the express image of His Person"; but we could not have loved him as "bearing our sins in his own body on the tree." We could not have loved the Holy Ghost, as revealing to us the Father and the Son; as opening the eyes of our understanding; bringing us out of darkness into his marvellous light; renewing the image of God in our soul, and sealing us unto the day of redemption.

And as our faith, both in God the Father and the Son, receives an unspeakable increase from this grand event, as does also our love both of the Father and the Son; so does the love of our neighbour also, our benevolence to all mankind, which cannot but increase in the same proportion with our faith and love of God. For who does not apprehend the force of that inference drawn by the loving Apostle: "Beloved, if God so loved us, we ought also to love one another." If God SO loved us—observe, the stress of the argument lies on this very point—if God SO loved us, how ought we to love one another! But this motive to brotherly love had been totally wanting if Adam had not fallen. Consequently, we could not then have loved one another in so high a degree as we may now.

But there is another grand point, which though little adverted to, deserves our deepest consideration. By that one act of our first parent, not only "sin entered into the world," but pain also, and was alike entailed on his whole posterity. And herein appeared not only the justice but the unspeakable goodness of God. For how much good does he continually bring out of this evil! How much holiness and happiness out of pain!

Indeed, had there been no suffering in the world, a considerable part of religion, yea and in some respects the most excellent part, could have had no place therein; since the very existence of it depends on our suffering. Upon this foundation, even our suffering, it is evident all our passive graces are built; yea the noblest of all Christian graces—*love enduring all things*. Here is the ground for resignation to God, enabling us to say from the heart in every trying hour, "It is the Lord: let him do what seemeth him good." Here is the ground for confidence in God, both with regard to what we feel, and with regard to what we should fear were it not that our soul is calmly stayed on him. It is in the day of trouble that we have occasion to say, "Though he slay me, yet will I trust in him." And this is well pleasing to God, that we should own him in the face of danger; in defiance of sorrow, sickness, pain, or death.

Again: had there been neither natural nor moral evil in the world, what must have become of patience, meekness, gentleness, longsuffering? It is manifest they could have had no being, seeing all these have evil for their object. Will you say, "But all these graces might have been divinely infused into the hearts of men"? Undoubtedly they might. But if they had, there would have been no use or exercise for them. Whereas in the present state of things, we can never long want occasion to exercise them. And the more they are exercised, the more all our graces are strengthened and increased. And in the same proportion as [our graces] increase, must our happiness increase, even in the present world.

Yet again: as God's permission of Adam's fall gave all his posterity a thousand opportunities of suffering, so it gives them opportunities of doing good in numberless instances; of exercising themselves in various good works, which otherwise could have had no being. And what exertions of benevolence, of compassion, of godlike mercy, had then been totally prevented! [And] the more good we do (other circumstances being equal), the happier we shall be. The more kind offices we do to those that groan under the various evils of human life, the more comfort we receive even in the present world, the greater the recompence we have in our own bosom.

To sum up what has been said under this head: as the more holy we are upon earth, the more happy we must be (seeing there is an inseparable connexion between holiness and happiness); therefore the fall of Adam may be of such advantage to the children of men, even in the present life, as they will not thoroughly comprehend till they attain life everlasting.

It is then we shall be enabled fully to comprehend, not only the advantages which accrue at the present time to the sons of men by the fall of their first parent, but the infinitely greater advantages which they may reap from it in eternity. There will be an abundant reward in heaven for *suffering* as well as for *doing* the will of God. Therefore that event which occasioned the entrance of suffering into the world has thereby occasioned to all the children of God an increase of glory to all eternity. For although the sufferings themselves will be at an end, yet the joys occasioned thereby shall never end, but flow at God's right hand for evermore.[26]

Away with our fears,
Our troubles and tears,
The Spirit is come,
The witness of Jesus returned to his home.
Our glorified Head
His Spirit hath shed,
With his people to stay,
And never again will he take him away.

Then let us rejoice
In heart and in voice,
Our leader pursue,
And shout as we travel the wilderness through;
With the Spirit remove
To Zion above,
Triumphant arise,
And walk with our God till we fly to the skies.[27]

WHAT ABOUT THE HEATHEN?

But it may be asked, "If there be no true love of our neighbour, but that which springs from the love of God; and if the love of God flows from no other fountain than faith in the Son of God; does it not follow, that the whole heathen world is excluded from all possibility of salvation—seeing they are cut off from faith; for faith cometh by hearing; and how shall they hear without a preacher?" I answer, St. Paul's words, spoken on another occasion, are applicable to this: "What the law speaketh, it speaketh to them that are under the law." Accordingly, that sentence, "He that believeth not shall be damned," is spoken of them to whom the gospel is preached. Others it does not concern; and we are not required to determine anything touching their final state. How it will please God, the Judge of all, to deal with *them,* we may leave to God himself. But this we know, that he is not the God of the Christians only, but the God of the Heathens also; that he is "rich in mercy to all that call upon him," according to the light they have; and that "in every nation, he that feareth God and worketh righteousness is accepted of him."[28]

> Lord over all, if thou hast made,
>   Hast ransomed every soul of man,
> Why is the grace so long delayed?
>   Why unfulfilled the saving plan?
> The bliss, for Adam's race designed,
> When will it reach to all mankind?
>
> Art thou the God of Jews alone?
>   And not the God of Gentiles too?
> To Gentiles make thy goodness known;
>   Thy judgments to the nations show;
> Awake them by the gospel call;
> Light of the world, illumine all!
>
> Jesus, for this we still attend,
>   Thy kingdom in the isles to prove;
> The law of sin and death to end,
>   We wait for all the power of love,
> The law of perfect liberty,
> The law of life which is in thee.
>
> O might it now from thee proceed,
>   With thee, into the souls of men!
> Throughout the world thy gospel spread;
>   And let thy glorious Spirit reign,
> On all the ransomed race bestowed;
> And let the world be filled with God![29]

IV

The Experience of Grace

THE MEANING OF GRACE

All the blessings which God hath bestowed upon man are of his mere grace, bounty, or favour; his free, undeserved favour; favour altogether undeserved; man having no claim to the least of his mercies. It was free grace that "formed man of the dust of the ground, and breathed into him a living soul," and stamped on that soul the image of God, and "put all things under his feet." The same free grace continues to us at this day, life and breath and all things. For there is nothing we are, or have, or do, which can deserve the least thing at God's hand. "All our works, thou, O God, hast wrought in us." These, therefore, are so many more instances of free mercy. And whatever righteousness may be found in man, this also is the gift of God.

Wherewithal then shall a sinful man atone for any the least of his sins? With his own works? No. Were they ever so many or holy, they are not his own, but God's. But indeed they are all unholy and sinful themselves, so that every one of them needs a fresh atonement. Only corrupt fruit grows on a corrupt tree. And his heart is altogether corrupt and abominable, being "come short of the glory of God," the glorious righteousness at first impressed on his soul after the image of his great Creator. Therefore, having nothing, neither righteousness nor works, to plead, his mouth is utterly stopped before God.

If then sinful men find favour with God, it is "grace upon grace!" If God vouchsafe still to pour blessings upon us, yea the greatest of all blessings, salvation, what can we say to these things but, "Thanks be unto God for his unspeakable gift!" And thus it is. Herein "God commendeth his love toward us, in that, while we were yet sinners, Christ died" to save us. "By grace," then, "are ye saved through faith." Grace is the source, faith the condition of salvation.[1]

By "the grace of God" is sometimes to be understood that free love, that unmerited mercy, by which I a sinner, through the merits of Christ, am now reconciled to God. But in this place it rather means that power of God the Holy Ghost, which "worketh in us both to will and to do of his good pleasure." As soon as ever the grace of God in the former sense, his pardoning love, is manifested to our souls, the grace of God in the latter sense, the power of his Spirit, takes place therein. And now we can perform, through God, what to man was impossible. Now we can order our conversation aright. We can do all things in the light and power of that love, through Christ which strengtheneth us.[2]

You assert [that the Methodists] "speak of grace, that it is as perceptible to the heart as sensible objects are to the senses; whereas the Scriptures speak of grace, that it is conveyed imperceptibly; and that the only way to be satisfied whether we have it or no is to appeal not to our inward feelings but our outward actions."

We do speak of grace (meaning thereby that power of God which worketh in us both to will and to do of his good pleasure), that it is "as perceptible to the heart" (while it comforts, refreshes, purifies, and sheds the love of God abroad therein) "as sensible objects are to the senses." And yet we do not doubt but it may frequently be "conveyed to us imperceptibly." But we know no Scripture which speaks of it as always conveyed and always working in an imperceptible manner. We likewise allow that outward actions are one way of satisfying us that we have grace in our hearts. But we cannot possibly allow that "the only way to be satisfied of this is to appeal to our outward actions and not our inward feelings." On the contrary, we believe that love, joy, peace are inwardly felt, or they have no being; and that men are satisfied they have grace, first by feeling these, and afterward by their outward actions.[3]

> Father of everlasting grace,
> Thy goodness and thy truth we praise,
>   Thy goodness and thy truth we prove;
> Thou hast, in honour of thy Son,
> The gift unspeakable sent down,
>   The Spirit of life, and power, and love.
>
> Send us the Spirit of thy Son,
> To make the depths of Godhead known,
>   To make us share the life divine;
> Send him the sprinkled blood to apply,
> Send him our souls to sanctify,
>   And show and seal us ever thine.[4]

THE PLAN OF SALVATION

The salvation which is here spoken of is not what is frequently understood by that word, the going to heaven, eternal happiness. It is not a blessing which lies on the other side of death; or, as we usually speak, in the other world. The very words of the text itself put this beyond all question: "Ye *are saved*" [Eph. 2:8]. It is not something at a distance: it is a present thing; a blessing which, through the free mercy of God, ye are now in possession of. Nay, the words may be rendered, and that with equal propriety, "Ye *have been* saved": so that the salvation which is here spoken of might be extended to the entire work of God, from the first dawning of grace in the soul, till it is consummated in glory.

If we take this in its utmost extent, it will include all that is wrought in the soul by what is frequently termed natural conscience, but more properly, preventing grace—all the drawings of the Father; the desires after God, which, if we yield to them, increase more and more—all that light wherewith the Son of God "enlighteneth everyone that cometh into the world"; showing every man "to do justly, to love mercy, and to walk humbly with his God"—all the convictions which his Spirit, from time to time, works in every child of man; although, it is true, the generality of men stifle them as soon as possible, and after a while forget, or at least deny, that they ever had them at all.

But we are at present concerned only with that salvation which the Apostle is directly speaking of. And this consists of two general parts, justification and sanctification.

Justification is another word for pardon. It is the forgiveness of all our sins; and, what is necessarily implied therein, our acceptance with God. The price whereby this hath been procured for us (commonly termed the meritorious cause of our justification) is the blood and righteousness of Christ; or, to express it a little more clearly, all that Christ hath done and suffered for us, till he "poured out his soul for the transgressors." The immediate effects of justification are, the peace of God, a "peace that passeth all understanding," and a "rejoicing in the hope of the glory of God" "with joy unspeakable and full of glory."

And at the same time that we are justified, yea, in that very moment, sanctification begins. In that instant we are born again, born from above, born of the Spirit; there is a *real* as well as a *relative* change. We are inwardly renewed by the power of God. We feel "the love of God shed abroad in our hearts by the Holy Ghost which is given unto us"; producing love to all mankind, and more especially to the children of God; expelling the love of the world, the love of pleasure, of ease, of honour, of money, together with pride, anger, self-will, and every other evil temper; in a word, changing the earthly, sensual, devilish mind, into "the mind which was in Christ Jesus."

How naturally do those who experience such a change imagine that all sin is gone; that it is utterly rooted out of their heart, and has no more any place therein! How easily do they draw that inference, "I *feel* no sin; therefore I *have* none: it does not *stir;* therefore it does not *exist:* it has no *motion;* therefore it has no *being!*"

But it is seldom long before they are undeceived, finding sin was only suspended, not destroyed. Temptations return, and sin revives; showing it was but stunned before, not dead. They now feel two principles in themselves, plainly contrary to each other; "the flesh" lusting against "the Spirit"; nature opposing the grace of God. They cannot deny that although they still feel power to believe in Christ, and to love God; and although his Spirit still "witnesses with their spirits that they are children of God"; yet they feel in themselves sometimes pride or self-will, sometimes anger or unbelief. They find one or more of these frequently *stirring* in their heart, though not *conquering;* yea, perhaps, "thrusting sore at them that they may fall"; but the Lord is their help.

From the time of our being born again, the gradual work of our sanctification takes place. We are enabled "by the Spirit" to "mortify the deeds of the body," of our evil nature; and as we are more and more dead to sin, we are more and more alive to God. We go on from grace to grace, while we are careful to "abstain from all appearance of evil," and are "zealous of good works," as we have opportunity, doing good to all men; while we walk in all His ordinances blameless, therein worshipping him in spirit and in truth; while we take up our cross, and deny ourselves every pleasure that does not lead us to God.

It is thus that we wait for entire sanctification; for a full salvation from all our sins—from pride, self-will, anger, unbelief; or, as the Apostle expresses it, "go on unto perfection." But what is perfection? The word has various senses: here it means perfect love. It is love excluding sin; love filling the heart, taking up the whole capacity of the soul. It is love "rejoicing evermore, praying without ceasing, in everything giving thanks."[5]

THE FAITH THAT SAVES

What faith is it then through which we are saved? It may be answered, first, in general, it is a faith in Christ. Christ, and God through Christ, are the proper objects of it. Herein therefore it is sufficiently, absolutely, distinguished from the faith either of ancient or modern Heathens. And from the faith of a devil it is fully distinguished by this: it is not barely a speculative, rational thing, a cold, lifeless assent, a train of ideas in the head; but also a disposition of the heart. For thus saith the Scripture, "With the heart man believeth unto righteousness"; and "If thou shalt confess with thy mouth the Lord Jesus, and shalt believe with thy heart that God hath raised him from the dead, thou shalt be saved."

And herein does it differ from that faith which the Apostles themselves had while our Lord was on earth, that it acknowledges the necessity and merit of his death, and the power of his resurrection. It acknowledges his death as the only sufficient means of redeeming man from death eternal, and his resurrection as the restoration of us all to life and immortality; inasmuch as he "was delivered for our sins, and rose again for our justification." Christian faith is, then, not only an assent to the whole gospel of Christ, but also a full reliance on the blood of Christ; a trust in the merits of his life, death, and resurrection; a recumbency upon him as our atonement and our life, as *given for us,* and *living in us.*[6]

Faith, in general, is a divine, supernatural ἔλεγχος, *evidence* or *conviction,* "of things not seen," not discoverable by our bodily senses, as being either past, future, or spiritual. Justifying faith implies, not only a divine evidence or conviction that "God was in Christ, reconciling the world unto himself," but a sure trust and confidence that Christ died for *my* sins, that he loved *me,* and gave himself for *me.* And at what time soever a sinner thus believes, be it in early childhood, in the strength of his years, or when he is old and hoary-haired, God justifieth that ungodly one.

God, for the sake of his Son, pardoneth and absolveth him who had in him, till then, no good thing. Repentance, indeed, God had given him before; but that repentance was neither more nor less than a deep sense of the want [lack] of all good, and the presence of all evil. And whatever good he hath or doeth from that hour when he first believes in God through Christ, faith does not *find,* but *bring.* This is the fruit of faith. First the tree is good, and then the fruit also.

I cannot describe the nature of this faith better than in the words of our own Church: "The only instrument of salvation" (whereof justification is one branch) "is faith; that is, a sure trust and confidence that God both hath and will forgive our sins, that he hath accepted us again into his favour, for the merits of Christ's death and passion. . . . Therefore, have a sure and constant faith, not only that the death of Christ is available for all the world, but that he hath made a full and sufficient sacrifice for *thee,* a perfect cleansing of *thy* sins, so that thou mayest say with the Apostle, he loved *thee,* and gave himself for *thee.*

For this is to make Christ *thine own,* and to apply his merits unto *thyself.*"[7]

[You charge that the Methodists] "represent faith as a supernatural principle, altogether precluding the judgment and understanding, and discerned by some internal signs; not as a firm persuasion founded on the evidence of reason, and discernible only by a conformity of life and manners to sucha persuasion."

We do not represent faith "as altogether precluding," or at all "precluding, the judgment and understanding"; rather as enlightening and strengthening the understanding, as clearing and improving the judgment. But we do represent it as the gift of God—yea, and a "supernatural gift": yet it does not preclude "the evidence of reason"; though neither is this its whole foundation. "A conformity of life and manners" to that persuasion "Christ loved me and gave himself for me" is doubtless one mark by which it is discerned, but not the only one. It is likewise discerned by internal signs: both by the witness of the Spirit, and the fruit of the Spirit—namely,"love, peace, joy, meekness, gentleness," by all "the mind which was in Christ Jesus."[8]

> Author of faith, eternal Word,
>   Whose Spirit breathes the active flame;
> Faith, like its Finisher and Lord,
>   To-day as yesterday the same;
>
> To thee our humble hearts aspire,
>   And ask the gift unspeakable;
> Increase in us the kindled fire,
>   In us the work of faith fulfil.
>
> By faith we know thee strong to save;
>   (Save us, a present Saviour thou!)
> Whate'er we hope, by faith we have,
>   Future and past subsisting now.
>
> The things unknown to feeble sense,
>   Unseen by reason's glimmering ray,
> With strong, commanding evidence,
>   Their heavenly origin display.
>
> Faith lends its realising light,
>   The clouds disperse, the shadows fly;
> The Invisible appears in sight,
>   And God is seen by mortal eye.[9]

ONLY BELIEVE!

It does not become poor, guilty, sinful worms, who receive whatsoever blessings they enjoy (from the least drop of water that cools our tongue, to the immense riches of glory in eternity) of grace, of mere favour, and not of debt, to ask of God the reasons of his conduct. It is not meet for us to call Him in question, "who giveth account to none of his ways"; to demand, Why didst thou make faith the condition, the only condition of justification? Wherefore didst thou decree, *He that believeth,* and he only, *shall be saved?*

One reason, however, we may humbly conceive, of God's fixing this condition of justification, "If thou believest in the Lord Jesus Christ, thou shalt be saved," was to *hide Pride from man.* pride had already destroyed the very angels of God, had cast down "a third part of the stars of heaven." It was likewise in great measure owing to this, when the tempter said, "Ye shall be as gods," that Adam fell from his own steadfastness, and brought sin and death into the world. It was therefore an instance of wisdom worthy of God, to appoint such a condition of reconciliation for him and all his posterity, as might effectually humble, might abase them to the dust. And such is faith. It is peculiarly fitted for this end. For he that cometh unto God by this faith must fix his eye singly on his own wickedness, on his guilt and helplessness, without having the least regard to any supposed good in himself, to any virtue or righteousness whatsoever. He must come as a *mere sinner,* inwardly and outwardly, self-destroyed and self-condemned, bringing nothing to God but ungodliness only, pleading nothing of his own but sin and misery. Thus it is, and thus alone, when his *mouth is stopped,* and he stands utterly *guilty before* God, that he can *look unto Jesus* as the whole and sole propitiation for his sins. Thus only can he be *found in him,* and receive the "righteousness which is of God by faith."[10]

Whosoever therefore thou art who desirest to be forgiven and reconciled to the favour of God, do not say in thy heart, "I must *first do this;* I must *first* conquer every sin; break off every evil word and work, and do good to all men"; or, "I must *first* go to church, receive the Lord's Supper, hear more sermons, and say more prayers." Alas, my brother! Thou art clean gone out of the way. Thou art still "ignorant of the righteousness of God," and art "seeking to establish thy own righteousness," as the ground of thy reconciliation. Knowest thou not that thou canst do nothing but sin, till thou art reconciled to God?

Neither say in thy heart, "I cannot be accepted yet because I am not *good enough.*" Who is *good enough*—who ever was—to merit acceptance at God's hands? Was ever any child of Adam *good enough* for this? Or will any till the consummation of all things? And as for thee, thou art not good at all: there dwelleth in thee no good thing. And thou never wilt be, till thou believe in Jesus. Rather thou wilt find thyself worse and worse. But is there any need of being worse, in order to be accepted? Art thou not *bad enough* already?

Do not say, "But I am not *contrite enough:* I am not *sensible enough* of my sins." I know it. I would to God thou wert more *sensible* of them, more *contrite* a thousandfold than thou art. But do not stay for this. It may be God will make thee so, not before thou believest, but by believing. It may be thou wilt not weep much till thou lovest much because thou hast had much forgiven. In the meantime, look unto Jesus. Behold, how he loveth thee! What could he haved one more for thee which he hath not done?

> O Lamb of God, was ever pain,
> Was ever love like thine?

Look steadily upon him, till he looks on thee and breaks thy hard heart.

Nor yet do thou say, "I must *do* something *before* I come to Christ." I grant, supposing thy Lord should delay his coming, it were meet and right to wait for his appearing, in doing so far as thou hast power whatsoever he hath commanded thee. But there is no necessity for making such a supposition. How knowest thou that he will delay? Perhaps he will appear, as the day-spring from on high, before the morning light. O do not set him a time! Expect him every hour. Now he is nigh! Even at the door!

And to what end wouldest thou wait for *more sincerity before* thy sins are blotted out? To make thee more worthy of the grace of God? Alas, thou art still "establishing thy own righteousness." He will have mercy, not because thou art worthy of it, but because his compassions fail not; not because thou art righteous but because Jesus Christ hath atoned for thy sins.[11]

> Entered the holy place above,
>   Covered with meritorious scars,
> The tokens of his dying love
>   Our great High-priest in glory bears;
> He pleads his passion on the tree,
> He shows himself to God for me.
>
> Before the throne my Saviour stands,
>   My Friend and Advocate appears;

My name is graven on his hands,
And him the Father always hears;
While low at Jesu's cross I bow,
He hears the blood of sprinkling now.

This instant now I may receive
The answer of his powerful prayer:
This instant now by him I live,
His prevalence with God declare;
And soon my spirit, in his hands,
Shall stand where my Forerunner stands.[12]

GOD'S PART AND OURS

With regard to [your assertion], "If man has any free-will, then God cannot have the whole glory of his salvation," is your meaning this: "If man has any power to 'work out his own salvation,' then God cannot have the whole glory"? If it be, I must ask again, What do you mean by God's "having the whole glory"? Do you mean "His doing the whole work, without any concurrence on man's part"? If so, your assertion is, "If man do at all 'work together with God' in 'working out his own salvation,' then God does not do the whole work, without man's 'working together with him.' " Most true, most sure. But cannot you see how God nevertheless may have all the glory? Why, the very power to "work together with him" was from God. Therefore to him is all the glory. Has not even experience taught you this? Have you not often felt, in a particular temptation, power either to resist or yield to the grace of God? And when you have yielded to "work together with him," did you not find it very possible, notwithstanding, to give him all the glory? So that both experience and Scripture are against you here, and make it clear to every impartial inquirer that though man has freedom to work or not "work together with God," yet may God have the whole glory of his salvation.

If then you say, "We ascribe to God alone the whole glory of our salvation"; I answer, So do we too. If you add, "Nay, but we affirm that God alone does the whole work, without man's working at all"; in one sense we allow this also. We allow it is the work of God alone to justify, to sanctify, and to glorify; which three comprehend the whole of salvation. Yet we cannot allow that man can only resist, and not in any wise "work together with God"; or that God is so the whole worker of our salvation, as to exclude man's working at all. This I dare not say, for I cannot prove it by Scripture; nay, it is flatly contrary thereto, for the Scripture is express, that (having received power from

God) we are to "work out our own salvation"; and that (after the work of God is begun in our souls) we are "workers together with him." [13]

Many of the greatest maintainers of election [predestination] do not allow that even natural free-will in man is repugnant to God's glory. These accordingly assert that every man living has a measure of natural free-will. So the [Westminster] Assembly of Divines (and therein the body of Calvinists both in England and Scotland): "God hath endued the will of man with that natural liberty that is neither forced, nor by an absolute necessity of nature determined to do good or evil." And this they assert of man in his fallen state even before he receives the grace of God.

But I do not carry free-will so far. (I mean, not in moral things.) Natural free-will, in the present state of mankind, I do not understand. I only assert that there is a measure of free-will supernaturally restored to every man, together with that supernatural light which "enlightens every man that cometh into the world."[14]

Allowing [then] that all the souls of men are dead in sin by *nature,* this excuses none, seeing there is no man that is in a state of mere nature; there is no man, unless he has quenched the Spirit, that is wholly void of the grace of God. No man living is entirely destitute of what is vulgarly called *natural conscience.* But this is not natural; it is more properly termed *preventing grace.* Every man has a greater or lesser measure of this, which waiteth not for the call of man. Everyone has, sooner or later, good desires; although the generality of men stifle them before they can strike deep root, or produce any considerable fruit. Everyone has some measure of that light, some faint, glimmering ray, which sooner or later, more or less, enlightens every man that cometh into the world.[15]

> Father, I dare believe
> Thee merciful and true:
> Thou wilt my guilty soul forgive,
> My fallen soul renew.
>
> Come then for Jesu's sake,
> And bid my heart be clean;
> An end of all my troubles make,
> An end of all my sin.
>
> I will, through grace, I will,
> I do, return to thee;
> Take, empty it, O Lord, and fill
> My heart with purity.

For power I feebly pray:
Thy kingdom now restore,
To-day, while it is called to-day,
And I shall sin no more.[16]

TWO LEVELS OF FAITH

What is the faith which is properly saving, which brings eternal salvation to all those that keep it to the end? It is such a divine conviction of God and the things of God, as even in its infant state enables everyone that possesses it to "fear God and work righteousness." And whosoever in every nation believes thus far, the Apostle declares, is "accepted of him" (Acts 10:35). He actually is, at that very moment, in a state of acceptance. But he is at present only a *servant* of God, not properly a *son*. Meantime, let it be well observed that "the wrath of God" no longer "abideth on him."

Indeed, nearly fifty years ago, when the Preachers commonly called Methodists began to preach that grand scriptural doctrine, salvation by faith, they were not sufficiently apprised of the difference between a servant and a child of God. They did not clearly understand that even one "who feareth God and worketh righteousness, is accepted of him." In consequence of this, they were apt to make sad the hearts of those whom God had not made sad. For they frequently asked those who feared God, "Do you know that your sins are forgiven?" And upon their answering "No," immediately replied, "Then you are a child of the devil." No; that does not follow. It might have been said (and it is all that can be said with propriety), "Hitherto you are only a *servant,* you are not a *child* of God. You have already great reason to praise God that he has called you to his honourable service. Fear not. Continue crying unto him, 'and you shall see greater things than these."

And indeed, unless the servants of God halt by the way, they will receive the adoption of sons. They will receive the *faith* of the children of God, by his *revealing* his only begotten Son in their hearts. Thus the faith of a child is, properly and directly, a divine conviction whereby every child of God is enabled to testify, "The life that I now live, I live by faith in the Son of God, who loved me and gave himself for me." And whosoever hath this, the Spirit of God witnesseth with his spirit that he is a child of God. So the Apostle writes to the Galatians: "Ye are the sons of God by faith. And because ye are sons, God hath sent forth the Spirit of his Son into your hearts, crying, Abba, Father"; that is, giving you a childlike confidence in him, together with a kind affection towards him. This then it is that (if St. Paul was taught of God, and wrote as he was moved by the Holy Ghost) properly constitutes the difference between a servant of God and a child of God. "He that believeth," as a child of God, "hath the witness in himself." This the servant hath not. Yet let no man discourage him; rather, lovingly exhort him to expect it every moment.[17]

> Thou great mysterious God unknown,
> Whose love hath gently led me on,
>   Even from my infant days,
> Mine inmost soul expose to view,
> And tell me, if I ever knew
>   Thy justifying grace.
>
> Whate'er obstructs thy pardoning love,
> Or sin, or righteousness, remove,
>   Thy glory to display;
> Mine heart of unbelief convince,
> And now absolve me from my sins,
>   And take them all away.
>
> Father, in me reveal thy Son,
> And to my inmost soul make known
>   How merciful thou art:
> The secret of thy love reveal,
> And by thine hallowing Spirit dwell
>   For ever in my heart![18]

THE ASSURANCE OF SALVATION

I believe every Christian who has not yet received it should pray for the witness of God's Spirit with his spirit that he is a child of God. In being a child of God, the pardon of his sins is included; therefore I believe the Spirit of God will witness this also. That this witness is from God, the very terms imply; and this witness I believe is necessary for my salvation. How far invincible ignorance may excuse others I know not. But this, you say, is delusive and dangerous, because it encourages and abets idle visions and dreams. It encourages, true—accidentally, but not essentially. And that it does this accidentally, or that weak minds may pervert it to an idle use, is no objection against it; for so they may pervert every truth in the oracles of God.[19]

The gospel promises to you and me, and our children, and all that are afar off, even as many of those whom the Lord our God shall call as are not disobedient unto the heavenly vision, "the witness of God's Spirit with their spirit that they are the children of God"; that they are now at this hour all accepted in the Beloved; but it witnesses not that they shall be. It is an assurance of present salvation only; therefore not necessarily perpetual, neither irreversible.[20]

I believe a few, but very few, Christians have an assurance from God of everlasting salvation; and that this is the thing which the Apostle terms the plerophory or full assurance of hope.

I believe more have such an assurance of being now in the favour of God as excludes all doubt and fear. And this, if I do not mistake, the Apostle means by the plerophory or full assurance of faith.

I believe a consciousness of being in the favour of God (which I do not term plerophory or full assurance, since it is frequently weakened, nay perhaps interrupted, by returns of doubt or fear) is the common privilege of Christians fearing God and working righteousness.

Yet I do not affirm there are no exceptions to this general rule. Possibly some may be in the favour of God, and yet go mourning all the day long. But I believe this is usually owing either to disorder of body, or ignorance of the gospel promises.

Therefore I have not for many years thought a consciousness of acceptance to be essential to justifying faith.[21]

Many of our brethren and sisters in London, during that great outpouring of the Spirit,[22] spoke of several *new* blessings which they had attained. But after all, they could find nothing higher than *pure love,* on which the full assurance of hope generally attends. This the inspired writings always represent as the highest point; only there are innumerable *degrees* of it. The plerophory (or full assurance) of faith is such a clear conviction that I *am now* in the favour of God as excludes all doubt and fear concerning it. The full assurance of hope is such clear confidence that I *shall enjoy* the glory of God as excludes all doubt and fear concerning this. And this confidence is totally different from an opinion that "no saint shall fall from grace." It has no relation to it. Bold, presumptuous men often substitute this base counter in the room of that precious confidence. But it is observable the *opinion* remains just as strong while men are sinning and serving the devil as while they are serving God. Holiness or unholiness does not affect it in the least degree. Whereas, the giving way to anything unholy, either in life or heart, clouds the full assurance of hope; which cannot subsist any longer than the heart cleaves steadfastly to God.[23]

On the subject of your last I can but observe, first, with regard to the assurance of faith, I apprehend that the whole Christian Church in the first centuries enjoyed it. For though we have few points of doctrine explicitly taught in the small remains of the ante-Nicene Fathers, yet I think none that carefully reads Clemens Romanus, Ignatius, Polycarp, Origen, or any other of them, can doubt whether either the writer himself possessed it or all whom he mentions as real Christians. And I really conceive, both from the *Harmonia Confessionum* and whatever else I have occasionally read, that all the Reformed Churches in Europe did once believe, "Every true Christian has the divine evidence of his being in favour with God."[24]

> Come, Holy Ghost, all quickening fire!
> Come, and my hallowed heart inspire,
>   Sprinkled with the atoning blood;
> Now to my soul thyself reveal,
> Thy mighty working let me feel,
>   And know that I am born of God.
>
> Thy witness with my spirit bear,
> That God, my God, inhabits there;
>   Thou, with the Father, and the Son,
> Eternal light's co-eval beam;
> Be Christ in me, and I in him,
>   Till perfect we are made in one.
>
> My will be swallowed up in thee;
> Light in thy light still may I see,
>   Beholding thee with open face;
> Called the full power of faith to prove,
> Let all my hallowed heart be love,
>   And all my spotless life be praise.[25]

VARYING DEGREES OF FAITH

I blame no one for not believing he is in the favour of God till he is in a manner constrained to believe it. But laying all circumstances together, I can make no doubt of your having a measure of faith. Many years ago, when one was describing the glorious privilege of a believer, I cried out, "If this be so, I have no faith." But he replied *"Habes fidem, sed exiguam:* 'You have faith, but it is weak.'"* The very same thing I say to you, my dear friend. You have faith, but it is only as a grain of mustard seed. Hold fast what you have, and ask for what you want [lack]. There is an irreconcilable variability in the operations of the Holy Spirit on the souls of men, more especially as to the manner of justification. Many find him rushing upon them like a torrent, while they experience

> The o'erwhelming power of saving grace.

This has been the experience of many; perhaps of more in this late visitation than in any other age since the time of the Apostles. But in others he works in a very different way:

> He deigns his influence to infuse,
> Sweet, refreshing, as the silent dews.

It has pleased him to work in the latter way in you from the beginning; and it is not improbable he will continue (as he has begun) to work in a gentle and almost insensible manner. Let him take his own way. He is wiser than you; he will do all things well. Do not reason against him, but let the prayer of your heart be,

> Mould as thou wilt thy passive clay!

I commit you and your dear sisters to his tender care; and am, my dear friend, Most affectionately yours.[26]

By weak faith I understand (1) that which is mixed with fear, particularly of not enduring to the end; (2) that which is mixed with doubt, whether we have not deceived ourselves, and whether our sins be indeed forgiven; (3) that which has not yet purified the heart fully, not from all its idols. And thus weak I find the faith of almost all believers to be, within a short time after they have first peace with God.

Yet that weak faith is faith appears (1) from St. Paul, "Him that is weak in faith, receive"; (2) from St. John, speaking of believers who were little children, as well as of young men and fathers; (3) from our Lord's own words, "Why are ye fearful, O ye of little faith?—O thou of little faith wherefore didst thou doubt?—I have prayed for thee (Peter), that thy faith fail thee not." Therefore he then had faith. Yet so weak was that faith that not only doubt and fear, but gross sin in the same night prevailed over him.

Nevertheless he was "clean, by the word" Christ had "spoken to him"; that is, justified, though it is plain he had not a clean heart.

Therefore, there are degrees in faith; and weak faith may yet be true faith.[27]

You have great reason to praise God for what he has done, and to expect what he has promised. That spark of faith which you have received is of more value than all the world. O cherish it with all your might! Continually stir up the gift that is in you, not only by continuing to hear his word at all opportunities, but by reading, by meditation, and above all by private prayer. Though sometimes it should be a grievous cross, yet bear your cross, and it will bear *you*. Your labour shall not be in vain. Is not our Lord just now ready to bless you, to increase your faith, and love, and patience, and gentleness? You have no need to be any more overcome of evil. Through him you shall overcome evil with good. Surely his grace is sufficient for you: sufficient to subdue all things to himself.[28]

It is a natural defect of your bodily weakness and of the turn of your mind that you are constantly inclined to write bitter things against yourself. Hence you are easily persuaded to believe him who tells you that you "are void of every degree of saving faith." No, that is not the case. For salvation is only by faith, and you have received a degree of salvation. You are saved from many outward sins—from the corruption that overspreads the land as a flood. You are saved in a degree from inward sin, from impenitence, for you know and feel yourself a sinner. You are saved in a degree from pride, for you begin to know yourself poor and helpless. You are saved from seeking happiness in the world: this is not a small thing. O praise God for all you have, and trust him for all you want [lack]! Peace be with your spirit![29]

It is lost time to consider whether you write well or ill; you speak from the heart, and that is enough. Unbelief is either total, the absence of faith, or partial, the want of more faith. In the latter sense every believer may complain of unbelief, unless when he is filled with faith and the Holy Ghost. Then it is all midday. Yet even then we may pray, "Lord, increase our faith."[30]

VARIETY IN GOD'S WORKING

It is doubtless the peculiar prerogative of God to reserve the "times and seasons in his own power." And we cannot give any reason why, of two persons equally athirst for salvation, one is presently taken into the favour of God and the other left to mourn for months or years. One, as soon as he calls upon God, is answered, and filled with joy and peace in believing; another seeks after him, and it seems with the same degree of sincerity and earnestness, and yet cannot find him, or any consciousness of his favour, for weeks or months or years. We know well, this cannot possibly be owing to any absolute decree, consigning one, before he was born, to everlasting glory, and the other to everlasting fire; but we do not know what is the reason for it. It is enough that God knoweth.

There is likewise great variety in the manner and time of God's bestowing his sanctifying grace, whereby he enables his children to give him their whole heart, which we can in no wise account for. We know not why he bestows this on some even before they ask for it (some unquestionable instances of which we have seen); on some after they had sought it but a few days: and yet permits other believers to wait for it, perhaps twenty, thirty, or forty years; nay, and others till a few hours, or even minutes, before their spirits return to him. For the various circumstances also which attend the fulfilling of that great promise, "I will circumcise thy heart, to love the Lord thy God with all thy heart and with all thy soul," God undoubtedly has reasons; but those reasons are generally hid from the children of men. Once more: some of those who are enabled to love God with all their heart and with all their soul retain the same blessing without any interruption, till they are carried to Abraham's bosom; others do not retain it, although they are not conscious of having grieved the Spirit of God. This also we do not understand: we do not herein "know the mind of the Spirit."[31]

Fainting soul, be bold, be strong,
    Wait the leisure of thy Lord;
Though it seem to tarry long,
    True and faithful is his word;
On his word my soul I cast,
    (He cannot himself deny)
Surely it shall speak at last;
    It shall speak, and shall not lie.

Every one that seeks shall find,
    Every one that asks shall have,
Christ, the Saviour of mankind,
    Willing, able, all to save;
I shall his salvation see,
    I in faith on Jesus call,
I from sin shall be set free,
    Perfectly set free from all.

Lord, my time is in thine hand,
    Weak and helpless as I am,

Surely thou canst make me stand;
I believe in Jesu's name:
Saviour in temptation thou;
Thou hast saved me heretofore,
Thou from sin dost save me now,
Thou shalt save me evermore.[32]

Notes to Part One

I. THE MYSTERY AND MAJESTY OF GOD

1 See next note for JW's view of the authenticity of this text.
2 *W*.VI.199f. (S. 55: "On the Trinity," 1775). JW goes on to discuss the question: "Is that text genuine? Was it originally written by the Apostle, or inserted in later ages?" He comes to the conclusion (on the basis of Bengel's arguments, which he summarizes) that it is genuine. See also his *Notes on the New Testament, ad loc.*, for a fuller discussion. More recent scholarship has led to the opposite view, and the text is omitted from modern versions of the New Testament, from the RV onwards. But the doctrine of the Trinity is not, of course, dependent on this or any other single text, as Wesley himself also was aware; and his own exposition of the doctrine is in no way affected by the fact that we can no longer use his text as our point of departure.
3 *Hymns on the Trinity* (1767), No. 4. Cf. Frank Baker, *Representative Verse of Charles Wesley*, (London, 1962), p. 240.
4 *W*.VI.201ff. (S.55: "On the Trinity").
5 *L*.VIII.83 = *W*.XII.336: to Lady Maxwell [8 Aug. 1788].
6 *HPCM* 259; *MHB* 39.
7 *W*.VII.239ff. (S.111: "On the Omnipresence of God"). The Verse quoted by JW ("Hail FATHER . . .") is from a hymn by his nephew, Samuel Wesley, Jr.
8 *HPCM*(S) 661; *MHB* 440.
9 *W*.VI.316ff.,320ff. (S.67: "On Divine Providence").
10 *HPCM* 233.
11 *W*.VI.506f. (S.85: "On Working out Our Own Salvation").
12 *HPCM* 493, 441.
13 *W*.VI.344ff. (S.69: "The Imperfection of Human Knowledge").
14 *HPCM* 240; *MHB* 42; Ernst Lange (1650–1727); tr. by JW.

II. THE GREATNESS AND LITTLENESS OF MAN

1 *W*.VII.168f. (S.103: "What is Man?").
2 JW adds here the following footnote: "What security is there against all this,

127

upon the infidel hypothesis? But upon the Christian, there is abundant
security. For the Scripture prophecies are not yet fulfilled."
3 *W*.XI.8ff. ("Serious Thoughts occasioned by the Late Earthquake at
Lisbon," 1755).
4 *W*.VII.266f. (S.114: "The Unity of the Divine Being").
5 *W*.VI.244,252 (S.60: "The General Deliverance").
6 *W*.VII.230 (S.109: "What is Man?").
7 *W*.VI.54f.,58 (S.44) = *SS*.II.210f., 215 (S.38: "original Sin").
8 *L*.VI.61f. = *W*.XII.462: to Samuel Sparrow [28 Dec. 1773].
9 *L*.III.107 = *W*.XII.198: to Dr. Robertson [24 Sept. 1753]; cf. *W*.IX.335
("The Doctrine of Original Sin"). JW, like most Christian thinkers till quite
recently, took the story of the Fall of Adam as historical, whereas nowadays
it is usually regarded as mythological. But the historicity of the story was
never its main point; for "Adam" means "Man"—all mankind and every
man—and the story of his Fall has always been understood essentially as a
revelation of the predicament in which Man is, rather than as an explanation
of how he got into it. So JW certainly understood it, for he saw that as an
explanation it raises more problems than it solves. And note how he
characteristically appeals to experience for confirmation of the doctrine of
the Fall—or as we might prefer to say, "Man's fallenness."
10 *W*.VII.89f. (S.95: "On the Education of Children").
11 *W*.VII.338ff.,341 (S.123: "The Deceitfulness of Man's Heart").
12 *W*.IX.221ff. ("The Doctrine of Original Sin").
13 *Op. cit.*, 235ff.
14 *Op. cit.*, 238.
15 *Op. cit.*, 293f., 311f., 313f.

III. THE MYSTERY OF GODLINESS

1 *W*.IX.194 (Preface to "The Doctrine of Original Sin").
2 *W*.VII.336 (S.123: "The Deceitfulness of Man's Heart").
3 *HPCM* 84; *MHB* 347; *WHB* 18.
4 *W*.V.77,79ff. (S.7) = SS.I.148-55 (S.7: "The Way to the Kingdom").
5 *W*.V.85 = *SS*.I.159f.
6 *HPCM* 134; *HHB* 349; *WHB* 19.
7 *W*.VI.253 (S.61: "The Mystery of Iniquity").
8 *W*.VI.273 (S.62: "The End of Christ's Coming").
9 *HPCM*(S) 684; *MHB* 134; *WHB* 75.
10 *W*.VI.273f.
11 *W*.VI.507 (S.85: "On Working out Our Own Salvation").
12 *W*.VI.274 (S.62).
13 *HPCM*(S) 808; *MHB* 66; *WHB* 89.
14 *W*.VI.274.
15 *HPCM*(S) 557; *MHB* 222.
16 *W*.VI.274.
17 A son of the Countess of Huntingdon and a "Freethinker" who did not share
his mother's devotion to the Evangelical Revival.
18 See *L*.III.345-51 = *W*.IX.480-94.

¹⁹ JW probably has in mind here *A Short and Easy Method with the Deists* by Charles Leslie (1650–1722).
²⁰ *L.*VI.297ff. = *W.*XIII.33f.: to Mary Bishop [7 Feb. 1778].
²¹ *HPCM* 201; *MHB* 371; *WHB* 83; *AMH* 229.
²² *W.*VI.274ff.
²³ *HPCM* 269; *MHB* 483.
²⁴ *W.*VII.351ff. (S.125: "On Living without God").
²⁵ *HPCM* 85; *MHB* 363; *WHB* 102; *AMH* 183.
²⁶ *W.*VI.232-38 (S.59: "God's Love to Fallen Man").
²⁷ *HPCM*(S) 760; *MHB* 278; *WHB* 98.
²⁸ *W.*VII.47f.(S.91: "On Charity").
²⁹ *HPCM* 444, 448.

IV. THE EXPERIENCE OF GRACE

¹ *W.*V.7f(S.1) = *SS.*I.37f.(S.1: "Salvation by Faith").
² *W.*V.141 (S.12) = *SS.*I.232 (S.11: "The Witness of Our Own Spirit").
³ *L.*IV.331f. = *W.*IX.103f.: to John Downes, Rector of St. Michael's [17 Nov. 1759].
⁴ *HPCM* 377; *MHB* 730.
⁵ *W.*VII.44ff.(S.43) = *SS.*II.444ff.(S.50: "The Scripture Way of Salvation").
⁶ *W.*V.9 (S.1) = *SS.*I.39ff.(S.1: "Salvation by Faith").
⁷ *W.*V.60f.(S.5) = SS.I.125f.(S.5: "Justification by Faith").
⁸ *L.*IV.331 = *W.*IX.103: to John Downes, Rector of St. Michael's *ut sup.*
⁹ *HPCM* 95; *MHB* 362; *WHB* 26.
¹⁰ *W.*V.63f.(S.5) = *SS.*I.127ff.(S.5: "Justification by Faith").
¹¹ *W.*V.74ff.(S.6) = *SS.*I.143ff.(S.6: "The Righteousness of Faith").
¹² *HPCM*(S) 726; *MHB* 232; *WHB* 94.
¹³ *W.*X.230f. ("Predestination Calmly Considered").
¹⁴ *W.*X.229f.(*op.cit.*).
¹⁵ *W.*VI.512 (S.85: "On Working out Our Own Salvation").
¹⁶ *HPCM* 410; *MHB* 564.
¹⁷ *W.*VII.198ff.(S.106: "On Faith").
¹⁸ *HPCM* 97; *MHB* 376; *WHB* 48.
¹⁹ *L.*I.274f. = *W.*XII.35: to his brother Samuel [30 Nov. 1738].
²⁰ *L.*I.308 = *W.*XII.35f.: to his brother Samuel [10 May 1739].
²¹ *L.*V.358 = *W.*XIV.360f.: to Dr. Rutherforth [28 Mar. 1768].
²² In 1762; see *W.*XI.406 ("A Plain Account of Christian Perfection").
²³ *L.*VII.57f. = *W.*XIII.64: to Hester Ann Roe [10 Apr. 1781].
²⁴ *L.*III.137f. = *W.*XII.452: to Richard Thompson [25 July 1755].
²⁵ *HPCM* 351; cf. *MHB* 553.
²⁶ *L.*VII.298 = *W.*XIII.72f.: to Mary Cooke [30 Oct. 1785].
²⁷ *W.*I.276 = *JWJ.*II.355 [22 June 1740].
²⁸ *L.*V.12: to Mrs. Woodhouse [17 May 1766].
²⁹ *L.*VI.315: to Alexander Knox [11 July 1778].
³⁰ *L.*V.326: to Miss March [1 July 1772].
³¹ *W.*VI.348f.(S.69: "The Imperfection of Human Knowledge").
³² *HPCM* 142; *MHB* 479.

PART TWO

Guidance to Glory

* * *

I

Waiting on God

THE MEANS OF GRACE

"By grace are ye saved." Ye are saved from your sins, from the guilt and power thereof, ye are restored to the favour and image of God, not for any works, merits, or deservings of yours, but by the free grace, the mere mercy of God, through the merits of his well-beloved Son. Ye are thus saved, not by any power, wisdom, or strength, which is in you or in any other creature; but merely through the power or grace of the Holy Ghost, which worketh all in all.

But the question remains: "We know this salvation is the gift and work of God; but how (may one say who is convinced that he hath it not) may I attain thereto?" If you say, "Believe, and thou shalt be saved!" he answers, "True; but how shall I believe?" You reply, "Wait upon God." "Well; but how am I to wait? In the means of grace, or out of them? Am I to wait for the grace of God which bringeth salvation, by using these means or by laying them aside?"

It cannot possibly be conceived that the word of God should give no direction in so important a point, or that the Son of God, who came down from heaven for us men and for our salvation, should have left us undetermined with regard to a question wherein our salvation is so nearly concerned. And in fact, he hath not left us so undetermined; he hath shown us the way wherein we should go. We have only to consult the oracles of God, to inquire what is written there.

According to this, all who desire the grace of God are to wait for it in the means which he hath ordained; in using, not in laying them aside.[1]

But what are the steps which the Scriptures direct us to take, in the working out of our own salvation? The Prophet Isaiah gives us a general answer, touching the first steps which we are to take; "Cease to do evil: learn to do well." If ever you desire that God should work in you that faith whereof cometh both present and eternal salvation, by the grace already given fly from all sin as from the face of a serpent; carefully avoid every evil word and work; yea, abstain from all appearance of evil. And "learn to do well." Be zealous of good works, of works of piety as well as of works of mercy; family prayer, and crying to God in secret. Fast in secret, and "your Father which seeth in secret, he will reward you openly." "Search the Scriptures": hear them in public, read them in private, and meditate therein. At every opportunity be a partaker of the Lord's Supper. "Do this in remembrance" of him; and he will meet you at his own table. Let your conversation be with the children of God; and see that it be in grace, seasoned with salt." As ye have time, do good unto all men; to their souls and to their bodies. And herein "be ye steadfast, unmovable, always abounding in the work of the Lord." It then only remains that ye deny yourselves and take up your cross daily. Deny yourselves every pleasure which does not prepare you for taking pleasure in God, and willingly embrace every means of drawing near to God, though it be a cross, though it be grievous to flesh and blood. Thus when you have redemption in the blood of Christ, you will "go onto perfection"; till, "walking in the light as he is in the light," you are enabled to testify that "he is faithful and just," not only to "forgive" your "sins," but to "cleanse" you "from all unrighteousness."[2]

THE INITIATORY SACRAMENT

[Baptism] is the initiatory sacrament, which enters us into covenant with God. It was instituted by Christ, who alone has power to institute a proper sacrament, a sign, seal, pledge and means of grace, perpetually obligatory on all Christians.

By baptism we enter into that everlasting covenant which he hath commanded for ever (Ps. 111:9), that new covenant which he promised to make with the spiritual Israel [Ezek. 36:25f.; Jer. 31:31ff.]; in a word, to be their God, as he promised to Abraham in the evangelical covenant which he made with him and all his spiritual offspring (Gen. 17:7f.). And as circumcision was then the way of entering into this covenant, so baptism is now.

By baptism we are admitted into the Church, and consequently made members of Christ its Head. From which spiritual, vital union with him, proceeds the influence of his grace on those that are baptised.

By baptism, we who were "by nature children of wrath" are made the children of God. Being "grafted into the body of Christ's Church, we are made the children of God by adoption and grace." Herein a principle of grace is infused, which will not be wholly taken away, unless we quench the Holy Spirit of God by long continued wickedness.

In consequence of our being made children of God, we are heirs of the kingdom of heaven. Herein we receive a title to, and an earnest of, "a kingdom which cannot be moved." Baptism doth now save us, if we live answerable thereto; if we repent, believe, and obey the gospel. Supposing this, as it admits us into the Church here, so into glory hereafter.[3]

Baptism is the outward sign of this inward grace, which is supposed by our Church to be given with and through that sign to all infants, and to those of riper years if they repent and believe the gospel. But how extremely idle are the common disputes on this head! I tell a sinner, "You must be born again." "No," say you; "he was born again in baptism. Therefore he cannot be born again now." Alas, what trifling is this! What if he was *then* a child of God? He is *now* manifestly a child of the devil; for the works of his father he doeth. Therefore, do not play upon words. He must go through an entire change of heart. In one not yet baptised, you yourself would call that change the new birth. In him, call it what you will; but remember meantime that if either he or you die without it, your baptism will be so far from profiting you that it will greatly increase your damnation.[4]

> Father, Son, and Holy Ghost,
>   In solemn power come down!
> Present with thy heavenly host,
>   Thine ordinance to crown:
> See a sinful woman of earth!
>   Bless to him the cleansing flood,
> Plunge him, by a second birth,
>   Into the depth of God.

Let the promised inward grace
Accompany the sign;
On his new-born soul impress
The character divine;
Father, all thy name reveal!
Jesus, all thy name impart!
Holy Ghost, renew, and dwell
Forever in his heart![5]

WORKS OF PIETY

(1) Prayer.

Thus saith the Lord, "Ask, and it shall be given you"; "if any of you lack wisdom, let him ask of God." Here God plainly ordains prayer as the means of receiving whatsoever grace we want [need]; particularly that wisdom from above, which is the chief fruit of the grace of God. Here likewise, God commands all to pray who desire to receive any grace from him. Here is no restriction as to believers or unbelievers; but least of all as to unbelievers. For such, doubtless, were most of those to whom he said, "Ask, and it shall be given you." We know, indeed, that the prayer of an unbeliever is full of sin. Yet let him remember that which is written of one who could not then believe, for he had not so much as heard the gospel: "Cornelius, thy prayers and thine alms are come up for a memorial before God."[6]

Jesus, thou sovereign Lord of all,
    The same through one eternal day,
Attend thy feeblest followers' call,
    And O instruct us how to pray!
The power out the supplicating grace,
And stir us up to seek thy face.

We cannot think a gracious thought,
    We cannot feel a good desire,
Till thou, who call'dst a world from nought,
    The power into our hearts inspire:
The promised Intercessor give,
And let us now thyself receive.

Come in thy pleading Spirit down
    To us who for thy coming stay;

Of all thy gifts we ask but one,
We ask the constant power to pray:
Indulge us, Lord, in this request;
Thou canst not then deny the rest.[7]

(2) The Scriptures.

Under the general term of searching the Scriptures, both hearing, reading, and meditating are contained. And that this is the means whereby God not only gives, but also confirms and increases true wisdom, we learn from the words of St. Paul to Timothy: "From a child thou hast known the Holy Scriptures, which are able to make thee wise unto salvation through faith which is in Christ Jesus" (II Tim. 3:15). It should be observed that this is spoken primarily and directly of the Scriptures which Timothy had known from a child; which must have been those of the Old Testament, for the New was not then wrote. How far, then, was St. Paul from making light of the Old Testament! Behold this, lest ye one day "wonder and perish," ye who make so small account of one half of the oracles of God![8]

It is no part of my design to save either learned or unlearned men from the trouble of thinking. On the contrary, my intention is to make them think, and to assist them in thinking. This is the way to understand the things of God: "Meditate thereon day and night"; so shall you attain the best knowledge, even to "know the only true God, and Jesus Christ whom he hath sent."

If you desire to read the Scriptures in such a manner as may most effectually answer this end, would it not be advisable (1) to set apart a little time, if you can, every morning and evening for that purpose? (2) At each time, if you have leisure, to read a chapter out of the Old, and one out of the New Testament; if you cannot do this, to take a single chapter, or a part of one? (3) To read this with a single eye to know the whole will of God, and a fixed resolution to do it? In order to know his will, you should (4) have a constant eye to the analogy of faith, the connexion and harmony there is between those grand, fundamental doctrines, original sin, justification by faith, the new birth, inward and outward holiness. (5) Serious and earnest prayer should be constantly used before we consult the oracles of God, seeing "Scripture can only be understood through the same Spirit whereby it was given." Our reading should likewise be closed with prayer, that what we read may be written in our hearts. (6) It might also be of use, if while we read we were frequently to pause and examine ourselves by what we read, both with regard to our hearts and lives.[9]

The general role of interpreting Scripture is this: the literal sense of every text is to be taken, if it be not contrary to some other texts; but in that case the obscure text is to be interpreted by those which speak more plainly.[10]

> Inspirer of the ancient seers,
>   Who wrote from thee the sacred page,
> The same through all succeeding years,
>   To us, in our degenerate age,
> The spirit of thy word impart,
> And breathe thy life into our heart.
>
> The sacred lessons of thy grace,
>   Transmitted through thy word, repeat,
> And train us up in all thy ways,
>   To make us in thy will complete;
> Fulfil thy love's redeeming plan,
> And bring us to a perfect man.[11]

(3) The Lord's Supper.

In latter times many have affirmed that the Lord's Supper is not a converting, but a confirming ordinance. And among us it has been diligently taught that none but those who are converted, who have received the Holy Ghost, who are believers in the full sense, ought to communicate. But experience shows the gross falsehood of that assertion, that the Lord's Supper is not a converting ordinance. Ye are the witnesses. For many now present know, the very beginning of your conversion to God (perhaps in some, the first deep conviction [of sin]) was wrought at the Lord's Supper. Now, one single instance of this kind overthrows the whole assertion.

The falsehood of the other assertion appears both from Scripture precept and example. Our Lord commanded those very men who were then unconverted, who had not yet received the Holy Ghost, who (in the full sense of the word) were not yet believers, to "do this in remembrance of" him. Here the precept is clear. And to these he delivered the elements with his own hands. Here is example equally indisputable.

The Lord's Supper was ordained by God to be a means of conveying to men either preventing, or justifying, or sanctifying grace, according to their several necessities. The persons for whom it was ordained are all those who know and feel that they want [need] the grace of God, either to restrain them from sin, or to show their sins forgiven, or to renew their souls in the image of God. Inasmuch as we come to his Table, not to give him anything, but to receive whatever he sees best for us, there is no previous preparation indispensably necessary, but a desire to receive whatsoever he pleases to give. And no fitness is required at the time of communicating, but a sense of our state, of our utter sinfulness and helplessness; everyone who knows he is just fit for hell, being just fit to come to Christ, in this as well as all other ways of his appointment.[12]

Come to the feast, for Christ invites,
And promises to feed;
'Tis here his closest love unites
The members to their Head.

'Tis here he nourishes his own
With living bread from heaven,
Or makes himself to mourners known,
And shows their sins forgiven.

Still in his instituted ways
He bids us ask the power,
The pardoning or the hallowing grace,
And wait the appointed hour.[13]

And shall I let him go?
If now I do not *feel*
The streams of living water flow,
Shall I forsake the well?

He bids me eat the bread
He bids me drink the wine;
No other motive, Lord, I need
No other word than thine.[14]

Our hearts we open wide,
To make the Saviour room;
And lo! the Lamb, the Crucified,
The sinner's Friend, is come!

His presence makes the feast;
And now our spirits feel
The glory not to be expressed,
The joy unspeakable[15]

(4) Fasting.

Of all the means of grace there is scarce any concerning which men have run into greater extremes, than that of which our Lord speaks [in Matt. 6:16–18], I mean religious fasting. How have some exalted this beyond all Scripture and reason, and others utterly disregarded it—as it were revenging themselves by undervaluing as much as the former had overvalued it! Those have spoken of it as if it were all in all—if not the end itself, yet infallibly connected with it; these, as if it were just nothing, as if it were a fruitless labour, which had no relation at all thereto. Whereas it is certain, the truth lies between them both. It is not all, nor yet is it nothing. It is not the end, but it is a precious means thereto; a means which God himself has ordained, and in which, therefore, when it is duly used, he will surely give us his blessing.

"But is it not mere superstition" (so it has been objected) "to imagine that God regards such little things as these?" If you say it is, you condemn all the generations of God's children. But will you say these were all weak, superstitious men? Can you be so hardy as to affirm this, both of Moses and Joshua, of Samuel and David, of Jehoshaphat, Ezra, Nehemiah, and all the prophets; yea, of a greater than all, the Son of God himself? It is certain, both our Master and all these his servants did imagine that fasting is not a little thing, and that He who is higher than the highest doth regard it. Of the same judgment, it is plain, were all his Apostles. Nor would they attempt anything wherein the glory of God was nearly concerned, such as the sending forth labourers into the harvest, without solemn fasting as well as Prayer.

Not that we are to imagine the performing the bare outward act will receive any blessing from God. If it be a mere external service, it is all but lost labour. Such a performance may possibly afflict the body; but as to the soul, it profiteth nothing.

Yea, the body may sometimes be afflicted too much, so as to be unfit for the work of our calling. This also we are diligently to guard against; for we ought to preserve our health, as a good gift of God. Therefore, care is to be taken, whenever we fast, to proportion the fast to our strength. For we may not offer God murder for sacrifice, or destroy our bodies to help our souls.

But at these solemn seasons, we may, even in great weakness of body, avoid that other extreme, for which God condemns those who of old expostulated with him for not accepting their fasts. "Wherefore have we fasted, say they, and thou seest not?—Behold, in the day of your fast you find pleasure, saith the Lord" [Isa. 58:3]. If we cannot wholly abstain from food, we may at least abstain from pleasant food; and then we shall not seek his face in vain.

But let us take care to afflict our souls as well as our bodies. Let every season, either of public or private fasting, be a season of exercising all those holy affections which are implied in a broken and contrite heart. Let it be a season of devout mourning, of godly sorrow for sin.

And with fasting let us always join fervent prayer, pouring out our whole souls before God, confessing our sins with all their aggravations, humbling ourselves under his mighty hand, laying open before him all our wants, all our guiltiness and helplessness. This is a season for enlarging our prayers, both in behalf of ourselves and of our brethren. Let us now bewail the sins of our people; and cry aloud for the city of our God, that the Lord may build up Zion, and cause his face to shine on her desolations. Thus, we may observe, the man of God in ancient times always joined prayer and fasting together.

It remains only, in order to our observing such a fast as is acceptable to the Lord, that we add alms thereto; works of mercy, after our power, both to the bodies and souls of men. "With such sacrifices" also "God is well pleased." Thus the angel declared to Cornelius, "Thy prayers and thine alms are come up for a memorial before God" (Acts 10:4). And thus God himself expressly and largely declares [Isa. 58:6ff.].[16]

> Jesus, I fain would find
>   Thy zeal for God in me,
> Thy yearning pity for mankind,
>   Thy burning charity.
>
> In me thy Spirit dwell;
>   In me thy mercies move:
> So shall the fervour of my zeal
>   Be the pure flame of love.[17]

(5)"Christian Confidence."[18]

In the evening three women agreed to meet together weekly, with the same intention as those at London, viz., "To confess their faults one to another, and pray for one another, that they may be healed"

[Jas. 5:16]. At eight, four young men agreed to meet in pursuance of the same design. How dare any man deny this to be (as to the substance of it) a means of grace, ordained by God? Unless he will affirm (with Luther in the fury of his Solifidianism) that St. James's Epistle is an epistle of straw."[19]

[You allege that the Methodists] "use private confession, in which everyone is to speak the state of his heart, with his several temptations and deliverances, and answer as many searching questions as may be. And what a scene," say you, "is hereby disclosed! What a filthy jakes opened, when the most searching questions are answered without reserve!" Hold, sir, unless you are answering for yourself: this undoubtedly you have a right to do. You can tell best what is in your own heart. And I cannot deny what you say: it may be a very "filthy jakes," for aught I know. But pray do not measure others by yourself. The hearts of believers "are purified through faith." When these open their hearts to one another, there is no such scene disclosed. Yet temptations to pride in various kinds, to self-will, to unbelief in many instances, they often feel in themselves (whether they give any place to them or no) and occasionally disclose them to their brethren.

But this has no resemblance to Popish confession. There is no analogy between the Popish confession to a priest and our confessing our faults to one another and praying for one another, as St. James directs.[20]

It is true that the Leader "sees each person once a week, to inquire how their souls prosper"; and that when they meet, "the Leader or Teacher asks each a few questions relating to the present situation of their minds." So then, that questions are actually asked, yea and inquiries made, cannot be denied. But what kind of questions or inquiries? None that expose the answerer to any danger; none that they would scruple to answer before Dr. E[rskine], or any other person that fears God.[21]

> Jesus, Lord, we look to thee,
> Let us in thy name agree;
> Show thyself the prince of peace,
> Bid our strife for ever cease.
>
> Let us for each other care,
> Each the other's burden bear,

To thy church the pattern give,
Show how true believers live.

Free from anger and from pride,
Let us thus in God abide;
All the depths of love express,
All the heights of holiness!

Let us then with joy remove
To the family above;
On the wings of angels fly;
Show how true believers die.[22]

WORKS OF MERCY

(1) Faith and Good Works.

It is generally supposed that the means of grace and the ordinances of God are equivalent terms. We commonly mean by that expression, those that are usually termed works of piety; viz., hearing and reading the Scripture, receiving the Lord's Supper, public and private prayer, and fasting. And it is certain, these are the ordinary channels which convey the grace of God to the souls of men. But are they the only means of grace? Are there no other means than these, whereby God is pleased, frequently, yea ordinarily, to convey his grace to them that either love or fear him? Surely there are works of mercy, as well as works of piety, which are real means of grace. They are more especially such to those that perform them with a single eye. And those that neglect them do not receive the grace which otherwise they might. Yea, and they lose, by a continual neglect, the grace which they had received. Is it not hence, that many who were once strong in faith are now weak and feeble-minded? And yet they are not sensible whence that weakness comes, as they neglect none of the ordinances of God. But they might see whence it comes, were they seriously to consider St. Paul's account of all true believers: "We are his workmanship, created anew in Christ Jesus unto good works, which God hath before prepared, that we might walk therein" (Eph. 2:10).

The walking herein is essentially necessary, as to the continuance of that faith whereby we are already saved by grace, so to the attainment of everlasting salvation. Of this we cannot doubt, if we seriously consider that these are the very words of the great Judge himself:

"Come, ye blessed children of my Father, inherit the kingdom prepared for you from the foundation of the world. For I was hungry, and ye gave me meat: thirsty, and ye gave me drink: I was a stranger, and ye took me in: naked, and ye clothed me: I was sick, and ye visited me: I was in prison, and ye came unto me" (Matt. 25:34ff.). "Verily, I say unto you, inasmuch as ye have done it to the least of these my brethren, ye have done it unto me." If this do not convince you that the continuance in works of mercy is necessary to salvation, consider what the Judge of all says to those on the left hand: "Depart, ye cursed, into everlasting fire, prepared for the devil and his angels. For I was hungry, and ye gave me no meat: thirsty, and ye took me not in: naked, and ye clothed me not: sick and in prison and ye visited me not. Inasmuch as ye have not done it unto one of the least of these, neither have ye done it unto me." You see, were it for this alone, they must "depart" from God "into everlasting punishment."

Is it not strange that this important truth should be so little understood, or at least should so little influence the practice of them that fear God? Suppose this representation be true, suppose the Judge of all the earth speaks right, those, and those only, that feed the hungry, give a drink to the thirsty, clothe the naked, relieve the stranger, visit those that are in prison, according to their power and opportunity, shall "inherit the everlasting kingdom." And those that do not, shall "depart into everlasting fire, prepared for the devil and his angels."

> When, my Saviour, shall I be
> Perfectly resigned to thee?
> Poor and vile in my own eyes,
> Only in thy wisdom wise:
>
> Only thee content to know,
> Ignorant of all below,
> Only guided by thy light,
> Only mighty in thy might!
>
> So I may thy Spirit know,
> Let him as he listeth blow;
> Let the manner be unknown,
> So I may with thee be one.
>
> Fully in my life express
> All the heights of holiness,
> Sweetly let my spirit prove
> All the depths of humble love.[23]

(2) The Reward of the Righteous.

I am not insensible that many, even serious people, are jealous of all that is spoken upon this subject. Nay, and whenever the necessity of good works is strongly insisted on, take for granted that he who speaks in this manner is but one remove from Popery. But should we, for fear of this or of any other reproach, refrain from speaking "the truth as it is in Jesus"? Should we on any consideration "shun to declare the whole counsel of God"? Nay, if a false prophet could utter that solemn word, how much more may the ministers of Christ, "We cannot go beyond the word of the Lord to speak either more or less!"

Is it not to be lamented that any who fear God should desire us to do otherwise; and that by speaking otherwise themselves, they should occasion the way of truth to be evil spoken of? I mean, in particular, the way of salvation by faith; which on this very account is despised, nay, had in abomination, by many sensible men. It is now above forty years since this grand scriptural doctrine, "By grace ye are saved through faith," began to be openly declared by a few Clergymen of the Church of England. And not long after, some who heard but did not understand attempted to preach the same doctrine, but miserably mangled it; wresting the Scripture, and "making void the law through faith."

Some of these, in order to exalt the value of faith, have utterly deprecated good works. They speak of them as not only not necessary to salvation, but as greatly obstructive to it. They represent them as abundantly more dangerous than evil ones, to those who are seeking to save their souls. One cries aloud, "More people go to hell by praying, than by thieving." Another screams out, "Away with your works! Have done with your works, or you cannot come to Christ!" And this unscriptural, irrational, heathen declamation is called *preaching the gospel!*

But "shall not the Judge of all the earth" speak, as well as "do, right"? Will not he "be justified in his saying, and clear when he is judged"? Assuredly he will. And upon his authority we must continue to declare that whenever you do good to any for his sake; when you feed the hungry, give drink to the thirsty; when you assist the stranger, or clothe the naked; when you visit them that are sick or in prison; these are not *splendid sins,* as one marvellously calls them, but "sacrifices wherewith God is well pleased."

Not that our Lord intended we should confine our beneficence to the bodies of men. He undoubtedly designed that we should be equally abundant in works of spiritual mercy. He died "to purify unto himself a peculiar people, zealous of" *all* "good works"; zealous, above all, to "save souls from death," and thereby "hide a multitude of sins." And this is unquestionably included in St. Paul's exhortation: "As we have time, let us do good unto all men"; good in every possible kind, as well as in every possible degree. But why does our blessed Lord not mention works of spiritual mercy? He could not do it with any propriety. It was not for him to say, "I was in error, and ye convinced me; I was in sin, and you brought me back to God." And it needed not; for in mentioning *some,* he included *all* works of mercy.

But may I not add one thing more? (only he that heareth, let him understand): Good works are so far from being hindrances of our salvation; they are so far from being insignificant, from being of no account in Christianity; that, supposing them to spring from a right principle, they are the perfection of religion. They are the highest part of that spiritual building whereof Jesus Christ is the foundation. To those who attentively consider the thirteenth chapter of the First Epistle to the Corinthians, it will be undeniably plain, that what St. Paul there describes as the highest of all Christian graces is properly and directly the love of our neighbour. And to him who attentively considers the whole tenor both of the Old and New Testament, it will be equally plain that works springing from this love are the highest part of the religion therein revealed. Of these our Lord himself says, "Hereby is my Father glorified, that ye bring forth much fruit." Much *fruit!* (Does not the very expression imply the excellency of what is so termed? Is not the tree itself for the sake of the fruit? By bearing fruit, and by this alone, it attains the highest perfection it is capable of, and answers the end for which it was planted. Who, what, is he then, that is called a Christian, and can speak lightly of good works?[24]

> Holy Lamb, who thee confess,
> Followers of thy holiness,
> Thee they ever keep in view,
> Ever ask: What shall we do?
> Governed by thy only will,
> All thy words we would fulfil,
> Would in all thy footsteps go,
> Walk as Jesus walked below.
>
> While thou didst on earth appear,
> Servant to thy servants here,
> Mindful of thy place above,

All thy life was prayer and love.
Such our whole employment be,
Works of faith and charity;
Works of love on man bestowed.
Secret intercourse with God.[25]

THE RIGHT USE OF SUCH MEANS

The sure and general rule for all who groan for the salvation of God is this: whenever opportunity serves, use all the means which God has ordained; for who knows in which God will meet thee with the grace that bringeth salvation?

As to the manner of using them—whereon indeed it wholly depends whether they shall convey any grace at all to the user—it behooves us, first, always to retain a lively sense that God is above all means. Have a care, therefore, of limiting the Almighty. He doeth whatsoever and whensoever it pleaseth him. He can convey his grace either in or out of any of the means which he hath appointed. Look, then, every moment for his appearing! He is always ready, always able, always willing to save.

Secondly, before you use any means, let it be deeply impressed on your soul: there is no *power* in this. It is, in itself, a poor, dead, empty thing. Separate from God, it is a dry leaf, a shadow. Neither is there any *merit* in my using this; nothing intrinsically pleasing to God, nothing whereby I deserve any favour at his hands. But because God bids, therefore I do; because he directs me to wait in this way, therefore here I wait for his free mercy, whereof cometh my salvation.

Settle this in your heart, that the *opus operaturn,* the mere *work done,* profiteth nothing; that there is no *power* to save but in the Spirit of God, no *merit* but in the blood of Christ; that consequently, even what God ordains conveys no grace to the soul, if you trust not in him alone. On the other hand, he that does truly trust in him cannot fall short of the grace of God, even though he were cut off from every outward ordinance, though he were shut up in the center of the earth.

Thirdly, in using all means, seek God alone. In and through every outward thing, look singly to the *power* of his Spirit and the *merits* of his Son. Beware you do not stick in the *work* itself; if you do, it is all lost labour. Nothing short of God can satisfy your soul. Therefore eye him in all, through all, and above all.

Remember also to use all means *as means;* as ordained, not for their own sake, but in order to the renewal of your soul in righteousness and true holiness. If therefore they actually tend to this, well; but if not, they are dung and dross.

Lastly, after you have used any of these, take care how you value yourself thereon; how you congratulate yourself as having done some great thing. This is turning all to poison. Think, "If God was not there, what does this avail? Have I not been adding sin to sin? O Lord, save or I perish!" If God was there, if his love flowed into your heart, you have forgot, as it were, the outward work. You see, you know, you feel, God is all in all. Be abased. Sink down before him. Give him all the praise. "Let God in all things be glorified through Christ Jesus." [26]

Holy, and true, and righteous Lord,
   I wait to prove thy perfect will;
Be mindful of thy gracious word,
   And stamp me with thy Spirit's seal.

Confound, o'erpower me by thy grace,
   I would be by myself abhorred;
All night, all majesty, all praise,
   All glory, be to Christ my Lord.

Now let me gain perfection's height,
   Now let me into nothing fall,
Be less than nothing in thy sight,
   And feel that Christ is all in all. [27]

II

Christian Behavior

STEWARDSHIP

The relation which man bears to God, the creature to his Creator is exhibited to us in the oracles of God under various representations. Considered as a sinner, a fallen creature, he is there represented as a debtor to his Creator. He is also frequently represented as a servant, which indeed is essential to him as a creature. But no character more exactly agrees with the present state of man, than that of a steward. Our blessed Lord frequently represents him as such; and there is a peculiar propriety in the representation.

We are now indebted to him for all we have; but although a debtor is obliged to return what he has received, yet until the time of payment comes, he is at liberty to use it as he pleases. It is not so with a steward; he is not at liberty to use what is lodged in his hands as *he* pleases, but as his master pleases. He has no right to dispose of anything which is in his hands, but according to the will of his lord. For he is not the proprietor of any of these things, but barely entrusted with them by another; and entrusted on this express condition, that he shall dispose of all as his master orders. Now this is exactly the case of every man, with relation to God. We are not at liberty to use what he has lodged in our hands as we please, but as He pleases who alone is the possessor of heaven and earth, and the Lord of every creature.

We have no right to dispose of anything we have, but according to his will, seeing we are not proprietors of any of these things; they are all, as our Lord speaks, ἀλλότρια, *belonging to another person;* nor is anything *our own,* in the land of our pilgrimage. We shall not receive τὰ ἴδια, *our own things,* till we come to our own country. Eternal things only are our own; with all these temporal things we are barely entrusted by another, the Disposer and Lord of all. And he entrusts us

147

with them on this express condition, that we use them only as our Master's goods, and according to the particular directions which he has given us in his Word. On this condition he has entrusted us with our souls, our bodies, our goods, and whatever other talents we have received.

We learn from hence that there is no employment of our time, no action or conversation that is purely indifferent. All is good or bad, because all our time, as everything we have, is not our own. All these are the *property of another,* of God our Creator. Now, these either are or are not employed according to his will. If they are so employed, all is good; if they are not, all is evil.

We learn from hence [also] that there are no works of supererogation, that we can never do more than our duty; seeing all we have is not our own but God's; all we can do is due to him. We have not received this or that, or many things only, but everything from him; therefore, everything is his due. He that gives all must necessarily have a right to all.[1]

SELF-DENIAL

But what is self-denial? Wherein are we to deny ourselves? And whence does the necessity of this arise? I answer, the will of God is the supreme, unalterable role for every intelligent creature; equally binding every angel in heaven, and every man upon earth. Nor can it be otherwise. This is the natural, necessary result of the relation between creatures and their Creator. But if the will of God be our one role of action in everything, great and small, it follows, by undeniable consequence, that we are not to do our own will in anything. Here, therefore, we see at once the nature, with the ground and reason, of self-denial. We see the nature of self-denial: it is the denying or refusing to follow our own will, from a conviction that the will of God is the only rule of action to us. And we see the reason thereof, because we are creatures; because "it is he that hath made us, and not we ourselves."

This reason for self-denial must hold, even with regard to the angels of God in heaven; and with regard to man, innocent and holy, as he came out of the hands of his Creator. But a farther reason for it arises from the condition wherein all men are since the fall. We are all now "shapen in wickedness, and in sin did our mother conceive us." Our nature is altogether corrupt, in every power and faculty. And our will, depraved equally with the rest, is wholly bent to indulge our natural corruption. On the other hand, it is the will of God that we resist and counteract that corruption, not at some times or in some things only, but at all times and in all things. Here, therefore, is a farther ground for constant and universal self-denial.

To illustrate this a little further: the will of God is a path leading straight to God. The will of man, which once ran parallel with it, is now another path, not only different from it, but in our present state directly contrary to it: it leads from God. If, therefore, we walk in the one, we must necessarily quit the other. Indeed, a man "of faint heart and feeble hands" may "go in two ways," one after the other. But he cannot walk in two ways at the same time. He cannot, at one and the same time, follow his own will, and follow the will of God. He must choose the one or the other; denying God's will, to follow his own; or denying himself, to follow the will of God.

Now, it is undoubtedly pleasing, for the time, to follow our own will, by indulging, in any instance that offers, the corruption of our nature. But by following it in anything, we so far strengthen the perverseness of our will; and by indulging it, we continually increase the corruption of our nature. So, by the food which is agreeable to the palate, we often increase a bodily disease. It gratifies the taste, but it inflames the disorder; it brings pleasure, but it also brings death.

On the whole, then, to deny ourselves is to deny our own will, where it does not fall in with the will of God; and that however pleasing it may be. It is to deny ourselves any pleasure which does not spring from, and lead to, God; that is, in effect, to refuse going out of our way, though into a pleasant, flowery path; to refuse what we know to be deadly poison, though agreeable to the taste.[2]

TEMPERANCE

Some are wanting in temperance. They do not steadily use that kind and degree of food which they know, or might know, would most conduce to the health, strength, and vigour of the body. Or they are not temperate in sleep; they do not rigorously adhere to what is best both for body and mind; otherwise they would constantly go to bed and rise early, and at a fixed hour. Or they sup late, which is neither good for body nor soul. Or they use neither fasting nor abstinence. Or they prefer (which are so many sorts of intemperance) that preaching, reading, or conversation, which gives them transient joy and comfort, before that which brings godly sorrow, or instruction in righteousness. Such joy is not sanctified; it doth not tend to, or terminate in, the crucifixion of the heart. Such faith doth not centre in God, but rather in itself.[3]

[You allege that the Methodists] "value themselves upon extraordinary strictnesses and severities in life, and such as are beyond what the rules of Christianity require. They captivate the people by such professions and appearances of uncommon sanctity. But that which can never fail of a general respect is a quiet and exemplary life, free from the many follies and indiscretions which those restless and vagrant teachers are apt to fall into."

By "extraordinary strictnesses and severities," I presume your Lordship means the abstaining from wine and animal food; which it is sure, Christianity does not require. But if you do, I fear your Lordship is not thoroughly informed of the matter of fact. I began to do this about twelve years ago, when I had no thought of "annoying parochial ministers," or of "captivating" any "people" thereby, unless it were the Chicasaw or Choctaw Indians. But I resumed the use of them both, about two years after, for the sake of some who thought I made it a point of conscience; telling them, 'I *will* eat flesh while the world standeth," rather than "make my brother to offend." Dr. Cheyne advised me to leave them off again, assuring me, "Till you do, you will never be free from fevers." And since I have taken his advice, I have been free (blessed be God!) from all bodily disorders. Would to God I knew any method of being equally free from all "follies and indiscretions"! But this I never expect to attain till my spirit returns to God.[4]

I cannot subscribe to [Dr. Cadogan's] condemning of wine in general, several sorts of which, as Dr. Hoffman shows at large, are so far from being unwholesome, that they are some of the most powerful medicines yet known, in some very dangerous diseases. I myself was ordered by Dr. Cheyne (not the warmest advocate for liquors), after drinking only water for some years, to take a small quantity of wine every day. And I am persuaded, far from doing me any hurt, it contributed much to the recovery of my strength. But it seems we are to make a pretty large allowance for what the Doctor says on this head; seeing he grants it will do you little or no harm to take "a plentiful cup now and then." Enough, enough! Then it will certainly do you no harm if, instead of drinking that cup in one day (suppose once a week), you divide it into seven and drink one of them every day.

I cannot but think, if your wine is good in kind, suited to your constitution, and taken in small quantities, it is full as wholesome as any liquor in the world, except water. Yet the grievous abuse of it which almost universally prevails might easily prejudice a benevolent man against it, and make him endeavour to prevent the abuse by forbidding the use of it.[5]

Distilled liquors have their use, but are infinitely overbalanced by the abuse of them; therefore, were it in my power, I would banish them out of the world.[6]

I rejoice to hear that your health is so well re-established, and am in hopes it will continue. Your preaching frequently will be no hindrance, but rather a furtherance to it, provided you have the resolution always to observe the Methodist rule of concluding the service within the hour. The want of observing this has many times hurt you; and we must not offer murder for sacrifice. We are not at liberty to impair our own health in hopes of doing good to others.[7]

I am not afraid of your doing too little, but of your doing too much, either by preaching oftener than your strength will yet bear or by speaking too long or too loud.

Our preachers have as great a need of temperance in preaching as in eating or drinking; otherwise our grand enemy will carry his point, and soon disable us from preaching at all.[8]

THE CONDUCT OF BUSINESS

With what view, for what end, do you undertake and follow your worldly business? "To provide things necessary for myself and my family." It is a good answer, as far as it goes; but it does not go far enough. For a Turk or a Heathen goes so far—does his work for the very same ends. But a Christian may go abundantly farther. His end in all his labour is to please God; to do, not his own will, but the will of Him that sent him into the world—for this very purpose, to do the will of God on earth as angels do in heaven. He works for eternity. He "labours not for the meat that perisheth" (this is the smallest part of his motive), "but for that which endureth to everlasting life."

Again: in what *manner* do you transact your worldly business? I trust, with diligence, whatever your hand findeth to do, doing it with your might; in justice, rendering to all their due, in every circumstance of life; yea and in mercy, doing unto every man what you would he should do unto you. This is well. But a Christian is called to go still farther—to add piety to justice; to intermix prayer, especially the prayer of the heart, with the labour of his hands. Without this, all his diligence and justice only show him to be an honest Heathen; and many there are who profess the Christian religion that go no farther than honest Heathenism.

Yet again: in what *spirit* do you go through your business? In the spirit of the world, or in the spirit of Christ? I am afraid thousands of those who are called good Christians do not understand the question. If you act in the spirit of Christ, you carry the end you at first proposed through all your work from first to last. You do everything in the spirit of sacrifice, giving up your will to the will of God; and continually aiming not at ease, pleasure, or riches, not at anything "this short-enduring world can give," but merely at the glory of God. Now, can anyone deny that this is the most excellent way of pursuing worldly business?[9]

THE CHOICE OF A CAREER

Here is a father choosing an employment for his son. If his eye be not single; if he do not singly aim at the glory of God in the salvation of his soul—if it be not his one consideration, what calling is likely to secure him the highest place in heaven, not the largest share of earthly treasure or the highest preferment in the Church—the light which is in him is manifestly darkness. And O how great is that darkness! The mistake which he is in is not a little one, but inexpressibly great. What! do not you prefer his being a cobbler on earth, and a glorious saint in heaven, before his being a lord on earth, and a damned spirit in hell? If not, how great, unutterably great, is the darkness that covers your soul!

Let us consider another case, not far distant from this. Suppose a young man, having finished his studies at the University, is desirous to minister in holy things, and accordingly enters into orders. What is his intention in this? What is the end he proposes to himself? If his eye be single, his one design is to save his own soul and them that hear him; to bring as many sinners as he possibly can out of darkness into marvellous light. If on the other hand his eye be not single, if he aim at ease, honour, money, or preferment, the World may account him a wise man, but God says unto him, "Thou fool!" And while the light that is in him is thus darkness, "how great is that darkness!" What folly is comparable to his folly!—one peculiarly dedicated to the God of heaven, to "mind earthly things"! A worldly Clergyman is a fool above all fools, a madman above all madmen! Such vile, infamous wretches as these are the real ground of the contempt of the Clergy. Indolent Clergymen, pleasure-taking Clergymen, money-loving Clergymen, praise-loving Clergymen, preferment-seeking Clergymen—these are the wretches that cause the order in general to be condemned. These are the pests of the Christian world, the grand nuisance of mankind, a stink in the nostrils of God! Such as these were they who made St. Chrysostom to say, "Hell is paved with the souls of Christian priests."

Take another case. Suppose a young woman, of an independent

fortune, to be addressed at the same time by a man of wealth without religion, and a man of religion without wealth; in other words, by a rich child of the devil, and a poor child of God. What shall we say if, other circumstances being equal, she prefer the rich man to the good man? It is plain her eye is not single; therefore her foolish heart is darkened; and how great is that darkness which makes her judge gold and silver a greater recommendation than holiness; which makes a child of the devil with money appear more amiable to her than a Child of God without it! What words can sufficiently express the inexcusable folly of such a choice?[10]

TRUE COURTESY

See that you are courteous towards all men. It matters not, in this respect, whether they are high or low, rich or poor, superior or inferior to you. No, nor even whether good or bad, whether they fear God or not. Indeed, the *mode* of showing your courtesy may vary as Christian prudence will direct, but the thing itself is due to all; the lowest and the worst have a claim to our courtesy. It may either be inward or outward; either a temper or a mode of behaviour, such a mode of behaviour as naturally springs from courtesy of heart. Is this the same with good breeding, or politeness (which seems to be only a high degree of good breeding)? Nay, good breeding is chiefly the fruit of education; but education cannot give courtesy of heart. Mr. Addison's well known definition of politeness seems rather to be a definition of this: "A constant desire of pleasing all men, appearing through the whole conversation." Now this may subsist, even in a high degree, where there has been no advantage of education. I have seen as real courtesy in an Irish cabin, as could be found in St. James's or the Louvre.

Shall we endeavour to go a little deeper, to search the foundation of the matter? What is the source of that desire to please which we term courtesy? Let us look attentively into our heart, and we shall soon find an answer. The same Apostle that teaches us to be *courteous,* teaches us to *honour all men* [I Pet. 2:17]; and his Master teaches me to love all men. Join these together, and what will be the effect? A poor wretch cries to me for an alms. I look, and see him covered with dirt and rags. But through these I see one that has an immortal spirit, made to know and love and dwell with God to eternity. I honour him for his Creator's sake. I see through all these rags that he is purpled over with the blood of Christ. I love him for the sake of his Redeemer. The courtesy, therefore, which I feel and show towards him is a mixture of the honour and love which I bear to the offspring of God, the purchase of his Son's blood, and the candidate for immortality. This courtesy let us feel and show towards all men.[11]

THE CULTIVATION OF THE MIND

It cannot be that the people should grow in grace unless they give themselves to reading. A reading people will always be a knowing people. A people who talk much will know little. Press this upon them with your might, and you will soon see the fruit of your labours.[12]

Admonitions to preachers

What has exceedingly hurt you in time past, nay, and I fear to this day, is want of reading. I scarce ever knew a preacher read so little. And perhaps by neglecting it you have lost the taste for it. Hence your talent in preaching does not increase. It is just the same as it was seven years ago. It is lively, but not deep; there is little variety; there is no compass of thought. Reading only can supply this, with meditation and daily prayer. You wrong yourself greatly by omitting this. You can never be a deep preacher without it any more than a thorough Christian. O begin! Fix some part of every day for private exercises. You may acquire the taste which you have not; what is tedious at first will afterwards be pleasant. Whether you like it or no, read and pray daily. It is for your life; there is no other way; else you will be a trifler all your days and a pretty, superficial preacher.[13]

Read the most useful books, and that regularly and constantly. Steadily spend all the morning in this employ, or at least five hours in four-and-twenty.

"But I read only the Bible." Then you ought teach others to read only the Bible, and by parity of reason, to hear only the Bible. But if so, you need preach no more. Just so said George Bell. And what is the fruit? Why, now he reads neither the Bible nor anything else. This is rank enthusiasm. If you need no book but the Bible, you are got above St. Paul. He wanted others too. "Bring the books," says he, "but especially the parchments," those wrote on parchment. "But I have no taste for reading." Contract a taste for it by use, or return to your trade.[14]

Advice on study to a young lady

You want to know God, in order to enjoy him in time and in eternity. All that you want to know of him is contained in one book, the Bible.

Therefore your one point is to understand this. And all you learn is to be referred to this, as either directly or remotely conducive to it.

Might it not be well, then, to spend at least two hours every day in reading and meditating upon the Bible—reading every morning (if not every evening too) a portion of the Old and then of the New Testament?

Your studying hours (if your constitution will bear it) might be five or six hours a day; perhaps from nine to twelve in the morning, and from two to five in the afternoon. And whenever you begin to be tired with books that require a strong and deep attention, relax your mind by interposing history or poetry or something of a lighter nature.

[Wesley then goes on to list the subjects to be studied: Grammar, Arithmetic, Geography, Logic, Ethics, Natural Philosophy (Science), History, Metaphysics, Poetry, Divinity (Theology). He also recommends what he considers the best contemporary text-books. The range of his recommendations in History is particularly interesting. It covers Ancient History; Church History; the history of Europe, the Reformation, England, the Great Rebellion, the Puritans, New England, and the Conquest of Mexico. He concludes:]

This course of study, if you have the resolution to go through with it, will, I apprehend, take you up three, four, or five years, according to the degree of your health and of your application. And you will then have knowledge enough for any reasonable Christian. But remember, before all, in all, and above all, your great point is to know the only true God and Jesus Christ whom he hath sent.[15]

THE USE OF RICHES

Why is self-denial in general so little practised at present among the Methodists? Why is so exceedingly little of it to be found even in the oldest and largest societies? The more I observe and consider things, the more clearly it appears what is the cause of this. The Methodists grow more and more self-indulgent, because they *grow rich*. Although many of them are still deplorably poor, yet many others, in the space of twenty, thirty, or forty years, are twenty, thirty, yea a hundred times richer than they were when they first entered the society. And it is an observation which admits of few exceptions that nine in ten of these decreased in grace in the same proportion as they increased in wealth. Indeed, according to the natural tendency of riches, we cannot expect it to be otherwise.

But how astonishing a thing is this! How can we understand it? Does it not seem (and yet this cannot be) that Christianity, true, scriptural Christianity, has a tendency, in process of time, to undermine and destroy itself? For wherever true Christianity spreads, it must cause diligence and frugality, which in the natural course of things must beget riches; and riches naturally beget pride, love of the world, and every temper that is destructive of Christianity. Now, if there be no way to prevent this, Christianity is inconsistent with itself, and of consequence cannot stand, cannot continue long among any people; since wherever it generally prevails, it saps its own foundations.

But is there no way to prevent this—to continue Christianity among a people? Allowing that diligence and frugality must produce riches, is there no means to hinder riches from destroying the religion of those that possess them? I can see only one possible way; find out another who can. Do you gain all you can, and save all you can? Then you must in the nature of the case grow rich. Then if you have any desire to escape the damnation of hell, *give* all you can; otherwise I can have no more hope of your salvation, than of that of Judas Iscariot.

I call God to record upon my soul that I advise no more than I practise. I do, blessed be God, gain and save and give all I can. And so, I trust in God, I shall do, while the breath of God is in my nostrils. But what then? I count all things but loss for the excellency of the knowledge of Jesus my Lord! Still

> I give up every plea beside,
> "Lord, I am damned, but thou hast died!"[16]

Do you that possess more than food and raiment ask, "What shall we do? Shall we throw into the sea what God hath given us?" God forbid that you should! It is an excellent talent. It may be employed much to the glory of God. Your way lies plain before your face; if you have courage, walk in it. Having *gained,* in a right sense [i.e. without injuring either your own or your neighbour's body or soul], *all you can,* and *saved all you can;* in spite of nature and custom and worldly prudence, *give all you can.* I do not say, "Be a good Jew, giving a tenth of all you possess." I do not say, "Be a good Pharisee, giving a fifth of all your substance." I dare not advise you to give half of what you have; no, nor three-quarters; but all! Lift up your hearts, and you will see clearly in what sense this is to be done. If you desire to be "a faithful and wise steward," out of that portion of your Lord's goods which he has for the present lodged in your hands, but with the right of resumption whenever it pleaseth him, (1) Provide things needful for yourself; food to eat, raiment to put on; whatever nature moderately requires for preserving you both in health and strength. (2) Provide these for your wife, your children, your servants, or any others who pertain to your household. If when this is done there is an overplus left, then do good to "them that are of the household of faith." If there be an overplus still, "as you have opportunity, do good unto all men." In so doing, you *give all you can;* nay, in a sound sense, all you have. For all that is laid out in this manner is really given to God. You render unto God the things that are God's, not only by what you give to the poor, but also by that which you expend in providing things needful for yourself and your household.

O ye Methodists, hear the word of the Lord! I have a message from God to all men, but to *you* above all. For above forty years I have been a servant to you and to your fathers. And I have not been as a reed shaken with the wind. I have not varied in my testimony. I have testified to you the very same thing, from the first day even until now. But "who hath believed our report?" I fear not many rich. I fear there is need to apply to some of *you* those terrible words of the Apostle, "Go to now, ye rich men! Weep and howl for the miseries which shall come upon you. Your gold and silver is cankered, and the rust of them shall witness against you, and shall eat your flesh, as it were fire." Certainly it will, unless ye both save all you can and give all you can. But who of you hath considered this, since you first heard the will of the Lord concerning it? Who is now determined to consider and practise it? By the grace of God, begin today![17]

LEISURE AND PLEASURE

Leisure and I have taken leave of one another. I propose to be busy as long as I live, if my health is so long indulged to me.[18]

[The preceding is one of the first of Wesley's memorable sayings, often quoted since his time in an attempt to provoke Methodists, especially ministers, to greater busyness. But alongside it we should set the following.]

You do not at all understand my manner of life. Though I am always in haste, I am never in a hurry; because I never undertake any more work than I can go through with perfect calmness of spirit. It is true I travel four or five thousand miles in a year. But I generally travel alone in my carriage, and consequently am as retired ten hours a day as if I was in a wilderness. On other days I never spend less than three hours (frequently ten or twelve) in the day alone. Yet I find time to visit the sick and the poor; and I must do it if I believe the Bible, if I believe these are the marks whereby the Shepherd of Israel will know and judge his sheep at the great day; therefore, when there is time and opportunity for it, who can doubt but this is matter of absolute duty? When I was at Oxford, and lived almost like an hermit, I saw not how any busy man could be saved. I scarce thought it possible for a man to retain the Christian spirit amidst the noise and bustle of the world. God taught me better by my own experience. I had ten times more business in America (that is, at intervals) than ever I had in my life. But it was no hindrance to silence of spirit.[19]

Christianity is essentially a social religion, and to turn it into a solitary religion is indeed to destroy it. [By this] I mean not only that [Christianity] cannot subsist so well, but that it cannot subsist at all, without society—without living and conversing with other men. But if this be shown, then doubtless, to turn this religion into a solitary one is to destroy it.

Not that we can in anywise condemn the intermixing solitude or retirement with society. This is not only allowable, but expedient; nay, it is necessary, as daily experience shows, for every one that either already is, or desires to be, a real Christian. It can hardly be that we should spend one entire day in a continued intercourse with men, without suffering loss in our soul, and in some measure grieving the Holy Spirit of God. We have need daily to retire from the world, at least morning and evening, to converse with God, to commune more freely with our Father which is in secret. Nor indeed can a man of experience condemn even longer seasons of religious retirement, so they do not imply any neglect of the worldly employ wherein the providence of God has placed us.[20]

We cannot be always intent upon business. Both our bodies and minds require some relaxation. We need intervals of diversion from business. It will be necessary to be very explicit upon this head, as it is a point which has been much misunderstood.

Diversions are of various kinds. Some, which were formerly in great request, are now fallen into disrepute [such as hawking, broad-sword, quarterstaff, cudgelling, bear-baiting, bull-baiting]. It is not needful to say anything more of these foul remains of Gothic barbarity, than that they are a reproach, not only to all religion, but even to human nature. One would not pass so severe a censure on the sports of the field. Let those who have nothing better to do, still run foxes and hares out of breath. Neither need much be said about horseraces, till some man of sense will undertake to defend them. It seems a great deal more may be said in defence of seeing a serious tragedy. I could not do it with a clear conscience; at least not in an English theatre, the sink of all profaneness and debauchery; but possibly others can. I cannot say quite so much for balls or assemblies, which though more reputable than masquerades, yet must be allowed by all impartial persons to have exactly the same tendency. So undoubtedly have all public dancings. Of playing at cards I say the same as of seeing plays. I could not do it with a clear conscience. But I am not obliged to pass any sentence on those that are otherwise minded. I leave them to their own Master. To him let them stand or fall.[21]

I think you misunderstood what a Papist at Lisbon asked a Protestant, "Do you say I can't be saved in my religion?" He replied, "I say, Possibly you may be saved in that religion. But I could not." So I say in the present case to one that asks, "Can't I be saved if I dance or play at cards?" I answer, "Possibly you may be saved though you dance and play at cards. But I could not." So far you may safely speak; but no further. So much and no more I advise our preachers to speak. But I cannot advise them to speak this to unawakened people. It will only anger, not convince them. It is beginning at the wrong end. A plain preacher in London used to say, "If you take away his rattles from a child, he will be angry; nay, if he can he will scratch or bite you. But give him something better first and he will throw away the rattles of himself." Yet I do not remember that I call these things "innocent amusements." And you know we do not suffer any that use them to continue in our Society. Yet I make allowance for *those that are without.* Else I might send my own father and mother to hell, though they not only lived many years, but died in the full assurance of faith.[22]

I never myself bought a lottery ticket; but I blame not those that do.[23]

That bill was for the share of a lottery ticket. The remaining money you may pay to George Whitefield.[24]

CHEERFULNESS

You seem to apprehend that I believe religion to be inconsistent with cheerfulness and with a sociable, friendly temper. So far from it, that I am convinced, as true religion or holiness cannot be without cheerfulness, so steady cheerfulness, on the other hand, cannot be without holiness or true religion. And I am equally convinced that true religion has nothing sour, austere, unsociable, unfriendly in it; but on the contrary, implies the most winning sweetness, the most amiable softness and gentleness. Are you for having as much cheerfulness as you can? So am I. Do you endeavour to keep alive your taste for all the truly innocent pleasures of life? So do I likewise. Do you refuse no pleasure but what is a hindrance to some greater good or has a tendency to some evil? It is my very rule; and I know no other by which a sincere, reasonable Christian can be guided. In particular, I pursue this rule in eating, which I seldom do without much pleasure. And this I know is the will of God concerning me: that I should enjoy every pleasure that leads to my taking pleasure in him, and in such measure as most leads to it. I know that, as to every action which is naturally pleasing, it is his will that it should be so; therefore, in taking that pleasure so far as it tends to this end (of taking pleasure in God), I do his will. Though, therefore, that pleasure be in some sense distinct from the love of God, yet is the taking of it by no means distinct from his will.[25]

Good sort of men do not usually eat to excess; at least, not so far as to make themselves sick with meat, or to intoxicate themselves with drink. And as to the manner of taking it, it is usually innocent, mixed with a little mirth, which is said to help digestion. So far, so good. And provided they take only that measure of plain, cheap, wholesome food, which most promotes health of body and mind, there will be no cause of blame. Neither can I require you to take that advice of Mr. Herbert, though he was a good man:

> "Take thy meat; think it dust. Then eat a bit,
> And say with all, Earth to earth I commit."

This is too melancholy; it does not suit with that cheerfulness which is highly proper at a Christian meal. Permit me to illustrate this subject with a little story. The King of France, one day pursuing the chase, outrode all his company, who after seeking him some time, found him sitting in a cottage eating bread and cheese. Seeing them, he cried out,

"Where have I lived all my time? I never before tasted so good food in my life!" "Sire," said one of them, "you never had so *good sauce* before; for you were never hungry." Now it is true, hunger is a good sauce; but there is one that is better still: that is, thankfulness. Sure, that is the most agreeable food which is seasoned with this. And why should not yours at every meal? You need not then fix your eye on death; but receive every morsel as a pledge of eternal life. The Author of your being gives you, in this food, not only a reprieve from death, but an earnest that, in a little time, "death shall be swallowed up in victory."[26]

TWO ORDERS OF CHRISTIANS

It is the observation of an ancient writer that there have been from the beginning two orders of Christians. The one lived an innocent life, conforming in all things not sinful, to the customs and fashions of the world; doing many good works, abstaining from gross evils, and attending the ordinances of God. They endeavoured, in general, to have a conscience void of offence in their behaviour, but did not aim at any particular strictness, being in most things like their neighbours. The other Christians not only abstained from all appearance of evil, were zealous of good works in every kind, and attended all the ordinances of God, but likewise used all diligence to attain the whole mind that was in Christ, and laboured to walk in every point as their beloved Master. In order to do this they walked in a constant course of universal self-denial, trampling on every pleasure which they were not divinely conscious prepared them for taking pleasure in God. They took up their cross daily. They strove, they agonised without intermission, to enter in at the strait gate. This one thing they did, they spared no pains to arrive at the summit of Christian holiness; "leaving the first principles of the doctrine of Christ, to go on to perfection"; to "know all that love of God which passeth knowledge, and to be filled with all the fulness of God."

From long experience and observation I am inclined to think that whoever finds redemption in the blood of Jesus, whoever is justified, has then the choice of walking in the higher or the lower path. I believe the Holy Spirit at that time sets before him the "more excellent way," and incites him to walk therein; to choose the narrowest path in the narrow way; to aspire after the heights and depths of holiness—after the entire image of God. But if he does not accept this offer, he insensibly declines into the lower order of Christians. He still goes on in what may be called a good way, serving God in his degree, and finds mercy in the close of life, through the blood of the covenant.

I would be far from quenching the smoking flax—from discouraging those that serve God in a low degree. But I could not wish them to stop here. I would encourage them to come up higher. Without thundering hell and damnation in their ears, without condemning the way wherein they were, telling them it is the way that leads to destruction, I will endeavour to point out to them what is, in every respect,"a more excellent way."

Let it be well remembered, I do not affirm that all who do not walk in this way are in the high road to hell. But this much I must affirm, they will not have so high a place in heaven as they would have had if they had chosen the better part.[27]

THE SERVANT OF THE LORD

Behold the servant of the Lord!
   I wait thy guiding eye to feel,
To hear and keep thy every word,
   To prove and do thy perfect will,
Joyful from my own works to cease,
Glad to fulfil all righteousness.

Me, if thy grace vouchsafe to use,
   Meanest of all thy creatures, me:
The deed, the time, the manner choose,
   Let all my fruit be found of thee;
Let all my works in thee be wrought,
By thee to full perfection brought.

My every weak, though good design,
   O'errule, or change, as seems thee meet;
Jesus, let all my work be thine!
   Thy work, O Lord, is all complete,
And pleasing in thy Father's sight;
Thou only hast done all things right.

Here then to thee thy own I leave;
   Mould as thou wilt thy passive clay;
But let me all thy stamp receive,
   But let me all thy words obey,
Serve with a single heart and eye,
And to thy glory live and die.[28]

III

Growth in Grace

THE PURSUIT OF HOLINESS

None are or can be saved but those who are by faith made inwardly and outwardly holy. But this holy faith is the gift of God; and he is never straitened for time. He can as easily give this faith in a moment as in a thousand years. He frequently does give it on a death-bed, in answer to the prayer of believers, but rarely, if ever, to those who had continued unholy, upon the presumption that he would save them at last. But if he did, what unspeakable losers must they be! Could grief be in heaven, they would grieve to eternity, seeing everyone there shall receive his own reward according to his own labour.[1]

What, then, is that holiness which is the true "wedding garment" [Matt. 22:12], the only qualification for glory? "In Christ Jesus" (that is, according to the Christian Institution, whatever be the case of the heathen world) "neither circumcision availeth anything, nor uncircumcision; but a new creation"—the renewal of the soul "in the image of God wherein it was created." "In Christ Jesus neither circumcision availeth anything, nor uncircumcision, but faith which worketh by love." It first, through the energy of God, worketh love to God and all mankind; and by this love, every holy and heavenly temper—in particular, lowliness, meekness, gentleness, temperance, and long-suffering. "It is neither circumcision" (the attending on all the Christian ordinances) "nor uncircumcision" (the fulfilling of all heathen morality), but "the keeping the commandments of God," particularly those: "Thou shalt love the Lord thy God with all thy heart, and thy neighbour as thyself." In a word, holiness is the having "the mind that was in Christ," and the "walking as Christ walked."

Such has been my judgment for these threescore years, without any material alteration. Only, about fifty years ago I had a clearer view than before of justification by faith; and in this, from that very hour, I never varied, no, not an hair's breadth. Indeed, some have supposed that when I began to declare, "By grace ye are saved through faith," I retracted what I had before maintained: "Without holiness no man shall see the Lord." But it is an entire mistake. These Scriptures well consist with each other; the meaning of the former being plainly this: by faith we are saved from sin, and made holy. The imagination that faith *supersedes* holiness is the marrow of Antinomianism.

The sum of all this is: the God of love is willing to save all the souls that he has made. This he has proclaimed to them in his Word, together with the terms of salvation, revealed by the Son of his love, who gave his own life that they that believe in him might have everlasting life. And for these he has prepared a kingdom from the foundation of the world. But he will not force them to accept of it; he leaves them in the hands of their own counsel; he saith, "Behold, I set before you life and death, blessing and cursing. Choose life, that ye may live." Choose holiness by my grace, which is the way, the only way, to everlasting life.[2]

Q. Should we not have a care of depreciating justification, in order to exalt the state of full sanctification?

A. Undoubtedly we should beware of this; for one may insensibly slide into it.

Q. How shall we effectually avoid it?

A. When we are going to speak of entire sanctification, let us first describe the blessings of a justified state, as strongly as possible.[3]

Q. When does inward sanctification begin?

A. In the moment we are justified. The seed of every virtue is then sown in the soul. From that time the believer gradually dies to sin, and grows in grace. Yet sin remains in him, yea the seed of all sin, till he is sanctified throughout, in spirit, soul and body.

Q. In what manner should we preach entire sanctification?

A. Scarce at all to those who are not pressing forward. To those who are, always by way of promise; always drawing rather than driving.

Q. How should we wait for the fulfilling of the promise?

A. *In universal obedience; in keeping all the commnandments; in denying ourselves, and taking up our cross daily. These are the general means which God hath ordained for our receiving his sanctifying grace. The particular are, prayer, searching the Scripture, communicating and fasting.*[4]

> O come, and dwell in me,
>   Spirit of power within!
> And bring the glorious liberty
>   From sorrow, fear, and sin.
>   The seed of sin's disease,
>   Spirit of health, remove,
>   Spirit of finished holiness,
>   Spirit of perfect love.
>
> Hasten the joyful day
>   Which shall my sins consume,
> When old things shall be passed away,
>   And all things new become.
>   The original offence
>   Out of my soul erase,
>   Enter thyself, and drive it hence,
>   And take up all the place.[5]

STAGES IN THE SPIRITUAL LIFE

Love is the sum of Christian sanctificaion; it is the one *kind* of holiness which is found, only in various *degrees,* in the believers who are distinguished by St. John into "little children, young men, and fathers." The difference between one and the other lies properly in the degree of love. And herein there is as great a difference in the spiritual as in the natural sense, between fathers, young men, and babes.

Everyone that is born of God, though he be as yet only a"babe in Christ," has the love of God in his heart; the love of his neighbour; together with lowliness, meekness, and resignation. But all of these are then in a low degree, in proportion to the degree of his faith. The faith of a babe in Christ is weak, generally mingled with doubts or fears; with doubts, whether he has not deceived himself; or fear, that he shall not endure to the end. And if, in order to prevent those perplexing doubts, or to remove those tormenting fears, he catches hold of the opinion that a true believer cannot make shipwreck of the faith, experience will sooner or later show that it is merely the staff of a broken reed. But to return: in the same proportion as he grows in faith, he grows in holiness; he increases in love, lowliness, meekness, in every part of the image of God; till it pleases God, after he is thoroughly convinced of inbred sin, of the total corruption of his nature, to take it all away; to purify his heart and cleanse him from all unrighteousness; to fulfil that promise which he made first to his ancient people, and in them to the Israel of God in all ages: "I will circumcise thy heart, and the heart of thy seed, to love the Lord thy God with all thy heart, and with all thy soul."[6]

To those whom he styles *young men,* St. John says, "I have written unto you, young men, because ye are strong, and the word of God abideth in you, and ye have overcome the wicked one." These, the Apostle observes in the other verse, had "the word of God abiding in them." It may not improbably mean the pardoning word, the word which spake all their sins forgiven; in consequence of which, they have the consciousness of the divine favour without any intermission.

To these more especially we may apply the exhortation of the Apostle Paul: "Leaving the first principles of the doctrine of Christ," namely repentance and faith, "let us go on unto perfection." But in what sense are we to leave these principles? Not absolutely; for we are to retain both one and the other, the knowledge of ourselves and the knowledge of God, unto our lives' end. But only comparatively; not fixing, as we did at first, our whole attention upon them, thinking and talking perpetually of nothing else but either repentance or faith.

But what is the perfection here spoken of? It is not only a deliverance from doubts and fears, but from sin; from all inward as well as outward sin; from evil desires and evil tempers as well as from evil works. Yea and it is not only a negative blessing, a deliverance from all evil dispositions, implied in that expression, "I will circumcise thy heart"; but a positive one likewise; even the planting all good dispositions in their place, clearly implied in that other expression, "To love the Lord your God with all your heart, and with all your soul."

These are they to whom the Apostle John gives the venerable title of *Fathers,* who "have known him that is from the beginning," the eternal, Three-One God. One of these expresses himself thus: "I bear about with me an experimental verity and a plenitude of the presence of the ever-blessed Trinity." And those who are fathers in Christ, generally, though I believe not always, enjoy the plerophory, or "full assurance," of hope; having no more doubt of reigning with him in glory, than if they already saw him coming in the clouds of heaven. But this does not prevent their continually increasing in the knowledge and love of God. While they "rejoice evermore, pray without ceasing, and in everything give thanks," they pray in particular that they may never cease to watch, to deny themselves, to take up their cross daily, to fight the good fight of faith; and against the world, the devil, and their own manifold infirmities; till they are able to "comprehend, with all saints, what is the length, and breadth, and height, and depth, and to know that love of Christ which passeth knowledge"; yea, to be "filled with all the fulness of God."[7]

At many times our advances in the race that is set before us are clear and perceptible; at other times they are no more perceptible (at least to ourselves) than the growth of a tree. At any time you may pray—

> Strength and comfort from thy word,
> Imperceptibly supply.

And when you perceive nothing, it does not follow that the work of God stands still in your soul; especially while your desire is unto him, and while you choose him for your portion. He does not leave you to yourself, though it may seem so to your apprehension. The difference between temptation and sin is generally plain enough to all that are simple of heart; but in some exempt cases it is not plain. There we want the unction of the Holy One. Voluntary humility, calling every defect a sin, is not well-pleasing to God. Sin, properly speaking, is neither more nor less than "a voluntary transgression of a known law of God."[8]

It is a blessing indeed when God uncovers our hearts and clearly shows us what spirit we are of. But there is no manner of necessity that this self-knowledge should make us miserable. Certainly the highest degree of it is well consistent both with peace and joy in the Holy Ghost. Therefore how deeply soever you may be convinced of pride, self-will, peevishness, or any other inbred sin, see that you do not let go that confidence whereby you may still rejoice in God your Saviour. Some, indeed, have been quite unhappy, though they retained their faith, through desire on the one hand and conviction on the other. But that is nothing to you; you need never give up anything which you have already received.

It is a great thing to spend all our time to the glory of God. But you need not be scrupulous as to the precise time of reading and praying; I mean, as to the dividing it between one and the other. A few minutes one way or the other are of no great importance.

May He who loves you fill you with his pure love![9]

> Open, Lord, my inward ear,
>   And bid my heart rejoice;
> Bid my quiet spirit hear
>   Thy comfortable voice;
> Never in the whirlwind found
>   Or where earthquakes rock the place,
> Still and silent is the sound,
>   The whisper of thy grace.
>
> Show me, as my soul can bear,
>   The depth of inbred sin!
> All the unbelief declare,
>   The pride that lurks within;
> Take me, whom thyself hast bought,
>   Bring into captivity
> Every high aspiring thought,
>   That would not stoop to thee.
>
> Lord, my time is in thy hand,
>   My soul to thee convert:
> Thou canst make me understand,
>   Though I am slow of heart;
> Thine in whom I live and move,
>   Thine the work, the praise is thine;
> Thou art wisdom, power, and love,
>   And all thou art is mine.[10]

CHRISTIAN PERFECTION

"You make sinless perfection necessary after justification, in order to make us meet for glory." And who does not? Indeed, men do not agree in the time. Some believe it is attained before death; some, in the article of death; some, in an after-state, in the Mystic or Popish purgatory. But all writers whom I have ever seen till now (the Romish themselves not excepted) agree that we must be "fully cleansed from all sin" before we can enter into glory.[11]

The perfection I hold is so far from being contrary to the doctrine of our Church, that it is exactly the same which every Clergyman prays for every Sunday: "Cleanse the thoughts of our hearts by the inspiration of thy Holy Spirit, that we may perfectly love thee, and worthily magnify thy holy name." I mean neither more nor less than this.[12]

As to the *word* [perfection], it is scriptural; therefore neither you nor I can in conscience object against it, unless we would send the Holy Ghost to school, and teach Him to speak who made the tongue.

By that word I mean (as I have said again and again) "so loving God and our neighbour as to rejoice evermore, pray without ceasing, and in everything give thanks." He that experiences this is scripturally perfect. And if you do not yet, you may experience it. You surely will if you follow hard after it, for the Scripture cannot be broken.

What then does their arguing prove, who object against perfection? "Absolute and infallible perfection?" I never contended for it. *Sinless Perfection?* Neither do I contend for this, seeing the term is not scriptural. A perfection that perfectly fulfils the whole law, and so needs not the merit of Christ? I acknowledge none such—I do now, and always did protest against it.

"But is there not *sin* in those that are *perfect?*" I believe not; but be that as it may, they feel none, no temper but pure love, while they rejoice, pray, and give thanks continually. And whether sin is *suspended* or *extinguished,* I will not dispute; it is enough that they feel nothing but love. This you allow "we should daily press after"; and this is all I contend for.[13]

The perfection I teach is perfect love: loving God with all the heart; receiving Christ as Prophet, Priest and King, to reign alone over all our thoughts, words, and actions. The Papists neither teach nor believe this: give even the devil his due. They teach there is no perfection here on earth which is not consistent with venial sins; and among venial sins they commonly reckon simple fornication. Now I think this is so far from the perfection I teach that it does not come up to any but Mr. Relly's perfection. To say Christ will not reign alone in our hearts in this life will not enable us to give him all our hearts—this in my judgment is making him an half-Saviour. He can be no more if he does not quite save us from our sins. I pray, then, be not quite so peremptory. Who exalts Christ most? those who call on him to be the sole Monarch of the heart, or those who allow him only to share the power and to govern most of the thoughts and tempers? Who honour him most? those who believe he heals all our sicknesses, takes away all our ungodliness, or those who say he heals only the greater part of it, till death does what he cannot do? I know no creature (of us) who says, "Part of our salvation belongs to Christ and part to us." No; we all say Christ alone saves us from all sin; and your question is not about the Author but the measure of salvation. Both agree it is all Christ; but is it all salvation, or only half salvation he will give?[14]

You judge rightly. Perfect love and Christian liberty are the very same thing; and those two expressions are equally proper, being equally scriptural. "Nay, how can they and you mean the same thing? They say you insist on holiness in the creature, on good tempers, and sin destroyed." Most surely. And what is Christian liberty, but another word for holiness? And where is this liberty or holiness, if it is not in the creature? Holiness is the love of God and man, or the mind which was in Christ. Now, I trust the love of God is shed abroad in your heart, by the Holy Ghost which is given unto you. And if you are holy, is not that mind in you which was also in Christ Jesus?

And are not the love of God and our neighbour good tempers? And so far as these reign in the soul, are not the opposite tempers, worldly-mindedness, malice, cruelty, revengefulness, destroyed? Indeed, the unclean spirit, though driven out, may return and enter again; nevertheless he was driven out. I use the word *destroyed* because St. Paul does. *Suspended* I cannot find in my Bible. "But they say you do not consider this as the consequence of the power of Christ dwelling in us." Then what will they not say? My very words are: "None feel their need of Christ like these; none so entirely depend upon him. For Christ does not give light to the soul separate from, but in and with, himself. Hence his words are equally true of all men, in whatever state of grace they are: 'As the branch cannot bear fruit of itself, except it abide in the vine, no more can ye, except ye abide in me. Without' (or separate from) 'me, ye can do nothing.' For our perfection is not like that of a tree, which flourishes by the sap derived from its own root; but like that of a branch, which, united to the vine, bears fruit; but severed from it, is 'dried up and withered.'"[15]

> Give me the faith which can remove
>   And sink the mountain to a plain;
> Give me the child-like praying love,
>   Which longs to build thy house again;
> Thy love, let it my heart o'erpower
> And all my simple soul devour.
>
> I would the precious time redeem,
>   And longer live for this alone,

To spend, and to be spent, for them
  Who have not yet my Saviour known;
Fully on these my mission prove,
And only breathe, to breathe thy love.

Enlarge, inflame, and fill my heart
  With boundless charity divine;
So shall I all my strength exert,
  And love them with a zeal like thine;
And lead them to thy open side,
The sheep for whom their Shepherd died.[16]

THE IMPERFECTIONS OF THE PERFECT

Q. Do you affirm that this perfection excludes all infirmities, ignorance, and mistake?

A. I continually affirm quite the contrary, and aways have done so.

Q. But how can every thought, word, and work be governed by pure love, and the man be subject at the same time to ignorance and mistake?

A. I see no contradiction here: "A man may be filled with pure love, and still liable to mistake." Indeed I do not expect to be freed from actual mistakes, till this mortal puts on immortalilty. I believe this to be a natural consequence of the souls dwelling in flesh and blood. For we cannot now think at all, but by the mediation of those bodily organs which have suffered [from the Fall] equally with the rest of our frame. And hence we cannot avoid sometimes thinking wrong, till this corruptible shall have put on incorruption.

*   But we may carry this thought farther yet. A mistake in judgement may possibly occasion a mistake in practice. . . .Yet where every word and action springs from love, such a mistake is not properly a sin. However, it cannot bear the rigour of God's justice, but needs the atoning blood.*[17]

"You say, 'A mistake is not a sin, if love is the sole principle of action; yet it is a transgression of the perfect law.' Therefore, perfect love is not the perfect law!" Most sure. For by "the perfect law" I mean that given to Adam at his creation. But the loving God with all his heart was not the whole of that law. It implied abundantly more; even thinking, speaking and acting right in every instance, which he was then able, and therefore obliged, to do. But none of his descendants are able to do this [owing to the Fall]; therefore love is the fulfilling of their law.[18]

No man is able to perform the service which the Adamic law requires. And no man is obliged to perform it; God does not require it of any man. For Christ is the end of the Adamic as well as the Mosaic law. By his death he hath put an end to both; he hath abolished both the one and the other with regard to man; and the obligation to observe either the one or the other is vanished away. (I mean, it is not the condition either of present or future salvation.)

In the room of this, Christ has established another, namely the law of faith. Not everyone that doeth, but everyone that believeth, now receiveth righteousness in the full sense of the word; that is, he is justified, sanctified, and glorified.

Is love the fulfilling of this law? Unquestionably it is. The whole law under which we now are is fulfilled by love (Rom. 13:9f.). Faith working or animated by love is all that God now requires of man. He has substituted love in the room of angelic perfection.

And this distinction between the "law of faith" (or love) and the "law of works," is neither a subtle nor an unnecessary distinction. It is plain, easy, and intelligible to any common understanding. And it is absolutely necessary, to prevent a thousand doubts and fears, even in those who do "walk in love."[19]

Yet as, even in this case, there is not full conformity to the perfect law, so the most perfect do, on this very account, need the blood of atonement, and may properly, for themselves as well as for their brethren, say, "Forgive us our trespasses."

Q. *But if Church has put an end to that law, what need of any atoning for their transgressing it?*

A. *Observe in what sense he has put an end to it, and the difficulty vanishes. Were it nor for the abiding merit of his death, and his continual intercession for us, that law would condemn us still. These therefore we still need for every transgression of it.*[20]

To explain myself a little farther on this head: (1) not only sin properly so called (that is, a voluntary transgression of a known law), but sin improperly so called (that is, an involuntary transgression of a divine law, known or unknown), needs the atoning blood. (2) I believe there is no such perfection in this life as excludes these involuntary transgressions which I apprehend to be naturally consequent on the ignorance and mistakes inseparable from mortality. (3) Therefore sinless perfection is a term I never use, lest I should seem to contradict myself. (4) I believe a person filled with the love of God is still liable to these involuntary transgressions. (5) Such transgressions you may call sins, if you please. I do not, for the reasons above-mentioned.

Q. What advice would you give those that do and those that do not, call them so?

A. Let those that do not call them sins never think that themselves or any other persons are in such a state as that they can stand before infinite justice without a Mediator. This must argue either the deepest ignorance, or the highest arrogance and presumption.

Let those who do call them so beware how they confound these defects with sins properly so called. But how will they avoid it? How will these be distinguished from those, if they are all promiscuously called sins? I am much afraid, if we should allow any sins to be consistent with perfection, few would confine the idea to those defects concerning which only the assertion could be true.

Q. How shall we avoid setting perfection too high or too low?

A. By keeping to the Bible, and setting it just as high as the Scripture does. It is nothing higher and nothing lower than this—the pure love of God and man; the loving God with all our heart and soul, and our neighbour as ourselves. It is love governing the heart and life, running through at our tempers, words, and actions.[21]

Q. But do we not "in many things offend all," yea the best of us, even against the law?

A. In one sense we do not, while all our tempers, and thoughts, and words, and works spring from love. But in another we do, and shall do, more or less, as long as we main in the body. For neither love nor the "unction of the Holy One" makes us infallible. Therefore, through unavoidable defect of understanding, we cannot but mistake in many things. And these mistakes will frequently occasion something wrong, both in our temper, and words, and actions.

Q. Do we not then need Christ, even on this account?

A. The holiest of men still need Christ as their Prophet as "the light of the world." For he does not give them light, but from moment to moment. The instant he withdraws, all is darkness. They still need Christ as their King; for God does not give them a stock of holiness. But unless they receive a supply every moment nothing but unholiness would remain. They still need Christ as their Priest, to make atonement for their holy things. Even perfect holiness is acceptable to God only through Jesus Christ.

Q. May not, then, the very best of men adopt the dying martyr's confession: "I am in myself nothing but sin, darkness, hell; but thou art my light my holiness my heaven"?

A. Not exactly. But the best of men say. "Thou art my light, my holiness, my heaven. Through my union with thee, I am full of light, of holiness, and happiness. But if I were left to myself, I should be nothing but sin, darkness, hell."[22]

> Thou hidden Source of calm repose,
>   Thou all-sufficient Love divine,
> My help and refuge from my foes,
>   Secure I am, if thou art mine:
> And lo! from sin, and grief, and shame
> I hide me, Jesus, in thy name.
>
> Thy mighty name salvation is,
>   And keeps my happy soul above;
> Comfort it brings, and power, and peace,
>   And joy, and everlasting love:
> To me, with thy dear name, are given
> Pardon, and holiness, and heaven.
>
> Jesus, my all in all thou art;
>   My rest in toil, my ease in pain,
> The medicine of my broken heart,
>   In war my peace, in loss my gain,
> My smile beneath the tyrant's frown,
> In shame my glory and my crown;
>
> In want my plentiful supply,
>   In weakness my almighty power,
> In bonds my perfect liberty,
>   My light in Satan's darkest hour,
> In grief my joy unspeakable,
> My life in death, my heaven in hell.[23]

"TREASURE IN EARTHEN VESSELS"

What is this treasure [II Cor. 4:7] which Christian believers have? I say "believers"; for it is of these directly that the Apostle is here speaking. Part of this they have in common with other men, in the remains of the image of God. May we not conclude herein, first, an immaterial principle, a spiritual nature, endued with understanding, and affections, and a degree of liberty; of a self-moving, yea, and self-governing power? (Otherwise we were mere machines; stocks and stones.) And secondly, all that is vulgarly called natural conscience; implying some discernment of the difference between moral good and evil, with an approbation of the one, and disapprobation of the other, by an inward monitor excusing or accusing? Certainly, whether this is natural or superadded by the grace of God, it is found, at least in some small degree, in every child of man. Something of this is found in every human heart, passing sentence concerning good and evil, not only in all Christians, but in all Mahometans, all Pagans, yea, the vilest of savages.

Such treasure have all the children of men, more or less, even when they do not know God. But it is not these of whom the Apostle is here speaking; neither is this the treasure which is the subject of his discourse. The persons concerning whom he is here speaking are those that are born of God; those that "being justified by faith" have now redemption in the blood of Jesus, even the forgiveness of sins; those who enjoy that peace of God which passeth all understanding; whose soul doth magnify the Lord, and rejoice in him with joy unspeakable; and who feel the "love of God shed abroad in their hearts by the Holy Ghost which is given unto them." This, then, is the treasure which they have received: a faith of the operation of God; a peace which sets them above the fear of death, and enables them in everything to be content; an hope full of immortality, whereby they already "taste of the powers of the world to come"; the love of God shed abroad in their hearts, with love to every child of man, and a renewal in the whole image of God, in all righteousness and true holiness. This is properly and directly the treasure concerning which the Apostle is here speaking.

But this, invaluable as it is, "we have in earthen vessels." The word is exquisitely proper, denoting both the brittleness of the vessels, and the meanness of the matter they are made of. It directly means what we term earthenware; china, porcelain, and the like. How weak, how easily broken in pieces! Just such is the case with a holy Christian. We have the heavenly treasure in earthly, mortal, corruptible bodies. "Dust thou art," said the righteous Judge to his rebellious creature, till then incorruptible and immortal, "and to dust thou shalt return." From the moment that awful sentence was pronounced, the body received the sentence of death in itself; if not from the moment our first parents completed their rebellion by eating of the forbidden fruit. May we not probably conjecture that there was some quality naturally in this, which sowed the seeds of death in the human body, till then naturally incorruptible and immortal? Be this as it may, it is certain that from this time "the corruptible body has pressed down the soul." And no marvel, seeing the soul, during its vital union with the body, cannot exert any of its operations any otherwise than in union with the body, with its bodily organs. But all of these are more debased and depraved by the fall of man, than we can possibly conceive; and the brain, on which the soul more directly depends, not less than the rest of the body. Consequently, if these instruments, by which the soul works, are disordered, the soul itself must be hindered in its operations. Let a musician be ever so skilful, he will make but poor music if his instrument be out of tune. From a disordered brain (such as is, more or less, that of every child of man) there will necessarily arise confusedness of apprehension, showing itself in a thousand instances; false judgment, the natural result thereof; and wrong inferences; and from these, innumerable mistakes will follow, in spite of all the caution we can use. But mistakes in the judgment will frequently give occasion to mistakes in practice; they will naturally cause our speaking wrong in some instances, and acting wrong in others; nay, they may occasion not only wrong words or actions, but wrong tempers also. If I judge a man to be better than he really is, in consequence I really love him more than he deserves. If I judge another to be worse than he really is I shall in consequence love him less than he deserves. Now, both these are wrong tempers. Yet possibly it may not be in my power to avoid either the one or the other.

Such are the unavoidable consequences of having these "treasures in earthen vessels"! Not only death, and its forerunners—sickness, weakness, and pain, and a thousand infirmities—but likewise error, in ten thousand shapes, will be always ready to attack us. Such is the present condition of humanity! Such is the state of the wisest men! Lord, "what is man that thou art still mindful of him; or the son of man, that thou regardest him?"[24]

Even those who "stand fast in the liberty wherewith Christ has made them free," who are now really perfect in love, are still encompassed with infirmities. They may be dull of apprehension; they may have a natural heedlessness, or a treacherous memory; they may have too lively an imagination. And any of these may cause little improprieties, either in speech or behaviour, which though not sinful in themselves, may try all the grace you have; especially if you impute to perverseness of will (as it is very natural to do) what is really owing to defect of memory or weakness of understanding— [i.e.,] if these appear to you to be voluntary mistakes, which are really involuntary. So proper was the answer which a saint of God (now in Abraham's bosom) gave me some years ago, when I said, "Jenny, surely now your mistress and you can neither of you be a trial to the other, as God has saved you both from sin!" "O, Sir," said she, "if we are saved from sin, we still have infirmities enough to try all the grace that God has given us!"[25]

It will be eternally true, "If thou canst believe, all things are possible to him that believeth." Have this faith, and you have salvation. And this is the very thing you want. When this is joined with a strong understanding, it is well. But it may exist with a very weak one. This is the case with Mrs. W. . . , whose understanding is extremely weak; and yet she has strong faith, and such as exceedingly profits me; though I take knowledge that the treasure is in an earthen vessel. I see all that is of nature; but this does not hinder my rejoicing in that which is of grace. This is one branch of Christian simplicity. While reason, assisted from above, enables me to discern the precious from the vile, I make my full use of the former, without losing one moment in thinking upon the latter. Perhaps reason enlightened makes me simple. If I knew less of human nature (forgive me for talking so much of myself), I should be more apt to stumble at the weaknesses of it.[26]

> Our life is hid with Christ in God;
>   Our Life shall soon appear,
> And shed his glory all abroad
>   In all his members here.
>
> The heavenly treasure now we have
>   In a vile house of clay;
> But he shall to the utmost save,
>   And keep it to that day.
>
> Then let us lawfully contend,
>   And fight our passage through;
> Bear in our faithful minds the end,
>   And keep the prize in view.[27]

VARIETIES OF EXPERIENCE

Q. Can those who are perfect grow in grace?

A. Undoubtedly they can; and that not only while they are in the body, but to all eternity.

Q. Can they fall from it?

A. I am well assured they can; matter of fact puts this beyond dispute. Formerly we thought one saved from sin could not fall; now we know the contrary. There is no such height or strength of holiness as it is impossible to fall from. If there be any that cannot fall, this wholly depends on the promise of God.

Q. Can those who fall from this state recover it?

A. Why not? We have many instances of this also. Nay, it is an exceeding common thing for persons to lose it more than once before they are established therein.[28]

God will do his own work in his own manner, and exceeding variously in different persons. It matters not whether it be wrought in a more pleasing or painful manner, so it is wrought; so nature is subdued, pride and self-will dethroned, and the will of God done in us and by us. Therefore, trouble yourself not about the experience of others; God knows you, and let him do with you as he sees best.

I judge your late distress to be partly the effect of disease, but chiefly preternatural. In the Third Journal there is a case nearly parallel, only the symptoms were more severe. For in a moment Lucretia Smith felt such a cloud spread over her that she could not believe there was a God or an after-state. You did right to pray as you could pray; and this is the best method which can be taken in heaviness or darkness of any kind. Then, if sin be the cause, it will be discovered. But take care that you do not refuse any help; even rough speakers may be of service. Only spread what they say before the Lord, and he will turn it to good.[29]

You are hindered chiefly by not understanding the freeness of the gift of God. You are perpetually seeking for something in yourself, to move him to love and bless you. But it is not to be found there; it is in himself, and in the Son of his love. He did then give you a proof of this in that fresh evidence of pardon; and he is ready to give it you again to-day; for he is not weary of well-doing. But even after this, you may or you may not use the power which attends that peace. And if you ask for more power, it shall be given you; for you have an Advocate with the Father. O cast yourself upon him; learn more of that lesson:

Thy salvation to obtain,
Out of myself I go:

> Freely thou must heal my pain,
> Thy unbought mercy show.

How much of it may you find in this hour! Look up, and see redemption near![30]

All who expect to be sanctified at all, expect to be sanctified by faith. But meantime, they know that faith will not be given but to them that obey. Remotely, therefore, the blessing depends on our works; although immediately, on simple faith.[31]

Conviction is not condemnation. You may be convinced, yet not condemned; convinced of useless thoughts or words, and yet not condemned for them. You are condemned for nothing, if you love God, and continue to give him your whole heart.

Certainly, spiritual temptations will pass through your spirit; else you could not feel them. I believe I understand your state better than you do yourself. Do not perplex yourself at all about what you shall call it. You are a child of God, a member of Christ, an heir of the kingdom. What you have, hold fast (whatever name is given to it), and you shall have all that God has prepared for them that love him. Certainly you do need more faith; for you are a tender, sickly plant. But see,

> Faith while yet you ask is given:
> God comes down, the God and Lord
> That made both earth and heaven!

You cannot live on what he did yesterday. Therefore he comes today! He comes to destroy that tendency to levity, to severe judging, to anything that is not of God. Peace be with your spirit![32]

A will steadily and uniformly devoted to God is essential to a state of sanctification, but not an uniformity of joy or peace or happy communion with God. These may rise and fall in various degrees; nay, and may be affected either by the body or by diabolical agency, in a manner which all our wisdom can neither understand nor prevent. As to wanderings, you would do right well to consider the sermon on Wandering Thoughts:[33] you might likewise profit by Elizabeth Harper's *Journal*, whose experience much resembled yours, only she was more simple; and you may learn from her to go straight to God as a little child, and tell him all your troubles and hindrances and doubts, and desire him to turn them all to good. You are not sent to Waterford to be useless. Stir up the gift of God which is in you; gather together those that have been scattered abroad, and make up a band, if not a class or two. Your best way would be to visit from house to house. By this means you can judge of their conduct and dispositions in domestic life, and may have opportunity to speak to the young of the family. By motion you will contract warmth; by imparting life you will increase it in yourself.

As to the circumstance mentioned in the postscript of your last, I should think you would do well to exert yourself in that matter as much as possible. It will be a cross: take up that cross, bear your cross, and it will bear you; and if you do it with a single eye, it will be no loss to your soul.[34]

I advise you frequently to read and meditate upon the 13th chapter of the First Epistle to the Corinthians. There is the true picture of Christian perfection! Let us copy after it with all our might. I believe it might likewise be of use to you to read more than once the *Plain Account of Christian Perfection*. Indeed, what is it more or less than humble, gentle, patient love! It is undoubtedly our privilege to "rejoice evermore," with a calm, still, heart-felt joy. Nevertheless this is seldom long at one stay. Many circumstances may cause it to ebb and flow. This, therefore, is not the essence of religion, which is no other than humble, gentle, patient love. I do not know whether these are not all included in that one word resignation. For the highest lesson our Lord (as man) learned on earth was to say, "Not as I will, but as Thou wilt." May he confirm you more and more![35]

I know not that you have anything to do with fear. Your continual prayer should be for faith and love. I admired a holy man in France who, considering the state of one who was full of doubts and fears, forbade him to think of *his sins* at all, and ordered him to think only of the love of God in Christ. The fruit was, all his fears vanished away and he lived and died in the triumph of faith.

Faith is sight—that is, spiritual sight: and it is light and not darkness; so that the famous Popish phrase, "The darkness of faith," is a contradiction in terms. O beware of all that talk or write in that unscriptural manner, or they will perplex if not destroy you. I cannot find in my Bible any such sin as *legality*. Truly we have been often afraid where no fear was. I am not half *legal* enough, not enough *under the law* of love. Sometimes there is painful conviction of sin preparatory to full sanctification; sometimes a conviction that has far more pleasure than pain, being mixed with joyful expectation. Always there should be a gradual growth in grace, which need never be intermitted from the time we are justified. Don't wait, therefore, for pain or anything else, but simply for all-conquering faith.[36]

> The Lord will save his people here;
> In times of need their Help is near,
>   To all by sin and hell oppressed;
> And they that know thy name will trust
> In thee, who to thy promise just
>   Hast never left a soul distressed.

> The Lord is by his judgments known;
> He helps his poor afflicted one.
>   His sorrows all he bears in mind;
> The mourner shall not always weep,
> Who sows in tears in joy shall reap,
>   With grief who seeks with joy shall find.

> A helpless soul that looks to thee
> Is sure at last thy face to see,
>   And all thy goodness to partake;
> The sinner who for thee doth grieve,
> And longs, and labours to believe,
>   Thou never, never wilt forsake.[37]

THE PATIENCE OF HOPE

"The doctrine of Perfection," you say, "has perplexed me much since some of our preachers have placed it in so dreadful a light: one of them affirming, A believer till perfect is under the curse of God and in a state of damnation; another, If you die before you have attained it, you will surely perish."

By "perfection" I mean "perfect love," or the loving God with all our heart, so as to rejoice evermore, to pray without ceasing, and in everything to give thanks. I am convinced every believer may attain this; yet I do not say he is in a state of damnation or under the curse of God till he does attain. No, he is in a state of grace and in favour with God as long as he believes. Neither would I say, "If you die without it, you will perish"; but rather, Till you are saved from unholy tempers, you are not ripe for glory. There will, therefore, more promises be fulfilled in your soul before God takes you to himself.

Were you to ask, "What if I should die this moment?" I should answer, I believe you would be saved, because I am persuaded none that has faith can die before he is made ripe for glory. This is the doctrine which I continually teach, which has nothing to do with justification by works. Nor can it discourage any who have faith, neither weaken their peace, nor damp their joy in the Lord. True believers are not distressed hereby, either in life or in death; unless in some rare instance, wherein the temptation of the devil is joined with a melancholy temper.

Upon the whole, I observe that your great argument turns all along a mistake of the doctrine. Whatever warm expressions may drop from young men, we do not teach that any believer is under condemnation. So that all the inferences drawn from this supposition fall to the ground at once.[38]

Q. *Does not the harshly preaching perfection tend to bring believers into a kind of bondage, or slavish fear?*

A. *It does. Therefore we should always place it in the most amiable light, so that it may excite only hope, joy and desire.*

Q. *Why may we not continue in the joy of faith even till we are made perfect?*

A. *Why indeed! since holy grief does not quench this joy; since even while we are under the cross, while we deeply partake of the sufferings of Christ, we may rejoice with joy unspeakable.*

Q. *Do we not discourage believers from rejoicing evermore?*

A. *We ought not so to do. Let them all their life long rejoice unto God, so it be with reverence. And even if lightness or pride should mix with their joy, let us not strike at the joy itself—this is the gift of God—but at that lightness or pride, that the evil may cease and the good remain.*

Q. *Ought we to be anxiously careful about perfection, lest we should die before we have attained?*

A. *In no wise. We ought to be thus careful for nothing, neither spiritual nor temporal.*

Q. *But ought we not to be troubled on account of the sinful nature which still remains in us?*

A. *It is good for us to have a deep sense of this, and be much ashamed before the Lord. But this should only incite us the more earnestly to turn unto Christ every moment, and to draw light and life and strength from him, that we may go on conquering and to conquer. And therefore, when the sense of our sin most abounds, the sense of his love should much more abound.*

Q. *Will our joy or our trouble increase as we grow in grace?*

A. *Perhaps both. But without doubt our joy in the Lord will increase as our love increases.*

Q. *Is not the teaching believers to be continually poring upon their inbred sin the ready way to make them forget that they were purged from their former sins?*

A. *We find by experience it is; or to make them undervalue and account it a little thing; whereas indeed (though there are still greater gifts behind), this is inexpressibly great and glorious.*[39]

One point I advise you to hold fast, and let neither men nor devils tear it from you. You are a child of God; you are justified freely, through the redemption which is in Christ Jesus. Your sins are forgiven! Cast not away that confidence, which hath great recompence of reward.

Now, can any be justified, but by faith? None can. Therefore you are a believer; you have faith in Christ; you know the Lord; you can say, "My Lord and my God." And whoever denies this may as well deny that the sun shines at noonday.

> Yet still ten thousand lusts remain,
>   And vex your soul, absolved from sin;
> Still rebel nature strives to reign,
>   And you are all unclean, unclean!

This is equally clear and undeniable. And this is not only your experience, but the experience of a thousand believers besides, who yet are sure of God's favour, as of their own existence. To cut off all doubt on this head, I beg you to give another serious reading to those two sermons, "Sin in Believers," and "The Repentance of Believers."[40]

"But is there no help? Is there no deliverance, no salvation from this inbred enemy?" Surely there is; else many great and precious promises must fall to the ground. "I will sprinkle clean water upon you and ye shall be clean; from all your filthiness and from all your idols will I cleanse you." "I will circumcise thy heart" (from all sin), "to love the Lord thy God with all thy heart, and with all thy soul." This I term sanctification (which is both an instantaneous and a gradual work), or perfection, the being perfected in love, filled with love, which still admits of a thousand degrees. But I have no time to throw away in contending for words; especially where the thing is allowed. And you allow the whole thing which I contend for: an entire deliverance from sin, a recovery of the whole image of God, the loving God with all our heart, soul and strength. And you believe God is able to give you this; yea, to give it you in an instant. You trust he will. O hold fast this also; this blessed hope which he has wrought in your heart! And with all zeal and diligence confirm the brethren (1) in holding fast that whereto they have attained; namely, the remission of all their sins, by faith in a bleeding Lord; (2) in expecting a second change, whereby they shall be saved from all sin and perfected in love.

If they like to call this "receiving the Holy Ghost," they may. Only, the phrase in that sense is not scriptural, and not quite proper; for they all "received the Holy Ghost" when they were justified. God then "sent forth the Spirit of his Son into their hearts, crying, Abba, Father."

O Joseph, keep close to the Bible, both as to sentiment and expression![41]

The plerophory (or full assurance) of faith is such a divine testimony that we are reconciled to God as excludes all doubt and fear concerning it. This refers only to what is present. The plerophory (or full assurance) of hope is a divine testimony that we shall endure to the end; or more directly, that we shall enjoy God in glory. This is by no means essential to or inseparable from perfect love. It is sometimes given to those that are not perfected in love, as it was to Mr. Grimshaw. And it is not given (at least not for some time) to many that are perfected in love. I do not say you ought not to pray for it; but I think you may, only with absolute resignation. In this, as in all things, "His manner and his time are best."[42]

> Come, let us anew
> Our journey pursue,
> Roll round with the year,
> And never stand still till the Master appear.

His adorable will
Let us gladly fulfil,
And our talents improve,
By the patience of hope and the labour of love.

Our life is a dream
Our time as a stream
Glides swiftly away,
And the fugitive moment refuses to stay.

The arrow is flown,
The moment is gone;
The millennial year
Rushes on to our view, and eternity's here.

O that each in the day
Of His coming may say:
I have fought my way through,
I have finished the work thou didst give me to do!

O that each from his Lord
May receive the glad word:
Well and faithfully done;
Enter into my joy, and sit down on my throne![43]

IV

Looking Towards Eternity

THE SHADOW OF DEATH

"O that death" (said a gentleman of large possessions, of good health, and a cheerful natural temper), "I do not love to think of it! It comes in and spoils all!" So it does indeed. It comes with its "miscreated front" and spoils all your mirth, diversions, pleasures! It turns all into the silence of a tomb, into rottenness and dust; and many times it will not stay till the trembling hand of old age beckons to it; but it leaps upon you while you are in the dawn of life, in the bloom and strength of your years.

> The morning flowers display their sweets,
>   And gay their silken leaves unfold,
> Unmindful of the noontide heats,
>   And fearless of the evening cold.
> Nipped by the wind's unkindly blast,
>   Parched by the sun's directed ray,
> The momentary glories waste,
>   The short-lived beauties die away.

And where are you then? Does your soul disperse and dissolve into the common air? Or does it share the fate of its former companion [the body], and moulder into dust? Or does it remain conscious of its own existence, in some distant, unknown world? It is all unknown! A black, dreary, melancholy scene! Clouds and darkness rest upon it.

But the case is far otherwise with a Christian. To him life and immortality are brought to light. His eye pierces through the vale of the shadow of death, and sees into the glories of eternity. His view does not terminate on that black line, "the verge 'twixt mortal and immortal

187

being," but extends beyond the bounds of time and place, to the house of God eternal in the heavens. Hence he is so far from looking upon death as an enemy that he longs to feel his welcome embrace. He groans (but they are pleasing groans) to have mortality swallowed up of life.

Perhaps you will say, "But all this is a dream. He is only in a fool's paradise!" Supposing he be, it is a pleasing dream. *Maneat mentis gratissimus error* ["Let the mind's pleasant error remain"]. If he is only in a fool's paradise, yet it is a paradise; while you are wandering in a wide, weary, barren world. Be it folly, his folly gives him that present happiness which all your wisdom cannot find. So that he may now turn the tables upon you and say,

> Whoe'er can ease by folly get,
> With safety may despise
> The wretched unenjoying wit,
> The miserable wise.

Such unspeakable advantage (even if there is none beyond death) has a Christian over an Infidel! It is true, he has given up some pleasures before he could attain to this. But what pleasures? Those of eating till he is sick, till he weakens a strong, or quite destroys a weak, constitution. He has given lip the pleasure of drinking a man into a beast, and that of ranging from one worthless creature to another, till he brings a canker upon his estate, and perhaps rottenness into his bones. But in lieu of these, he has now (whatever may be hereafter) a continual serenity of mind, a constant evenness and composure of temper, "a peace which passeth all understanding." He has learned in every state wherein he is, therewith to be content; nay, to give thanks, as being clearly persuaded, it is better for him than any other. He feels continual gratitude to his Supreme Benefactor, Father of Spirits. Parent of Good; and tender, disinterested benevolence to all the children of this common Father. May the Father of your spirit, and the Father of our Lord Jesus Christ, make you such a Christian! May he work in your soul a divine conviction of things not discerned by eyes of flesh and blood! May he give you to see Him that is invisible, and to taste of the powers of the world to come! May he fill you with all peace and joy in believing, that you may be happy in life, in death, in eternity![1]

Hark! a voice divides the sky,
  Happy are the faithful dead!
In the Lord who sweetly die,
  They from all their toils are freed;
Them the Spirit hath declared
  Blest, unutterably blest;
Jesus is their great reward,
  Jesus is their endless rest.

Followed by their works, they go
  Where their Head hath gone before;
Reconciled by grace below,
  Grace hath opened mercy's door;
Justified through faith alone,
  Here they knew their sins forgiven,
Here they laid their burden down,
  Hallowed, and made meet for heaven.

Who can now lament the lot
  Of a saint in Christ deceased?
Let the world, who know us not,
  Call us hopeless and unblest;
When from flesh the spirit freed
  Hastens homeward to return,
Mortals cry, "A man is dead!"
  Angels sing, "A child is born!"[2]

THE INTERMEDIATE STATE

What kind of existence shall I then enter upon, when my spirit has launched out of the body? What can we know of those innumerable objects which properly belong to the invisible world which mortal "eye hath not seen nor ear heard, neither hath it entered into our hearts to conceive"? What a scene will then be opened, when the regions of Hades are displayed without a covering! Our English translators seem to have been much at a loss for a word to render this. Indeed, two hundred years ago, it was tolerably expressed by the word *hell,* which then signified much the same with the word *hades,* namely, the invisible world. Accordingly, by Christ descending into hell, they meant, his body remained in the grave, his soul remained in Hades (which is the receptacle of separate spirits) from death to the resurrection. Here we cannot doubt but the spirits of the righteous are inexpressibly happy. They are, as St. Paul expresses it, "with the Lord"; favoured with so intimate a communion with him, as "is far better" than whatever the chief of the Apostles experienced while in this world. On the other hand, we learn from our Lord's own account of Dives and Lazarus that the rich man, from the moment he left the world, entered into a state of torment. And "there is a great gulf fixed" in Hades, between the place of the holy and that of unholy spirits, which it is impossible for either the one or the other to pass over.

But who can inform us, in what part of the universe Hades is situated—this abode of both happy and unhappy spirits, till they are reunited to their bodies? It has not pleased God to reveal anything concerning it in the Holy Scripture; and consequently, it is not possible for us to form any judgment, or even conjecture, about it. Neither are we informed how either the one or the other are employed, during the time of their abode there. Yet may we not probably suppose that the Governor of the world may sometimes permit wicked souls "to do his gloomy errands in the deep," or perhaps, in conjunction with evil angels, to inflict vengeance on wicked men? Or will many of them be shut up in chains of darkness, unto the judgment of the great day? In the meantime, may we not probably suppose that the spirits of the just, though generally lodged in Paradise, yet may sometimes, in conjunction with the holy angels, minister to the heirs of salvation? May they not

> Sometimes, on errands of love,
> Revisit their brethren below?

It is a pleasing thought that some of these human spirits, attending us with, or in the room of, angels, are of the number of those that were dear to us while they were in the body.

But be this as it may, it is certain, human spirits swiftly increase in knowledge, in holiness, and in happiness; conversing with all the wise and holy souls that lived in all ages and nations from the beginning of the world; with angels and archangels, to whom the children of men are not more than infants; and above all, with the eternal Son of God, "in whom are hid all the treasures of wisdom and knowledge."

And shall not we then, as far as angels ken, survey the bounds of creation, and see every place where the Almighty?

> Stopped his rapid wheels, and said,
> "This be thy just circumference, O world"?

Yea, shall we not be able to move, quick as thought, through the wide realms of uncreated night? Above all, the moment we step into eternity, shall we not feel ourselves swallowed up of Him who is in this and every place—who filleth heaven and earth? It is only the veil of flesh and blood which now hinders us from perceiving that the great Creator cannot but fill the whole immensity of space. He is every moment above us, beneath us, and on every side. Indeed, in this dark abode, this land of shadows, this region of sin and death, the thick cloud which is interposed between conceals him from our sight. But the veil will disappear; and he will appear in unclouded majesty, "God over all, blessed for ever!"[3]

> Come on, my partners in distress,
> My comrades through the wilderness,
>   Who still your bodies feel;
> Awhile forget your griefs and fears,
> And look beyond this vale of tears,
>   To that celestial hill.
>
> Beyond the bounds of time and space,
> Look forward to that heavenly place,
>   The saints' secure abode:
> On faith's strong eagle-pinions rise,
> And force your passage to the skies,
>   And scale the mount of God.
>
> That great mysterious Deity
> We soon with open face shall see;
>   The beatific sight
> Shall fill heaven's sounding courts with praise
> And wide diffuse the golden blaze
>   Of everlasting light.
>
> The Father shining on his throne,
> The glorious co-eternal Son,
>   The Spirit, one and seven,
> Conspire our rapture to complete;
> And lo! we fall before his feet,
>   And silence heightens heaven.[4]

A PROSPECT OF PARADISE

It is, indeed, very generally supposed that the souls of good men, as soon as they are discharged from the body, go directly to heaven; but this opinion has not the least foundation in the oracles of God. On the contrary, our Lord says to Mary, after the resurrection, "Touch me not; for I am not yet ascended to my Father" in heaven. But he had been in paradise, according to his promise to the penitent thief: "This day shalt thou be with me in paradise." Hence it is plain, that paradise is not heaven. It is indeed (if we may be allowed the expression) the ante-chamber of heaven, where the souls of the righteous remain till, after the general judgment, they are received into glory.[5]

St. Paul teaches that it is in heaven we are to be joined with "the spirits of just men made perfect," in such a sense as we cannot be on earth or even in paradise. In paradise the souls of good men rest from their labours and are with Christ from death to the resurrection. This bears no resemblance at all to the Popish purgatory, wherein wicked men are supposed to be tormented in purging fire till they are sufficiently purified to have a place in heaven. But we believe (as did the ancient Church) that none suffer after death but those who suffer eternally. We believe that we are to be *here* saved from sin and enabled to love God with all our heart.[6]

In what part of the universe [paradise] is situated, who can tell or even conjecture, since it has not pleased God to reveal anything concerning it? But we have no reason to think [those blessed spirits] are confined to this place, or indeed to any other. May we not rather say that, "servants of his,"as well as the holy angels, they "do his pleasure," whether among the inhabitants of the earth or in any other part of his dominions? And as we easily believe that they are swifter than the light, even as swift as thought, they are well able to traverse the whole universe in the twinkling of an eye, either to execute the divine commands or to contemplate the works of God. What a field is here open before them! And how immensely may they increase in knowledge, while they survey his works of creation or providence, or his manifold wisdom in the Church! What depth of wisdom, of power, and of goodness do they discover in his methods of "bringing many sons to glory"! Especially while they converse on any of these subjects with the illustrious dead of ancient days!

Meantime, how will they advance in holiness; in the whole image of God wherein they were created; in the love of God and man; gratitude to their Creator and benevolence to all their fellow-creatures! Yet it does not follow (what some earnestly maintain) that this general benevolence will at all interfere with that peculiar affection which God himself implants for our relations, friends and benefactors. O no! Had you stood by his bed-side, when that dying saint was crying out, "I have a father and mother gone to heaven" (to paradise, the receptacle of happy spirits); "I have ten brothers and sisters gone to heaven; and now I am going to them that am the eleventh! Blessed be God that I was born!" would you have replied, "What if you are going to them? They will be no more to you than any other persons; for you will not know them"? *Not know them!* Nay, does not all that is in you recoil at that thought?

Indeed, sceptics may ask, "How do disembodied spirits know each other?" I answer plainly, I cannot tell; but I am certain that they do. This is as plainly proved from one passage of Scripture as it could be from a thousand. Did not Dives and Lazarus know each other in Hades, even afar off? Can we doubt, then, whether the souls that are together in paradise shall know one another? The Scripture, therefore, clearly decides this question. And so does the very reason of the thing; for we know every holy temper which we carry with us into paradise will remain in us for ever. But such is gratitude to our benefactors. This, therefore, will remain forever. And this implies that the knowledge of our benefactors will remain, without which it cannot exist.[7]

THE COMMUNION OF SAINTS

It has in all ages been allowed that the communion of saints extends to those in Paradise as well as those upon earth, as they are all one body united under one Head. And

> Can death's interposing tide
> Spirits one in Christ divide?

But it is difficult to say either what kind or what degree of union may be between them. It is not improbable their fellowship with us is far more sensible than ours with them. Suppose any of them are present, they are hid from our eyes, but we are not hid from *their* sight. They no doubt clearly discern all our words and actions, if not all our thoughts too; for it is hard to think these walls of flesh and blood can intercept the view of an angelic being. But we have in general only a faint and indistinct perception of their presence, unless in some particular instances, where it may answer some gracious ends of Divine Providence. Then it may please God to permit that they should be perceptible, either by some of our outward senses or by an internal sense for which human language has not any name. But I suppose this is not a common blessing. I have known but few instances of it. To keep up constant and close communion with God is the most likely means to obtain this also.[8]

There is nothing strange in a particular union of spirit between two persons who truly fear God. It is not at all uncommon: within a few years I have known many instances of this kind. And I see not any reason why this union should be destroyed by death: I cannot conceive it is. I have myself, since her death, found a wonderful union of spirit with Fanny Cooper; and have sometimes looked on one or the other side, not knowing whether I should not see her. So you may remember Mr. de Renty says to his friends, "To die is not to be lost: our union with each other shall hereafter be more complete than it can be here." And I have heard my mother say that she had many times been "as sensible of the presence of the spirit of my grandfather as she could have been if she had seen him standing before her face."[9]

And how much will that add to the happiness of those spirits who are already discharged from the body, that they are permitted to minister to those whom they have left behind! An indisputable proof of this we have in the twenty-second chapter of the Revelation. When the Apostle fell down to worship the glorious spirit which he seems to have mistaken for Christ, he told him plainly, "I am of thy fellow-servants the prophets"; not God, not an angel, but a human spirit. And in how many ways may they "minister to the heirs of salvation!" Sometimes by counteracting wicked spirits, whom we cannot resist because we cannot see them; sometimes by preventing our being hurt by men, or beasts, or inanimate creatures. How often may it please God to answer the prayer of good Bishop Ken—

> O may thine angels, while I sleep,
> Around my bed their vigils keep;
> Their love angelical instil;

Stop all the avenues of ill!
May they celestial joys rehearse,
And thought to thought with me converse;
Or, in my stead, the whole night long,
Sing to my God a grateful song!

And may not the Father of spirits allot this office jointly to angels, and human spirits waiting to be made perfect?

It may indeed be objected that God has no need of any subordinate agents, of either angelical or human spirits, to guard his children in their waking or sleeping hours; seeing "He that keepeth Israel doth neither slumber nor sleep."And certainly he is able to preserve them by his own immediate power; yea and he is able, by his own immediate power only, without any instruments at all, to supply the wants of all his creatures both in heaven and earth. But it is and ever was his pleasure, not to work by his own immediate power only, but chiefly by subordinate means, from the beginning of the world. And how wonderfully is his wisdom displayed in adjusting all these to each other! So that we may well cry out, "O Lord, how manifold are thy works! In wisdom hast thou made them all!"[10]

Come, let us join our friends above
   That have obtained the prize,
And on the eagle wings of love
   To joys celestial rise:
Let all the saints terrestrial sing,
   With those to glory gone:
For all the servants of our King,
   In earth and heaven, are one.

One family we dwell in him,
   One Church, above, beneath,
Though now divided by the stream,
   The narrow stream of death:
One army of the living God,
   To his command we bow;
Part of his host have crossed the flood,
   And part are crossing now.

Ten thousand to their endless home
   This solemn moment fly;
And we are to the margin come,
   And we expect to die;

Ev'n now by faith we join our hands
    With those that went before,
And greet the blood-besprinkled bands
    On the eternal shore.

Our spirits too shall quickly join,
    Like theirs with glory crowned,
And shout to see our Captain's sign,
    To hear his trumpet sound.
O that we now might grasp our Guide!
    O that the word were given!
Come, Lord of hosts, the waves divide,
    And land us all in heaven.[11]

JUDGMENT

Q. Do not some of our assistants preach too much of the wrath, and too little of the love, of God?

A. We fear they have leaned to that extreme; and hence some of their hearers may have lost the joy of faith.

Q. Need we ever preach the terrors of the Lord to those who know they are accepted of him?

A. No. It is folly so to do; for love is to them the strongest of all motives.[12]

But may not love itself constrain us to lay before men "the terrors of the Lord"? And is it not better that sinners "should be terrified now, than that they should sleep on, and awake in hell"? I have known exceeding happy effects of this, even upon men of strong understanding; yet I agree with you, that there is little good to be done by "the profuse throwing about hell and damnation."[13]

We shall all, I that speak and you that hear, "stand at the judgment-seat of Christ." There we are to give an account of all our works, from the cradle to the grave; of all our words; of all our desires and tempers, all the thoughts and intents of our hearts; of all the use we have made of our various talents, whether of mind, body, or fortune, till God said, "Give an account of thy stewardship, for thou mayest be no longer steward." In [an earthly] court it is possible some who are guilty may escape for want of evidence; but there is no want of evidence in that court. All men, with whom you had the most secret intercourse, who were privy to all your designs and actions, are ready before your face. So are all the spirits of darkness, who inspired evil designs and assisted in the execution of them. So are all the angels of God; those eyes of the Lord that run to and fro over all the earth, who watched over your soul and laboured for your good, so far as you would permit. So is your own conscience, a thousand witnesses in one, now no more capable of being either blinded or silenced, but constrained to know and to speak the naked truth touching all your thoughts and words and actions. And is conscience as a thousand witnesses? Yea, but God is as a thousand consciences! O who can stand before the face of the great God, even our Saviour Jesus Christ!

"What manner of persons then ought we to be, in all holy conversation and godliness!" We know it cannot be long before the Lord will descend with the voice of the archangel and the trumpet of God; when every one of us shall appear before him, and give account of his own works. "Wherefore, beloved, seeing ye look for these things," seeing ye know he will come and will not tarry, "be diligent, that ye may be found of him in peace, without spot and blameless." Why should ye not? My should one of you be found on the left hand at his appearing? He willeth not that any should perish, but that all should come to repentance; by repentance to faith in a bleeding Lord; by faith to spotless love, to the full image of God renewed in the heart and producing all holiness of conversation. Can you doubt of this, when you remember the Judge of all is likewise the Saviour of all? Hath he not bought you with his own blood, that ye might not perish, but have everlasting life? O make proof of his mercy rather than his justice, of his love rather than the thunder of his power![14]

> Thou Judge of quick and dead,
> Before whose bar severe,
> With holy joy, or guilty dread,
> We all shall soon appear:
> Our cautioned souls prepare
> For that tremendous day,
> And fill us now with watchful care,
> And stir us up to pray.
>
> To pray, and wait the hour,
> That awful hour unknown,
> When robed in majesty and power,

Thou shalt from heaven come down.
The immortal Son of Man,
To judge the human race,
With all thy Father's dazzling train,
With all thy glorious grace.

O may we thus be found
Obedient to his word,
Attentive to the trumpet's sound,
And looking for our Lord.
O may we thus ensure
A lot among the blest;
And watch a moment to secure
An everlasting rest.[15]

THE FATEFUL CHOICE

What is the choice which God proposes to his creatures? It is not, "Will you be happy threescore years, and then miserable for ever; or will you be miserable threescore years, and then happy for ever?" It is not, "Will you have first a temporary heaven, and then hell eternal; or will you have first a temporary hell, and then heaven eternal?" But it is simply this: "Will you be miserable threescore years, and miserable ever after; or will you be happy threescore years, and happy ever after? Will you have a foretaste of heaven now, and then heaven for ever; or will you have a foretaste of hell now, and then hell for ever? Will you have two hells, or two heavens?"[16]

Sir, you put me in mind of an eminent man who, preaching at St. James's said, "If you do not repent, you will go to a place which I shall not name before this audience." I cannot promise so much, either in preaching or writing, before any audience or to any person whatsoever. Yet I am not conscious of doing this very often—of "profusely flinging about everlasting fire"—though it is true I mentioned it in my last letter to you, as I have done now a second time; and perhaps I may mention it yet again. For, to say the truth, I desire to have both heaven and hell ever in my eye, while I stand on this isthmus of life between these two boundless oceans; and I verily think the daily consideration of both highly becomes all men of reason and religion.[17]

Thou God of glorious majesty,
   To thee, against myself, to thee,
   A worm of earth I cry;
A half-awakened child of man,
An heir of endless bliss or pain;
   A sinner born to die!

Lo! on a narrow neck of land,
   'Twixt two unbounded seas I stand,
   Secure, insensible;
A point of time, a moment's space,
Removes me to that heavenly place,
   Or shuts me up in hell.

O God, mine inmost soul convert!
   And deeply on my thoughtful heart
   Eternal things impress:
Give me to feel their solemn weight,
And tremble on the brink of fate,
   And wake to righteousness.[18]

A FORETASTE OF HELL

Are you then to go to heaven or hell? It must be either to one or the other. I pray God you may not go to hell! For who can dwell with everlasting burnings? Who can bear the fierceness of that flame, without even a drop of water to cool his tongue? Yea, and that without end; for as the worm dieth not, so the fire is not quenched. No; whoever is once cast into that lake of fire shall be tormented day and night for ever and ever. O eternity! eternity! Who can tell the length of eternity? I warn thee now, before God and the Lord Jesus Christ, that thou come not into that place of torment!

But alas! Is not hell now begun in thy soul? Does thy conscience never awake? Hast thou no remorse at any time; no sense of guilt; no dread of the wrath of God? Why, these (if thou art not saved from them in this life) are the worm that never dieth. And what else is thy carnal mind, thy enmity against God, thy foolish and hurtful lusts, thy inordinate affections? What are pride, envy, malice, revenge? Are they not vipers gnawing thy heart? May they not well be called the dogs of hell? Canst thou be out of hell while these are in thy soul, while they are tearing it in pieces, and there is none to help thee? Indeed, they are not fully let loose upon thee; and while thou seest the light of the sun, the things of the world that surround thee, or the pleasures of sense, divert thy thoughts from them. But when thou canst eat and drink no more, when the earth with the works thereof is burned up, when the sun is fallen from heaven and thou art shut up in utter darkness, what a state wilt thou be in then! Mayest thou never try! Seek thou a better habitation, a house of God, eternal in the heavens.

Will you reply to all this: "But I am a soldier, and have therefore nothing to do with these things?" Hold! Have soldiers nothing to do with death? How so? Do soldiers never die? Or do you fancy a soldier has nothing to do with judgment? Will you say, then, (as poor Captain Uratz did when he was asked, a few minutes before his death, whether he had made his peace with God), "I hope God will deal with me like a gentleman"? But God said unto him, "Thou fool! I will deal with thee as with all mankind. There is no respect of persons with me. I reward every man according to his works." Thou also shalt receive of the righteous Judge according to the things which thou hast done in the body. Death levels all; it mingles in one dust the gentleman, soldier, clown, and beggar; it makes all these distinctions void. When life ends, so do they. Holy or unholy is the one question then. Lo! the books are opened that all the dead may be judged according to the things that are written therein. O may thy name be found written in the book of life!

For have soldiers nothing to do with hell? Why, then, is it so often in thy mouth? Dost thou think God does not hear the prayer? And how often hast thou prayed to him to damn thy soul? Is his ear waxed heavy that it cannot hear? I fear thou wilt find it otherwise. For sin is the high road to hell. And have soldiers nothing to do with sin? Alas! how many of you wallow therein, yea and glory in your shame! How do you labour to work out your own damnation! O, poor work, for poor wages! The wages of sin is death; the wages of cursing, of swearing, of taking the name of God in vain, of Sabbath-breaking, drunkenness, revenge, of fornication, adultery, and all uncleanness. Now, art thou clear of these? Does not thy own heart smite thee? Art thou not condemned already? What voice is that which sounds in thine ears? Is it not the voice of God? "Shall I not visit for these things? saith the Lord."

But if there were no other hell, thou hast hell enough within thee. An awakened conscience is hell. Pride, envy, wrath, hatred, malice, revenge—what are these but hell upon earth? And how often art thou tormented in these flames—flames of lust, envy, or proud wrath! Are not these to thy soul, when blown up to the height, as it were a lake of fire, burning with brimstone? Flee away, before the great gulf is fixed; escape, escape for thy life! If thou hast not strength, cry to God, and thou shalt receive power from on high; and he whose name is rightly called Jesus, shall save thee from thy sins.

And why should he not? Has a soldier nothing to do with heaven? God forbid that you should think so! Heaven was designed for you also. God so loved your soul, that he gave his only-begotten Son, that you believing in him might not perish, but have everlasting life. Receive then, the kingdom prepared for you from the foundation of the world! This, this is the time to make it sure; this short, uncertain day of life. Arise, and call upon thy God. Call upon the Lamb, who taketh away the sins of the world, to take away thy sins. Believe in him and thou shalt be saved.[19]

O believe the record true,
   God to you his Son hath given!
Ye may now be happy too,
   Find on earth the life of heaven,
Live the life of heaven above,
All the life of glorious love.

Find in Christ the way of peace,
   Peace unspeakable, unknown;
By his pain he gives you ease,
   Life by his expiring groan;
Rise, exalted by his fall,
Find in Christ your all in all.

This the universal bliss,
   Bliss for every soul designed,
God's original promise this,
   God's great gift to all mankind:
Blest in Christ this moment be!
Blest to all eternity![20]

A VISION OF HEAVEN

Some writers make a distinction which seems not improper. They speak of the essential part of heaven and the accessory parts. A man without any learning is naturally led into the same distinction. So the poor dying peasant in Frederica: "To be sure heaven is a fine place, a very fine place; but I do not care for that: I want to *see* God and to *be with Him."* I do not know whether the usual question be well stated, "Is heaven a state or a place?" There is no opposition between these two: it is both the one and the other. It is the *place* wherein God more immediately dwells with those saints who are in a glorified *state.* Homer could only conceive of the place that it was paved with brass. Milton in one place makes heaven's pavement beaten gold; in another he defines it more sublimely "the house of God, star-paved." As full an account of this house of God as it can yet enter into our hearts to conceive is given us in various parts of the Revelation. There we have a fair prospect into the holiest, where are, first, He that sitteth upon the throne; then the four living creatures; next, the twenty-four elders; afterwards the great multitude which no man can number; and, surrounding them all, the various myriads of angels, whom God hath constituted in a wonderful order.

"But what is the essential part of heaven?" Undoubtedly it is to see God, to know God, to love God. We shall then know both his nature, and his works of creation, of providence, and of redemption. Even in paradise, in the intermediate state between death and the resurrection, we shall learn more concerning these in an hour than we could in an age during our stay in the body. We cannot tell, indeed, how we shall then exist or what kind of organs we shall have: the soul will not be encumbered with flesh and blood; but probably it will have some sort of ethereal vehicle, even before God clothes us "with our nobler house of empyrean light."[21]

> Away with our sorrow and fear!
>   We soon shall recover our home,
> The city of saints shall appear,
>   The day of eternity come;
> From earth we shall quickly remove,
>   And mount to our native abode,
> The house of our Father above,
>   The palace of angels and God.
>
> By faith we already behold
>   That lovely Jerusalem here;
> Her walls are of jasper and gold,
>   As crystal her buildings are clear;

Immovably founded in grace,
  She stands as she ever hath stood,
And brightly her Builder displays,
  And flames with the glory of God.[22]

THE NEW CREATION

Thus saith the Creator and Governor of the universe: "Behold, I make all things new"—all which are included in that expression of the Apostle, "A new heaven and a new earth." A *new heaven.* The original word in Genesis (chap. 1.) is in the plural number; and indeed, this is the constant language of Scripture; not *heaven,* but *heavens.* Accordingly, the ancient Jewish writers are accustomed to reckon three heavens; in conformity to which, the Apostle Paul speaks of his being caught up "into the third heaven." It is this, the third heaven, which is usually supposed to be the more immediate residence of God; so far as any residence can be ascribed to his omnipresent Spirit, who pervades and fills the whole universe. It is here (if we speak after the manner of men) that the Lord sitteth upon his throne, surrounded by angels and archangels, and by all his flaming ministers.

We cannot think that this heaven will undergo any change, any more than its Great Inhabitant. Surely this palace of the Most High was the same from eternity, and will be, world without end. Only the inferior heavens are liable to change; the highest of which we usually call the starry heavens. This, St. Peter informs us, "is reserved unto fire, against the day of judgment and destruction of ungodly men." In that day, "being on fire," it shall first "shrivel as a parchment scroll"; then it "shall be dissolved, and shall pass away with a great noise"; lastly, it shall "flee from the face of Him that sitteth on the throne, and there shall be found no place for it."

At the same time "the stars shall fall from heaven"; the secret chain being broken which had retained them in their several orbits from the foundation of the world. In the meanwhile, the lower or sublunary heaven, with the elements (or principles that compose it), "shall melt with fervent heat"; while "the earth, with the works that are therein, shall be burned up." This is the introduction to a far nobler state of things, such as it has not yet entered into the heart of men to conceive—the universal restoration, which is to succeed the universal destruction. For "we look," says the Apostle, "for new heavens and a new earth, wherein dwelleth righteousness" (II Pet. 3:7f.).[23]

> Righteous God! whose vengeful phials
>   All our fears and thoughts exceed,
> Big with woes and fiery trials,
>   Hanging, bursting o'er our head;
> While thou visitest the nations,
>   Thy selected people spare;
> Arm our cautioned souls with patience,
> Fill our humbled hearts with prayer.
>
> If thy dreadful controversy
>   With all flesh is now begun,
> In thy wrath remember mercy,
>   Mercy first and last be shown;
> Plead thy cause with sword and fire,
>   Shake us till the curse remove,
> Till thou com'st, the world's desire,
>   Conquering all with sovereign love.
>
> Every fresh alarming token
>   More confirms the faithful word;
> Nature (for its Lord hath spoken)
>   Must be suddenly restored:
> From this national confusion,
>   From this ruined earth and skies,
> See the times of restitution,
>   See the new creation rise!
>
> Vanish, then, this world of shadows,
>   Pass the former things away:
> Lord appear! appear to glad us
>   With the dawn of endless day!
> O conclude this mortal story,
>   Throw this universe aside!
> Come, eternal King of glory,
>   Now descend, and take thy bride![24]

Let us next take a view of those changes which we may reasonably suppose will then take place in the earth. It will no more be bound up with intense cold, nor parched up with extreme heat, but will have such a temperature as will be most conducive to its fruitfulness. And it will then contain no jarring or destructive principles within its own bosom. It will no more be shaken or torn asunder by the impetuous force of earthquakes, and will therefore need neither Vesuvium nor Etna, nor any burning mountains, to prevent them. There will be no more horrid rocks or frightful precipices; no wild deserts or barren sands; no impassable morasses or unfruitful bogs, to swallow up the unwary traveller. There will, doubtless, be inequalities on the surface of the earth; which are not blemishes, but beauties.

And what will the general produce of the earth be? Not thorns, briers, or thistles; not any useless or fetid weed; not any poisonous, hurtful, or unpleasant plant; but every one that can be conducive in any wise to our use or pleasure. How far beyond all that the most lively imagination is now able to conceive! We shall no more regret the loss of the terrestrial paradise; for all the earth shall be a more beautiful paradise than Adam ever saw.

Such will be the state of the new earth with regard to the meaner, the inanimate, parts of it. But great as this change will be, it is nothing in comparison of that which will take place throughout all animated nature. In the living part of the creation were seen the most deplorable effects of Adam's apostasy. The whole animated creation, from leviathan to the smallest mite, was thereby made subject to such vanity as the inanimate creatures could not be. They were [made] subject to that fell monster DEATH, the conqueror of all that breathe. They were made subject to its forerunner, pain, in its ten thousand forms; although "God made not death, neither hath he pleasure in the death of any living."

How many millions of creatures in the sea, in the air, and on every part of the earth can now no otherwise preserve their lives than by taking away the lives of others; by tearing in pieces and devouring their poor, innocent, unresisting fellow-creatures! Miserable lot of such innumerable multitudes who, insignificant as they seem, are the offspring of one common Father; the creatures of the same God of love! It is probable not only two-thirds of the animal creation, but ninety-nine parts of a hundred, are under a necessity of destroying others in order to preserve their own life!

But it shall not always be so. He that sitteth upon the throne will soon change the face of all things, and give a demonstrative proof to all his creatures that "his mercy is over all his works." The horrid state of things which at present obtains will soon be at an end. On the new earth no creature will kill, or hurt, or give pain to any other. The scorpion will have no poisonous sting, the adder no venomous teeth. The lion will have no claws to tear the lamb, no teeth to grind his flesh and bones. Nay, no creature, no beast, bird, or fish will have any inclination to hurt any other; for cruelty will be far away, and savageness and fierceness be forgotten. So that violence shall be heard no more, neither wasting or destruction seen on the face of the earth. "The wolf shall dwell with the lamb" (the words may be literally as well as figuratively understood), "and the leopard shall lie down with the kid. They shall not hurt or destroy" from the rising up of the sun to the going down of the same.

But the most glorious of all will be the change which then will take place on the poor, sinful, miserable children of men. These had fallen in many respects, as from a greater height, so to a lower depth, than any other part of the creation. But they shall "hear a great voice out of heaven, saying, Behold, the tabernacle of God is with men. And he will dwell with them; and they shall be his people; and God himself shall be their God" (Rev. 21:3f.). Hence will arise an unmixed state of holiness and happiness, far superior to that which Adam enjoyed in Paradise. In how beautiful a manner is this described by the Apostle: "God shall wipe away all tears from their eyes; and there shall be no more death, neither sorrow nor crying. Neither shall there be any more pain; for the former things are done away!" As there will be no more death, and no more pain or sickness preparatory thereto; as there will be no more grieving for, or parting with, friends; so there will be no more sorrow or crying. Nay, but there will be a greater deliverance than all this; for there will be no more sin. And to crown all, there will be a deep, an intimate, an uninterrupted union with God; a constant communion with the Father and his Son Jesus Christ, through the Spirit; a continual enjoyment of the Three-One God, and of all the creatures in him![25]

Notes to Part Two

I. WAITING ON GOD

1. *W. V. 189f.(S.16) = SS.I.244f.(S.12: "The Means of Grace").*
2. *W.VI.510f.(S.85: "On Working out Our Own Salvation").*
3. *W.X.188-92 ("A Treatise on Baptism").*
4. *W.VIII.48f. ("An Earnest Appeal to Men of Reason and Religion").*
5. *HPCM* 477; *WHB* 128.
6. *W.I.278f. = JWJ.II.360* [25 June 1740].
7. *HPCM* 294; *MHB* 534.
8. *W.V.193 (S.16) = SS.I.294f.(S.12: "The Means of Grace").*
9. *W.XIV.267 (Preface to "Notes on the Old Testament").*
10. *L.III.129:* to Samuel Furly [10 May 1735].
11. *HPCM* 89; *WHB* 126.
12. *W.I.279f. = JWJ.II.361f.* [27-28 June 1740].
13. *HLS* 60; *WHB* 144.
14. *HLS* 86.
15. *HLS* 81; *WHB* 761; *WHB* 145.
16. *W.V.345-60 (S.27) = SS.I.451-70 (S.22: "Sermon on the Mount, VII").*
17. *HPCM* 300; *MHB* 385.
18. Cf. *W.VIII.323 (Large Minutes)*, where "Christian Conference" is listed among the means of grace.
19. *JWJ.II.174 = W.I.185f.* [4 Apr. 1739]. JW is clearly quoting Luther without knowledge of the context here. In his *Preface to the New Testament* Luther says the Epistle of James is "an epistle of straw" *by comparison with* the Fourth Gospel, Romans, Galatians, Ephesians, I John and I Peter; and in his *Preface to James and Jude* he says James is "a good book," though for several reasons he cannot regard it as apostolic. Such judgments hardly display the "fury of Solifidianism"!
20. *L.III.327 = W.IX.55:* to Dr. Lavington, Bishop of Exeter [Dec. 1751].
21. *W.X.352:* (Remarks on Aspasio Vindicated").
22. *HPCM* 509; *WHB* 113.
23. *HPCM* 381; *MHB* 555; *WHB* 45.
24. *W.VII.129ff. (S.99: "The Reward of the Righteous").*
25. *HPCM* 529; *MHB* 598; *WHB* 55.

²⁶ *W.V.*200f. (S.16) = *SS.*I.159f.(S.12: "The Means of Grace").
²⁷ *HPCM* 393; *MHB* 570.

II. CHRISTIAN BEHAVIOUR

¹ *W.*VI.136f.,148 (S.51) = *SS.*II.463f.,478f.(S.51: "The Good Steward").
² *W.*VI.106ff.(S.48: "Self-Denial").
³ *W.*XI.426 ("A Plain Account of Christian Perfection").
⁴ *L.*II.285 = *W.*VIII.489f.: to Dr. Gibson, Bishop of London [June 1747]. JW later added a footnote to the published text of the letter, saying that he followed Dr. Cheyne's advice for about two years.
⁵ *W.*XIV.280 (Preface to "An Extract from Dr. Cadogan's Dissertation on the Gout, and all Chronic Diseases," 1774).
⁶ *L.*VIII.26: to Thomas Wride [11 Dec. 1787]. "Distilled liquors" are "hard liquors"—the "spirituous liquors which Wesley forbade his Methodists not only to drink but to buy or sell. The "Rules of the United Societies" containing this prohibition are still printed in the *Discipline* of the Methodist Church in America. The reason for it in Wesley's time was chiefly the nationwide curse of excessive gin drinking.
⁷ *L.*VII.90: to Robert Carr Brackenbury [19 Nov. 1781].
⁸ *L.*VII.351: to Joseph Taylor [11 Nov. 1786].
⁹ *W.*VII.31 (S.89: "The More Excellent Way").
¹⁰ *W.*VII.302, 303ff.(S.118: "On Worldly Folly").
¹¹ *W.*VII.145f.(S.100: "On Pleasing All Men").
¹² *L.*VIII.247: to George Holder, 8 Nov. 1790.
¹³ *L.*IV.103 = *W.*XII.238: to John Trembath [17 Aug. 1760].
¹⁴ *W.*VIII.315 (Large Minutes).
¹⁵ *L.*IV.247ff. = *W.*XII.244ff.: to Miss Lewen [June 1764]. Cf. the very similar letter to his niece, Sally Webster, *L.*IV.81ff. [8 Sept. 1781]. In this he adds to the historical studies the History of America.
¹⁶ *W.*VII.289f.(S.116: "Causes of the Inefficacy of Christianity").
¹⁷ *W.*VII.9f.(S.87: "The Danger of Riches").
¹⁸ *L.*I.34 = *W.*XII.20: to his brother Samuel [5 Dec. 1726].
¹⁹ *L.*VI.292 = *W.*XII.287f.: to Miss March [10 Dec. 1777].
²⁰ *W.*V.296f.(S.24) = *SS.*I.382 (S.19: "Sermon on the Mount, IV").
²¹ *W.*VII.33ff.(S.89: "The More Excellent Way").
²² *L.*VIII.12: to James Barry [26 Sept. 1787].
²³ *L.*VIII.20: to David Gordon [29 Oct. 1787].
²⁴ *L.*VIII.219: to Henry More [12 May 1790].
²⁵ *L.*I.218f. = *W.*XII.46f.: to Mrs. Chapman [29 Mar. 1737].
²⁶ *W.*VII.32f.(S.89: "The More Excellent Way").
²⁷ *W.*VII.28f.(S.89).
²⁸ *HPCM* 429; *MHB* 572; *WHB* 52.

III. GROWTH IN GRACE

1. *L.*V.338 = *W.*XII.431: to a Young Disciple [Philothea Briggs], [31 Aug. 1772].
2. *W.*VII.316f.(S.120: "The Wedding Garment").
3. *W.*VIII.284 (Minutes, 2 Aug. 1745).
4. *W.*VIII.285f.: *op. cit.* Cf.*W.*XI.387 ("A Plain Account of Christian Perfection").
5. *HPCM* 367; *MHB* 554; *AMH* 377.
6. *W.*VI.489f.(S.83: "On Patience").
7. *W.*VII.236ff.(S.110: "The Discoveries of Faith").
8. *W.*XII.432f.: to a Young Disciple [23 July 1772] = *L.*V.331 [23 July 1772] and 341 [19 Oct. 1772], to Philothea Briggs.
9. *L.*IV.85f.: to Miss March [4 Mar. 1760].
10. *HPCM* 358; *MHB* 465; *WHB* 38.
11. *W.*VIII.429 ("Principles of a Methodist Farther Explained").
12. *W.*X.450 ("Answer to Imposture Detected").
13. *L.*IV.212 = *W.*XII.241: to Mrs. Maitland [12 May 1763].
14. *L.*IV.157f. = *W.*XII.224: to Alexander Coates [7 July 1761].
15. *W.*XII.397 = *L.*V.230f.: to Joseph Benson [5 Oct. 1770].
16. *HPCM* 433; *MHB* 390; *WHB* 119.
17. *W.*XI.394f. ("A Plain Account of Christian Perfection").
18. *L.*IV.155 = *W.*XII.233; to John Hosmer [7 June 1761].
19. *W.*XI.415ff. ("A Plain Account of Christian Perfection").
20. *W.*XI.419 (*op. cit.*).
21. *W.*XI.396f. (*op. cit.*).
22. *W.*XI.417 (*op. cit.*).
23. *HPCM* 209; *MHB* 98; *WHB* 40; *AMH* 339.
24. *W.*VII.345ff.(S.124: "The Heavenly Treasure in Earthen Vessels").
25. *W.*VI.479 (S.82: "On Temptation").
26. *W.*XII.243: to Miss T——— [29 Sept. 1764].
27. *HPCM* 537; *MHB* 823.
28. *W.*XI.426f.("A Plain Account of Christian Perfection").
29. *L.*III.230f. = *W.*XII.186f.: to Miss Furly [21 Oct. 1757].
30. *L.*IV.5f. = *W.*XII.187: to Miss Furly [9 Feb. 1758].
31. *L.*IV.71 = *W.*XII 190: to Miss Furly [19 Aug. 1759].
32. *L.*IV.109 = *W.*XII.260: to Miss March [11 Nov. 1760].
33. See *W.*VI.23-32 = *SS.*II.178-90.
34. *L.*VI.68f. = *W.*XII.381f.: to Mrs. Bennis [18 Jan. 1774].
35. *L.*VII.120 = *W.*XIII.105: to Ann Loxdale [12 Apr. 1782].
36. *L.*V.209f. = *W.*XIII.20: to Mary Bishop [27 Nov. 1770].
37. *HPCM* 545; *MHB* 80.
38. *L.*IV.10,13 = *W.*XII.212f.: to Elizabeth Hardy [5 Apr. 1758].
39. *W.*VIII.297f. (Minutes, 17 June 1747).
40. See *W.*V.144-70 = *SS.*II.360-97.
41. *L.*V.214f. = *W.*XII.399f.: to Joseph Benson [28 Dec. 1770].
42. *L.*VI.323 = *W.*XIII.47: to Elizabeth Ritchie [6 Oct. 1778].
43. *HPCM* 47; *MHB* 956; *WHB* 79; *AMH* 536.

IV. LOOKING TOWARDS ETERNITY

[1] *W.*XI.12f. ("Serious Thoughts Occasioned by the Late Earthquake at Lisbon").

[2] *HPCM* 51.

[3] *W.*VII.326ff. (S.122: "On Faith").

[4] *HPCM* 333; *MHB* 487; *WHB* 59.

[5] *W.*VII.246 (S.112: "Dives and Lazarus").

[6] *L.*VII.168 = *W.*XIII.112: to George Blackall [25 Feb. 1783].

[7] *W.*VII.331f. (S.122: "On Faith").

[8] *L.*VI.26 = *W.*XIII.24: to Mary Bishop [9 May 1773].

[9] *L.*VI.380f.: to Hannah Bell [17 Feb. 1780].

[10] *W.*VII.332f. (S. 112: "On Faith").

[11] *HPCM*(S) 949; *MHB* 824; *WHB* 104.

[12] *W.*VIII.284 (Minutes, 2 Aug. 1745).

[13] *L.*II.69 = *W.*XII.71f.: to "John Smith" [25 June 1746].

[14] *W.*V.183ff.(S.15) = *SS.*II.(S.48: "The Great Assize").

[15] *HPCM* 55; *MHB* 644; *WHB* 68.

[16] *W.*VI.505 (S.84: "The Important Question").

[17] *L.*II.97f. = *W.*XII.89: to "John Smith" [10 July 1747].

[18] *HPCM* 59.

[19] *W.*XI.199f. ("Advice to a Soldier").

[20] *HPCM* 20; *MHB* 319.

[21] *L.*VI.213f. = *W.*XIII.31: to Mary Bishop [17 Apr. 1776].

[22] *HPCM* 73; *MHB* 648.

[23] *W.*VII.117f.(S.98: "On Visiting the Sick"); *W.*VI.289f. (S.64: "The New Creation").

[24] *HPCM* 60.

[25] *W.*VI.293ff. (S.64).

A Meditation on
The Lord's Prayer[1]

OUR FATHER

If he is a father, then he is good, then he is loving, to his children. And here is the first and great reason for prayer. God is willing to bless; let us ask for a blessing.

"Our Father"—our Creator: the Author of our being: He who raised us from the dust of the earth; who breathed into us the breath of life, and we became living souls. But if he made us, let us ask, and he will not withhold any good thing from the work of his own hands.

"Our Father"—our Preserver; who day by day sustains the life he has given; of whose continuing love we now and every moment receive life and breath and all things. So much the more boldly let us come to him, and we shall "obtain mercy, and find grace to help in time of need."

Above all, the Father of our Lord Jesus Christ, and of all that believe in him; who justifies us "freely by his grace, through the redemption that is in Jesus"; who hath "blotted out all our sins, and healed all our infirmities"; who hath received us for his own children, by adoption and grace; and, "because" we "are sons, hath sent forth the Spirit of his Son into" our "hearts, crying, Abba, Father"; who "hath begotten us again of incorruptible seed", and "created us anew in Christ Jesus." Therefore we know that he heareth us always; therefore we pray to him without ceasing. We pray because we love; and "we love" him "because he first loved us."

"Our Father"—not *mine* only who now cry unto him, but ours in the most extensive sense. The God and "Father of the spirits of all flesh"; the Father of angels and men. So the very Heathens acknowledge him

211

to be, Πατὴρ ἀνδρῶν τε θεῶν τε. The Father of the universe, of all the families both in heaven and earth. Therefore with him there is no respect of persons. He loveth all that he hath made. "He is loving unto every man, and his mercy is over all his works." And the Lord's delight is in them that fear him, and put their trust in his mercy; in them that trust in him through the Son of his love, knowing they are "accepted in the Beloved." But "if God so loved us, we ought also to love one another," yea, all mankind; seeing "God so loved the world, that he gave his only begotten Son," even to die the death, that they "might not perish, but have everlasting life."

> Father of all, whose powerful voice
>   Called forth this universal frame;
> Whose mercies over all rejoice,
>   Through endless ages still the same:
> Thou by thy word upholdest all;
>   Thy bounteous love to all is showed;
> Thou hear'st thy every creature's call,
>   And fillest every mouth with good.

WHICH ART IN HEAVEN

High and lifted up, God over all, blessed for ever. Who, sitting on the circle of the heavens, beholdeth all things both in heaven and earth; whose eye pervades the whole sphere of created being; yea, and of uncreated night; unto whom "are known all his works" [Acts 15:18], and all the works of every creature, not only "from the beginning of the world" (a poor, low, weak translation), but ἀπ αἰῶνος, from all *eternity,* from everlasting to everlasting; who constrains the host of heaven as well as the children of men to cry out with wonder and amazement, "O the depth!" the depth "of the riches, both of the wisdom and of the knowledge of God!"

"Which art in heaven"—the Lord and Ruler of all, superintending and disposing all things; who art the King of kings, and Lord of lords, the blessed and only Potentate; who art strong and girded about with power, doing whatsoever pleaseth thee; the Almighty; for whensoever thou willest, to do is present with thee.

"In heaven"—eminently there. Heaven is thy throne, "the place where thine honour" particularly "dwelleth." But not there alone; for thou fillest heaven and earth, the whole expanse of space. "Heaven and earth are full of thy glory. Glory be to thee, O Lord most high!"

Therefore should we "serve the Lord with fear, and rejoice unto him with reverence." Therefore should we think, speak, and act as continually under the eye, in the immediate presence, of the Lord, the King.

> In heaven thou reign'st enthroned in light,
>   Nature's expanse beneath thee spread;
> Earth, air, and sea, before thy sight,
>   And hell's deep gloom, are open laid.
> Wisdom, and might, and love are thine;
>   Prostrate before thy face we fall,
> Confess thine attributes divine,
>   And hail thee Sovereign Lord of All!

HALLOWED BE THY NAME

This is the first of the six petitions whereof the prayer itself is composed. The name of God is God himself; the nature of God, so far as it can be discovered to man. It means, therefore, together with his existence, all his attributes or perfections:

His eternity, particularly signified by his great and incommunicable name, JEHOVAH, as the Apostle John translates it: τὸ Α καὶ τὸ Ω, ἀρχὴ καὶ τέλος, ὁ ὢν καὶ ὁ ἦ καὶ ὁ ἐρχόμενος—"The Alpha and Omega, the beginning and the end; He which is, and which was, and which is to come";

His fulness of Being, denoted by his other great name, I AM THAT I AM! His omnipresence; His omnipotence; who is indeed the only Agent in the material world; all matter being essentially dull and inactive, and moving only as it is moved by the finger of God; and he is the spring of action in every creature, visible and invisible, which could neither act nor exist, without the continual influx and agency of his almighty power;

His wisdom, clearly deduced from the things that are seen, from the goodly order of the universe; His Trinity in Unity and Unity in Trinity, discovered to us in the very first line of his written word (בָּרָא אֱלֹהִים, literally, *the Gods created,* a plural noun joined with a verb of the singular number) as well as in every part of his subsequent revelations, given by the mouth of all his holy prophets and Apostles;

His essential purity and holiness; and above all, his love, which is the very brightness of his glory.

In praying that God, or his name, may be hallowed or glorified, we pray that he may be known, such as he is, by all that are capable thereof, by all intelligent beings, and with affections suitable to that knowledge; that he may be duly honoured, and feared, and loved, by all in heaven above and in the earth beneath; by all angels and men, whom for that end he has made capable of knowing and loving him to eternity.

> Thee Sovereign Lord let all confess,
>   That moves in earth, or air, or sky;
> Revere thy power, thy goodness bless,
>   Tremble before thy piercing eye.
> All ye who owe to him your birth,
>   In praise your every hour employ:
> Jehovah reigns! Be glad, O earth!
>   And shout, ye morning-stars, for joy!

THY KINGDOM COME

This has a close connexion with the preceding petition. In order that the name of God might be hallowed, we pray that his kingdom, the kingdom of Christ, may come. This kingdom then comes to a particular person, when he "repents and believes the gospel"; when he is taught of God, not only to know himself, but to know Jesus Christ and him crucified. As "this is life eternal, to know the only true God, and Jesus Christ whom he hath sent"; so it is the kingdom of God begun below, set up in the believer's heart; "the Lord God Omnipotent" then "reigneth," when he is known through Christ Jesus. He taketh unto himself his mighty power, that he may subdue all things unto himself. He goeth on in the soul, conquering and to conquer, till he hath put all things under his feet, till "every thought is brought into captivity to the obedience of Christ."

When therefore God shall "give his Son the Heathen for his inheritance, and the uttermost parts of the earth for his possession"; when "all kingdoms shall bow before him, and all nations shall do him service"; when "the mountain of the Lord's house," the Church of Christ, "shall be established in the top of the mountains"; when "the fulness of the Gentiles shall come in, and all Israel shall be saved"; then shall it be seen that "the Lord is King, and hath put on glorious apparel," appearing to every soul of man as King of kings and Lord of lords. And it is meet for all those who love his appearing to pray that he would hasten the time; that this his kingdom, the kingdom of grace, may come quickly, and swallow up all the kingdoms of the earth; that all mankind, receiving him for their King, truly believing in his name, may be filled with righteousness, and peace, and joy, with holiness and happiness; till they are removed hence into his heavenly kingdom, there to reign with him for ever and ever.

For this also we pray in those words, "Thy kingdom come." We pray for the coming of his everlasting kingdom, the kingdom of glory in heaven, which is the continuation and perfection of the kingdom of grace on earth. Consequently this, as well as the preceding petition, is offered up for the whole intelligent creation, who are all interested in this grand event, the final renovation of all things, by God's putting an end to misery and sin, to infirmity and death, taking all things into his own hands, and setting up the kingdom which endureth throughout all ages.

Exactly answerable to all this are those awful words in the prayer at the burial of the dead: "Beseeching thee, that it may please thee of thy gracious goodness, shortly to accomplish the number of thine elect, and to hasten thy kingdom: that we, with all those that are departed in the true faith of thy holy name, may have our perfect consummation and bliss, both in body and soul, in thy everlasting glory."

> Son of thy Sire's eternal love,
>   Take to thyself thy mighty power;
> Let all earth's sons thy mercy prove,
>   Let all thy bleeding grace adore.
> The triumphs of thy love display;
>   In every heart reign thou alone;
> Till all thy foes confess thy sway,
>   And glory ends what grace begun.

THY WILL BE DONE IN EARTH AS IT IS IN HEAVEN

This is the necessary and immediate consequence wherever the kingdom of God is come; wherever God dwells in the soul by faith, and Christ reigns in the heart by love.

It is probable, many, perhaps the generality of men, at the first view of these words, are apt to imagine they are only an expression of, or petition for, resignation; for a readiness to suffer the will of God, whatsoever it be, concerning us. And this is unquestionably a divine and excellent temper, a most precious gift of God. But this is not what we pray for in this petition; at least, not in the chief and primary sense of it. We pray, not so much for a passive, as for an active, conformity to the will of God, in saying, "Thy will be done in earth as it is in heaven."

How is it done by the angels of God in heaven—those who now circle his throne rejoicing? They do it *willingly;* they love his commandments, and gladly hearken to his words. It is their meat and drink to do his will; it is their highest glory and joy. They do it *continually;* there is no interruption in their willing service. They rest not day nor night, but employ every hour (speaking after the manner of men; otherwise our measures of duration, days, and nights, and hours have no place in eternity) in fulfilling his commands, in executing his designs, in performing the counsel of his will. And they do it *perfectly.* No sin, no defect belongs to angelic minds. It is true, "the stars are not pure in his sight," even the morning-stars that sing together before him. "In his sight,"that is, in comparison of him, the very angels are not pure. But this does not imply that they are not pure *in themselves.* Doubtless they are; they are without spot and blameless. They are altogether devoted to his will, and perfectly obedient in all things.

If we view this in another light, we may observe, the angels of God in heaven do *all* the will of God. And they do nothing else, nothing but what they are absolutely assured is his will. Again, they do all the will of God as he willeth; in the manner which pleases him, and no other. Yea, and they do this only *because* it is his will; for this end, and no other reason.

When therefore we pray that the will of God may "be done in earth as it is in heaven," the meaning is that all the inhabitants of the earth, even the whole race of mankind, may do the will of their Father which is in heaven, as *willingly* as the holy angels; that these may do it *continually,* even as they, without any interruption of their willing service; yea, and that they may do it perfectly—that "the God of peace, through the blood of the everlasting covenant, may make them perfect in every good work to do his will, and work in them" all "which is well-pleasing in his sight."

In other words, we pray that we and all mankind may do the whole will of God in all things; and nothing else, not the least thing but what is the holy and acceptable will of God. We pray that we may do the whole will of God *as* he willeth, in the manner that pleases him. And lastly, that we may do it *because* it is his will; that this may be the sole reason and ground, the whole and only motive, of whatsoever we think, or whatsoever we speak or do.

> Spirit of grace, and health, and power,
>   Fountain of light and love below;
> Abroad thine healing influence shower,
>   O'er all the nations let it flow.
> Inflame our hearts with perfect love;
>   In us the work of faith fulfil;
> So not heaven's host shall swifter move
>   Than we on earth to do thy will.

GIVE US THIS DAY OUR DAILY BREAD

In the three former petitions we have been praying for all mankind. We come now more particularly to desire a supply for our own wants. Not that we are directed, even here, to confine our prayer altogether to ourselves; but this, and each of the following petitions, may be used for the whole Church of Christ upon earth.

By "bread" we may understand all things needful, whether for our souls or bodies—τὰ πρὸς ζωὴν καὶ εὐσέβειαν, *the things pertaining to life and godliness.* We understand not barely the outward bread, what our Lord terms "the meat which perisheth"; but much more the spiritual bread, the grace of God, the food "which endureth unto everlasting life." It was the judgment of many of the ancient Fathers that we are here to understand the sacramental bread also; daily received in the beginning by the whole Church of Christ, and highly esteemed, till the love of many waxed cold, as the grand channel whereby the grace of his Spirit was conveyed to the souls of all the children of God.

"Our daily bread." The word we render "daily" has been differently explained by different commentators. But the most plain and natural sense of it seems to be this, which is retained in almost all translations, as well ancient as modern: "what is sufficient for this day," and so for each day as it succeeds.

"Give us"—for we claim nothing of right, but only of free mercy. We deserve not the air we breathe, the earth that bears, or the sun that shines upon us. All our desert, we own, is hell; but God loves us freely;

therefore we ask him to give what we can no more procure for ourselves, than we can merit at his hands.

Not that either the goodness or the power of God is a reason for us to stand idle. It is his will that we should use all diligence in all things, that we should employ our utmost endeavours, as much as if our success were the natural effect of our own wisdom and strength; and then, as though we had done nothing, we are to depend on him, the Giver of every good and perfect gift.

"This day"—for we are to take no thought for the morrow. For this very end has our wise Creator divided life into these little portions of time, so clearly separated from each other, that we might look on every day as a fresh gift of God, another life, which we may devote to his glory; and that every evening may be as the close of life, beyond which we are to see nothing but eternity.

> Father, 'tis thine each day to yield
>   Thy children's wants a fresh supply:
> Thou cloth'st the lilies of the field,
>   And hearest the young ravens cry.
> On thee we cast our care; we live
>   Through thee, who know'st our every need;
> O feed us with thy grace, and give
>   Our souls this day the living bread!

AND FORGIVE US OUR TRESPASSES, AS WE FORGIVE THEM THAT TRESPASS AGAINST US

As nothing but sin can hinder the bounty of God from flowing forth upon every creature, so this petition naturally follows the former; that, all hindrances being removed, we may the more clearly trust in the love of God for every manner of thing which is good.

"Our trespasses"—the word properly signifies *our debts*. Thus our sins are frequently represented in Scripture; every sin laying us under a fresh debt to God, to whom we already owe, as it were, ten thousand talents. What, then, can we answer when he shall say, "Pay me that thou owest"? We are utterly insolvent; we have nothing to pay; we have wasted all our substance. Therefore, if he deal with us according to the rigour of his law, if he exact what he justly may, he must command us to be "bound hand and foot, and delivered over to the tormentors" [Matt. 18:24–35].

Indeed we are already bound hand and foot by the chains of our own sins. These, considered with regard to ourselves, are chains of iron and fetters of brass. They are wounds wherewith the world, the flesh, and the devil have gashed and mangled us all over. They are diseases that drink up our blood and spirits, that bring us down to the chambers of the grave. But, considered as they are here, with regard to God, they are debts immense and numberless. Well, therefore, seeing we have nothing to pay, may we cry unto him, that he would frankly forgive us all!

The word translated *forgive,* implies either to forgive a debt, or to unloose a chain. And, if we attain the former, the latter follows of course. If our debts are forgiven, the chains fall off our hands. As soon as ever, through the free grace of God in Christ, we "receive forgiveness of sins," we receive likewise "a lot among those which are sanctified, by faith which is in him." Sin has lost its power: it has no dominion over those who are under grace, that is, in favour with God. As "there is now no condemnation to them that are in Christ Jesus," so they are freed from sin as well as from guilt. "The righteousness of the law is fulfilled in" them, and they "walk not after the flesh but after the Spirit."

"As we forgive them that trespass against us." In these words our Lord clearly declares both on what condition, and in what degree or manner, we may look to be forgiven of God. All our trespasses and sins are forgiven us, *if* we forgive, and *as* we forgive, others. This is a point of the utmost importance. And our blessed Lord is so jealous lest at anytime we should let it slip out of our thoughts that he not only inserts it in the body of his prayer, but presently after repeats it twice over [Matt. 6:14f.]. Secondly, God forgives us *as* we forgive others. So that if any malice or bitterness, if any taint of unkindness or anger remains, if we do not clearly, fully, and from the heart, forgive all men their trespasses, we so far cut short the forgiveness of our own; God cannot clearly and fully forgive us; he may show us some degree of mercy, but we will not suffer him to blot out all our sins, and forgive all our iniquities.

In the meantime, while we do not from our hearts forgive our neighbour his trespasses, what manner of prayer are we offering to God whenever we utter these words? We are indeed setting God at open defiance; we are daring him to do his worst. "Forgive us our trespasses, as we forgive them that trespass against us!" That is, in plain terms, "Do not thou forgive us at all. We desire no favour at thy hands. We pray that thou wilt keep our sins in remembrance, and that thy wrath may abide upon us." But can you seriously offer such a prayer to God? And hath he not yet cast you quick [alive] into hell? O tempt him no longer! Now, even now, by his grace, forgive as you would be forgiven! Now have compassion on thy fellow-servant, as God hath had, and will have, pity on thee!

> Eternal, spotless Lamb of God
>   Before the world's foundation slain,
> Sprinkle us ever with thy blood;
>   O cleanse and keep us ever clean!
> To every soul (all praise to Thee!)
>   Our bowels of compassion move:
> And all mankind by this may see
>   God is in us; for God is love.

AND LEAD US NOT INTO TEMPTATION, BUT DELIVER US FROM EVIL

"And lead us not into temptation." The word translated *temptation* means trial of any kind. And so the English word temptation was formerly taken in an indifferent sense; although now it is usually understood of solicitation to sin. St. James uses the word in both these senses; first, in its general, then in its restrained, acceptation. He takes it in the former sense when he saith, "Blessed is the man that endureth temptation: for when he is tried," or approved of God,"he shall receive the crown of life" (Jas. 1:12f.). He immediately adds, taking the word in the latter sense, "Let no man say, when he is tempted, I am tempted of God: for God cannot be tempted with evil, neither tempteth he any man: But every man is tempted, when he is *drawn away* of his own lust," or *desire*—ἐξελκόμενος, drawn out of God; in whom alone he is safe—*"and enticed";* caught as a fish with a bait. Then it is, when he is thus *drawn away and enticed,* that he properly enters into temptation. Then temptation covers him as a cloud; it overspreads his whole soul. Then how hardly shall he escape out of the snare! Therefore we beseech God "not to lead us into temptation," that is (seeing God tempteth no man), not to suffer us to be led into it.

"But deliver us from evil": rather, *"from the evil one,"* ἀπὸ τοῦ πονηροῦ. Ὁ πονηρός is unquestionably *the wicked one,* emphatically so called, the prince and god of this world, who works with mighty power in the children of disobedience. But all those who are the children of God by faith are delivered out of his hands. He may fight against them; and so he will. But he cannot conquer, unless they betray their own souls. He may torment for a time, but he cannot destroy. For God is on their side, who will not fail, in the end, to "avenge his own elect, that cry unto him day and night." Lord, when we are tempted, suffer us not to enter into temptation! Do thou make a way for us to escape, that the wicked one touch us not!

> Giver and Lord of life, whose power
>   And guardian care for all are free;
> To thee in fierce temptation's hour,
>   From sin and Satan let us flee.
> Thine, Lord, we are, and ours thou art;
>   In us be all thy goodness showed;
> Renew, enlarge, and fill our heart
>   With peace, and joy, and heaven, and God.

FOR THINE IS THE KINGDOM, AND THE POWER, AND THE GLORY, FOR EVER. AMEN

The conclusion of this divine prayer, commonly called the Doxology, is a solemn thanksgiving, a compendious acknowledgement of the attributes and works of God.

"For thine is the kingdom"—the sovereign right of all things that are, or ever were, created; yea, thy kingdom is an everlasting kingdom, and thy dominion endureth throughout all ages.

"The power"—the executive power whereby thou governest all things in thy everlasting kingdom, whereby thou doest whatsoever pleaseth thee, in all places of thy dominion.

"And the glory"—the praise due from every creature, for thy power, and the mightiness of thy kingdom, and for all thy wondrous works which thou workest from everlasting, and shalt do, world without end, "for ever and ever! Amen!" So be it!

> Blessing and honour, praise and love,
>   Co-equal, co-eternal Three,
> In earth below, in heaven above,
>   By all thy works be paid to thee.
> Thrice Holy! thine the kingdom is,
>   The power omnipotent is thine;
> And when created nature dies,
>   Thy never-ceasing glories shine.

Note to Epilogue

[1] This exposition of the Lord's Prayer is taken from *W*.V.332-43 (S.26) = *SS*.I.432-47 (S.21: "Sermon on the Mount, VI"). The verses here interspersed through the text are appended to the sermon in the Standard edition.

Select Bibliography

Baker, Frank. *Charles Wesley as Revealed by His Letters* (Wesley Historical Society Lecture, No. 14). London, 1948.

———. *Representative Verse of Charles Wesley.* London, 1962.

Bett, Henry. *The Spirit of Methodism.* London, 1937.

Bowmer, J. C. *The Sacrament of the Lord's Supper in Early Methodism.* London, 1951.

Bready, J. W. *England Before and After Wesley.* London, New York, 1938.

Burtner, R. W., and Chiles, R. E., eds. *A Compend of Wesley's Theology.* New York, 1954.

Cannon, W. R. *The Theology of John Wesley.* New York, 1946.

Carter, Henry. *The Methodist, A Study in Discipleship.* London, 1955.

Cell, G. C. *The Rediscovery of John Wesley.* New York, 1935.

Doughty, W. L. *John Wesley, His Conferences and His Preachers* (Wesley Historical Society Lecture, No. 10). London, 1944.

———. *John Wesley, Preacher.* London, 1955.

Deschner, John. *Wesley's Christology.* Dallas (Tex.), 1960.

Edwards, M. L. *Family Circle: A Study of the Epworth Household in Relation to Jon and Charles Wesley.* London, 1949.

———. *John Wesley and the Eighteenth Century: A Study of His Social and Political Influence,* London, 1955.

Flew, R. N. *The Hymns of Charles Wesley: A Study of Their Structure.* London, 1963.

———. *The Idea of Perfection in Christian Theology.* Oxford, 1934.

Gill, F. C. *John Wesley's Prayers.* London, 1951, New York, 1952.

———. *Selected Letters of John Wesley.* New York, 1956.

Green, V. H. H. *The Young Mr. Wesley: A Study of John Wesley and Oxford.* London, 1961.

Haddal, Ingvar. *John Wesley, A Biography* (translated from the Norwegian). London, 1961.

Harrison, A. W. *The Separation of Methodism from the Church of England* (Wesley Historical Society Lecture, No. 11). London, 1945.

Hildebrandt, Franz. *Christianity According to the Wesleys.* London, 1956.

———. *From Luther to Wesley.* London, 1951.

Hobbs, E. C., ed. *The Wesley Orders of Common Prayer.* Nashville (Tenn.), 1957.

Kay, J. A. *Wesley's Prayers and Praises*. London, 1958.

Lawson, A. B. *John Wesley and the Christian Ministry*. London, 1963.

Lee, Umphrey. *John Wesley and Modern Religion*. Nashville (Tenn.), 1936.

————. *The Lord's Horseman: John Wesley the Man*. New York, 1944.

Lindström, Harald. *Wesley and Sanctification*. Stockholm, 1946.

Manning, B. L. *The Hymns of Wesley and Watts*. London, 1942.

Outler, A. C., ed. *John Wesley* (in "A Library of Protestant Thought"). London, New York, 1964.

Parris, J. R. *John Wesley's Doctrine of the Sacraments*. London, 1963.

Piette, Maximin. *John Wesley in the Evolution of Protestantism*. London, New York, 1937.

Rattenbury, J. E. *The Conversion of the Wesleys*. London, 1938.

————. *The Eucharistic Hymns of John and Charles Wesley*. London, 1948.

————. *The Evangelical Doctrines of Charles Wesley's Hymns*. London, 1941.

Schmidt, Martin. *John Wesley: A Theological Biography* (translated from the German). London, 1962, New York, 1963.

————. *The Young Wesley, Missionary and Theologian of Missions* (translated from the German). London, 1958.

Starkey, L. M. *The Work of the Holy Spirit: A Study in Wesleyan Theology*. New York, 1962.

Todd, J. M. *John Wesley and the Catholic Church*. London, 1958.

Urwin, E. C., and Wollen, D., eds. *John Wesley, Christian Citizen: Selections from His Social Teaching*. London, 1937.

Vulliamy, C. E. *John Wesley* [a biographical study]. London, 1931.

Williams, C. W. *John Wesley's Theology Today*. New York, 1960.

Wiseman, F. L. *Charles Wesley and His Hymns*. London, 1938.